Office for Disarmament Affairs
New York, 2012

The United Nations
DISARMAMENT YEARBOOK

Volume 36 (Part I): 2011

Disarmament Resolutions and Decisions
of the Sixty-sixth Session
of the United Nations General Assembly

Guide to the user

To facilitate early analysis of the resolutions and decisions on disarmament adopted at the sixty-sixth session of the General Assembly, UNODA offers Part I of the Yearbook as a handy, concise reference tool, containing the full texts of all the resolutions and decisions, the date of adoption by the Assembly and the First Committee, the agenda item number, the symbol number of the Report of the Rapporteur, the main sponsors and the voting patterns in the Assembly. For a snapshot of this information in a convenient chart, see "Quick view of votes by cluster". For a list of agenda items and their corresponding reports, see the Annex.

Bold type in the list of sponsors indicates the State that introduced the draft resolution or decision. Throughout the book, any deviation in introducing and/or voting on resolutions is asterisked, and explained in a corresponding footnote.

Electronically available in PDF or database format at
www.un.org/disarmament

UNITED NATIONS PUBLICATION
Sales No. E.12.IX.1

ISBN 978-92-1-142284-9

Contents

Page

Preface   vii

Quick view of votes by cluster (47 resolutions and 5 decisions).   viii

Resolutions

66/20   Objective information on military matters, including
         transparency of military expenditures   1

66/21   Prohibition of the development and manufacture of new types of
         weapons of mass destruction and new systems of such weapons:
         report of the Conference on Disarmament.   6

66/22   Implementation of the Declaration of the
         Indian Ocean as a Zone of Peace.   9

66/23   African Nuclear-Weapon-Free Zone Treaty.   12

66/24   Developments in the field of information and
         telecommunications in the context of international security . . .   14

66/25   Establishment of a nuclear-weapon-free zone
         in the region of the Middle East   18

66/26   Conclusion of effective international arrangements to assure
         non-nuclear-weapon States against the use or threat of use
         of nuclear weapons.   22

66/27   Prevention of an arms race in outer space   27

66/28   Follow-up to nuclear disarmament obligations agreed to at the
         1995, 2000 and 2010 Review Conferences of the Parties to the
         Treaty on the Non-Proliferation of Nuclear Weapons   32

66/29   Implementation of the Convention on the Prohibition of the Use,
         Stockpiling, Production and Transfer of Anti-personnel Mines
         and on Their Destruction.   38

66/30   Relationship between disarmament and development   42

66/31   Observance of environmental norms in the drafting and
         implementation of agreements
         on disarmament and arms control   45

66/32   Promotion of multilateralism in the area of disarmament
         and non-proliferation   47

66/33   2015 Review Conference of the Parties to the Treaty on the
         Non-Proliferation of Nuclear Weapons
         and its Preparatory Committee   52

66/34   Assistance to States for curbing the illicit traffic in small arms and light weapons and collecting them 56

66/35   Implementation of the Convention on the Prohibition of the Development, Production, Stockpiling and Use of Chemical Weapons and on Their Destruction 60

66/36   Regional disarmament 63

66/37   Conventional arms control at the regional and subregional levels 65

66/38   Confidence-building measures in the regional and subregional context 69

66/39   Transparency in armaments 72

66/40   Towards a nuclear-weapon-free world: accelerating the implementation of nuclear disarmament commitments 82

66/41   National legislation on transfer of arms, military equipment and dual-use goods and technology 91

66/42   Problems arising from the accumulation of conventional ammunition stockpiles in surplus 93

66/43   Treaty on the South-East Asia Nuclear-Weapon-Free Zone (Bangkok Treaty) 96

66/44   Treaty banning the production of fissile material for nuclear weapons or other nuclear explosive devices 99

66/45   United action towards the total elimination of nuclear weapons 104

66/46   Follow-up to the advisory opinion of the International Court of Justice on the *Legality of the Threat or Use of Nuclear Weapons* 115

66/47   The illicit trade in small arms and light weapons in all its aspects 120

66/48   Reducing nuclear danger 126

66/49   Compliance with non-proliferation, arms limitation and disarmament agreements and commitments 129

66/50   Measures to prevent terrorists from acquiring weapons of mass destruction 133

66/51   Nuclear disarmament 136

66/52   Prohibition of the dumping of radioactive wastes 146

66/53   United Nations regional centres for peace and disarmament 149

66/54 United Nations Regional Centre for Peace, Disarmament and Development in Latin America and the Caribbean 151

66/55 Regional confidence-building measures: activities of the United Nations Standing Advisory Committee on Security Questions in Central Africa. 154

66/56 United Nations Regional Centre for Peace and Disarmament in Asia and the Pacific. 159

66/57 Convention on the Prohibition of the Use of Nuclear Weapons. 161

66/58 United Nations Regional Centre for Peace and Disarmament in Africa 164

66/59 Report of the Conference on Disarmament 167

66/60 Report of the Disarmament Commission. 170

66/61 The risk of nuclear proliferation in the Middle East 172

66/62 Convention on Prohibitions or Restrictions on the Use of Certain Conventional Weapons Which May Be Deemed to Be Excessively Injurious or to Have Indiscriminate Effects . . . 179

66/63 Strengthening of security and cooperation in the Mediterranean region 183

66/64 Comprehensive Nuclear-Test-Ban Treaty 187

66/65 Convention on the Prohibition of the Development, Production and Stockpiling of Bacteriological (Biological) and Toxin Weapons and on Their Destruction. 192

66/66 Revitalizing the work of the Conference on Disarmament and taking forward multilateral disarmament negotiations 195

Decisions

66/514 Review of the implementation of the Declaration on the Strengthening of International Security. 198

66/515 Role of science and technology in the context of international security and disarmament. 199

66/516 Missiles. 200

66/517 Transparency and confidence-building measures in outer space activities. 201

66/518 The arms trade treaty 202

Annex

List of reports and notes of the Secretary-General 204

Preface

The *United Nations Disarmament Yearbook* is now in its thirty-sixth year of publication. Part I presents the official texts on all 47 resolutions and 5 decisions related to disarmament, arms control and international security that were debated in the First Committee and forwarded to the General Assembly for adoption at its sixty-sixth session.

Part I is issued as a separate publication to provide early access to the resolutions and decisions, each presented with key information: relevant agenda items, main sponsors and co-sponsors, vote counts, including voting patterns in the First Committee and the General Assembly, adoption and meeting number dates and the draft resolution numbers.

A *Quick view by cluster* gives the reader an easy handle (using the First Committee's "cluster" arrangement of agenda items) on resolution numbers, titles and votes in the First Committee and in the Assembly.

We hope that Part I furnishes the reader with a handy consolidated multilateral disarmament reference book, in print and electronic form.

Part II of the Yearbook will contain main multilateral issues under consideration, including their trends, summaries of First Committee and General Assembly actions taken on resolutions, full texts of principal multilateral agreements reached in 2011, declarations adopted by treaty review conferences and a convenient issue-oriented timeline. This book is forthcoming in early autumn, 2012.

Ed.

Quick view of votes by cluster (47 resolutions and 5 decisions)*

No.	Title	First Cttee action (vote, date)	GA action, 2 Dec. (vote)
Cluster 1: Nuclear weapons			
66/23	African Nuclear-Weapon-Free Zone Treaty	w/o vote 27 Oct.	w/o vote
66/25	Establishment of a nuclear-weapon-free zone in the region of the Middle East	w/o vote 26 Oct.	w/o vote
66/26	Conclusion of effective international arrangements to assure non-nuclear-weapon States against the use or threat of use of nuclear weapons	119-0-56 28 Oct.	120-0-57
66/28	Follow-up to nuclear disarmament obligations agreed to at the 1995, 2000 and 2010 Review Conferences of the Parties to the Treaty on the Non-Proliferation of Nuclear Weapons	105-52-10 110-7-47, p.p. 6 111-7-44, p.p. 9 26 Oct.	118-52-6 113-9-48, p.p. 6 118-7-43, p.p. 9
66/33	2015 Review Conference of the Parties to the Treaty on the Non-Proliferation of Nuclear Weapons and its Preparatory Committee	169-0-3 169-0-3, p.p. 7 28 Oct.	175-0-3 174-0-3, p.p. 7
66/40	Towards a nuclear-weapon-free world: accelerating the implementation of nuclear disarmament commitments	160-6-4 163-1-8, o.p. 1 160-5-3, o.p. 9 28 Oct.	169-6-6 170-1-7, o.p. 1 168-4-3, o.p. 9
66/43	Treaty on the South-East Asia Nuclear-Weapon-Free Zone (Bangkok Treaty)	w/o vote 28 Oct.	w/o vote
66/44	Treaty banning the production of fissile material for nuclear weapons or other nuclear explosive devices	151-2-23 149-3-16, o.p. 2 148-2-19, o.p. 3 28 Oct.	158-2-21 157-2-17, o.p. 2 160-2-16, o.p. 3
66/45	United action towards the total elimination of nuclear weapons	156-1-15 165-1-3, p.p. 9 166-3-2, o.p. 2 167-1-3, o.p. 8 161-3-7, o.p. 9 164-1-75, o.p. 15 26 Oct.	169-1-11 175-1-4, p.p. 9 174-3-2, o.p. 2 177-1-3, o.p. 8 169-3-6, o.p. 9 172-1-5, o.p. 15

---

* Abbreviations: o.p.= operative paragraph; p.p.= preambular paragraph.

No.	Title	First Cttee action (vote, date)	GA action, 2 Dec. (vote)
66/46	Follow-up to the advisory opinion of the International Court of Justice on the *Legality of the Threat or Use of Nuclear Weapons*	127-25-22 27 Oct.	130-26-23
66/48	Reducing nuclear danger	110-48-12 26 Oct.	117-49-13
66/51	Nuclear disarmament	113-44-18 157-0-14, o.p. 14 164-1-6, o.p. 16 27 Oct.	117-45-18 162-0-14, o.p. 14 172-1-7, o.p. 16
66/52	Prohibition of the dumping of radioactive wastes	w/o vote 27 Oct.	w/o vote
66/57	Convention on the Prohibition of the Use of Nuclear Weapons	113-48-10 26 Oct.	117-48-12
66/64	Comprehensive Nuclear-Test-Ban Treaty	170-1-3 168-1-3, p.p. 6 28 Oct.	175-1-3 174-1-3, p.p. 6
66/516	Missiles (decision)	w/o vote 26 Oct.	w/o vote

Cluster 2: Other weapons of mass destruction

No.	Title	First Cttee action (vote, date)	GA action, 2 Dec. (vote)
66/21	Prohibition of the development and manufacture of new types of weapons of mass destruction and new systems of such weapons: report of the Conference on Disarmament	173-1-1 27 Oct.	168-1-1
66/35	Implementation of the Convention on the Prohibition of the Development, Production, Stockpiling and Use of Chemical Weapons and on Their Destruction	w/o vote 26 Oct.	w/o vote
66/50	Measures to prevent terrorists from acquiring weapons of mass destruction	w/o vote 26 Oct.	w/o vote
66/65	Convention on the Prohibition of the Development, Production and Stockpiling of Bacteriological (Biological) and Toxin Weapons and on Their Destruction	w/o vote 26 Oct.	w/o vote

No.	Title	First Cttee action (vote; date)	GA action, 2 Dec. (vote)
Cluster 3: Outer space (disarmament aspects)			
66/27	Prevention of an arms race in outer space	171-0-2 26 Oct.	176-0-2
66/517	Transparency and confidence-building measures in outer space activities	w/o vote 26 Oct.	w/o vote
Cluster 4: Conventional weapons			
66/29	Implementation of the Convention on the Prohibition of the Use, Stockpiling, Production and Transfer of Anti-personnel Mines and on Their Destruction	155-0-17 28 Oct.	162-0-18
66/34	Assistance to States for curbing the illicit traffic in small arms and light weapons and collecting them	w/o vote 27 Oct.	w/o vote
66/42	Problems arising from the accumulation of conventional ammunition stockpiles in surplus	w/o vote 26 Oct.	w/o vote
66/47	The illicit trade in small arms and light weapons in all its aspects	w/o vote 27 Oct.	w/o vote
66/62	Convention on Prohibitions or Restrictions on the Use of Certain Conventional Weapons Which May Be Deemed to Be Excessively Injurious or to Have Indiscriminate Effects	w/o vote 27 Oct.	w/o vote
66/518	The arms trade treaty (decision)	155-0-13 28 Oct.	166-0-13
Cluster 5: Regional disarmament and security			
66/22	Implementation of the Declaration of the Indian Ocean as a Zone of Peace	124-4-45 26 Oct.	124-4-46
66/36	Regional disarmament	w/o vote 26 Oct.	w/o vote
66/37	Conventional arms control at the regional and subregional levels	165-1-3 133-1-31, o.p. 2 26 Oct.	175-1-2 141-1-31, o.p. 2
66/38	Confidence-building measures in the regional and subregional context	w/o vote 26 Oct.	w/o vote

No.	Title	First Cttee action (vote, date)	GA action, 2 Dec. (vote)
66/55	Regional confidence-building measures: activities of the United Nations Standing Advisory Committee on Security Questions in Central Africa	w/o vote 28 Oct.	w/o vote
66/63	Strengthening of security and cooperation in the Mediterranean region	w/o vote 27 Oct.	w/o vote

Cluster 6: Other disarmament measures and international security

No.	Title	First Cttee action (vote, date)	GA action, 2 Dec. (vote)
66/20	Objective information on military matters, including transparency of military expenditures	w/o vote 27 Oct.	w/o vote
66/24	Developments in the field of information and telecommunications in the context of international security	w/o vote 27 Oct.	w/o vote
66/30	Relationship between disarmament and development	w/o vote 27 Oct.	w/o vote
66/31	Observance of environmental norms in the drafting and implementation of agreements on disarmament and arms control	w/o vote 27 Oct.	w/o vote
66/32	Promotion of multilateralism in the area of disarmament and non-proliferation	120-4-49 27 Oct.	125-5-48
66/39	Transparency in armaments	149-0-25 150-0-24, o.p. 2 150-0-23, o.p. 3 151-0-23, o.p. 4 150-0-23, o.p. 5 (b) 149-0-25, o.p. 5 150-0-23, o.p. 7 27 Oct.	156-0-23 154-0-22, o.p. 2 154-0-20, o.p. 3 156-0-19, o.p. 4 157-0-21, o.p. 5 (b) 154-0-24, o.p. 5 156-0-22, o.p. 7
66/41	National legislation on transfer of arms, military equipment and dual-use goods and technology	w/o vote 27 Oct.	w/o vote
66/49	Compliance with non-proliferation, arms limitation and disarmament agreements and commitments	157-0-18 27 Oct.	161-0-18

No.	Title	First Cttee action (vote, date)	GA action, 2 Dec. (vote)
66/514	Review of the implementation of the Declaration on the Strengthening of International Security (decision)	w/o vote 27 Oct.	w/o vote
66/515	Role of science and technology in the context of international security and disarmament (decision)	w/o vote 27 Oct.	w/o vote

Cluster 7: Disarmament machinery

No.	Title	First Cttee action (vote, date)	GA action, 2 Dec. (vote)
66/53	United Nations regional centres for peace and disarmament	w/o vote 27 Oct.	w/o vote
66/54	United Nations Regional Centre for Peace, Disarmament and Development in Latin America and the Caribbean	w/o vote 31 Oct.	w/o vote
66/56	United Nations Regional Centre for Peace and Disarmament in Asia and the Pacific	w/o vote 31 Oct.	w/o vote
66/58	United Nations Regional Centre for Peace and Disarmament in Africa	w/o vote 28 Oct.	w/o vote
66/59	Report of the Conference on Disarmament	w/o vote 27 Oct.	w/o vote
66/60	Report of the Disarmament Commission	w/o vote 27 Oct.	w/o vote
66/61	The risk of nuclear proliferation in the Middle East	157-5-6 155-2-4, p.p. 5 160-2-2, p.p. 6 163-1-2, p.p. 7 26 Oct.	167-6-5 170-2-2, p.p. 5 171-2-2, p.p. 6 173-1-2, p.p. 7
66/66	Revitalizing the work of the Conference on Disarmament and taking forward multilateral disarmament negotiations	w/o vote 28 Oct.	w/o vote

RESOLUTIONS

Agenda item 87

66/20   Objective information on military matters, including transparency of military expenditures

Text

The General Assembly,

Recalling its resolutions 53/72 of 4 December 1998, 54/43 of 1 December 1999, 56/14 of 29 November 2001, 58/28 of 8 December 2003, 60/44 of 8 December 2005, 62/13 of 5 December 2007 and 64/22 of 2 December 2009 on objective information on military matters, including transparency of military expenditures,

Recalling also its resolution 35/142 B of 12 December 1980, which introduced the United Nations system for the standardized reporting of military expenditures, its resolutions 48/62 of 16 December 1993, 49/66 of 15 December 1994, 51/38 of 10 December 1996 and 52/32 of 9 December 1997, calling upon all Member States to participate in it, and its resolution 47/54 B of 9 December 1992, endorsing the guidelines and recommendations for objective information on military matters and inviting Member States to provide the Secretary-General with relevant information regarding their implementation,

Noting that, since then, national reports on military expenditures and on the guidelines and recommendations for objective information on military matters have been submitted by a number of Member States belonging to different geographical regions,

Convinced that the improvement of international relations forms a sound basis for promoting further openness and transparency in all military matters,

Convinced also that transparency in military matters is an essential element for building a climate of trust and confidence between States worldwide and that a better flow of objective information on military matters can help to relieve international tension and is therefore an important contribution to conflict prevention,

Noting the role of the standardized reporting system, as instituted through its resolution 35/142 B, as an important instrument to enhance transparency in military matters,

Conscious that the value of the standardized reporting system would be enhanced by a broader participation of Member States,

Noting that a periodic review of the Standardized Instrument for Reporting Military Expenditures could facilitate its further development and maintain its continued relevance and operation, and recalling resolution 62/13, in which the General Assembly established the Group of Governmental Experts on the Operation and Further Development of the United Nations Standardized Instrument for Reporting Military Expenditures,

Recalling, in that regard, the report of the Secretary-General on ways and means to implement the guidelines and recommendations for objective information on military matters, including, in particular, on how to strengthen and broaden participation in the standardized reporting system,[1]

Recalling also that the guidelines and recommendations for objective information on military matters recommended certain areas for further consideration, such as the improvement of the standardized reporting system,

Welcoming the report of the Group of Governmental Experts on further ways and means to implement the guidelines and recommendations for objective information on military matters, including, in particular, on how to strengthen and broaden participation in the standardized reporting system,[2]

Noting the efforts of several regional organizations to promote transparency of military expenditures, including standardized annual exchanges of relevant information among their member States,

Emphasizing the continuing importance of the Standardized Instrument under the current political and economic circumstances,

Mindful of the provisions of the Charter of the United Nations, including its Article 26,

1. *Endorses* the report of the Group of Governmental Experts on the Operation and Further Development of the United Nations Standardized Instrument for Reporting Military Expenditures,[2] the recommendations contained therein and the new title of the instrument, namely, the United Nations Report on Military Expenditures;

2. *Calls upon* Member States, with a view to achieving the broadest possible participation, to provide the Secretary-General, by 30 April annually, with reports on their military expenditures for the latest fiscal year for which data are available, using preferably and to the extent possible, one of the reporting forms, including a "nil" report if appropriate, on the basis of recommendations contained in paragraphs 68 to 71 of the report of the Group of Governmental Experts and annex II thereto, or as appropriate, any other format developed in the context of similar reporting on military expenditures to other international or regional organizations;

---

[1] See A/54/298.
[2] See A/66/89 and Corr.1–3.

3. *Recommends* that, for the purpose of reporting by Member States of their national military expenditures in the framework of the Report on Military Expenditures, "military expenditures" be commonly understood to refer to all financial resources that a State spends on the uses and functions of its military forces and information on military expenditures represents an actual outlay in current prices and domestic currency;

4. *Also recommends* the guidelines and recommendations for objective information on military matters to all Member States for implementation, fully taking into account specific political, military and other conditions prevailing in a region, on the basis of initiatives and with the agreement of the States of the region concerned;

5. *Invites* Member States in a position to do so to supplement their reports, on a voluntary basis, with explanatory remarks regarding submitted data to explain or clarify the figures provided in the reporting forms, such as the total military expenditures as a share of gross domestic product, major changes from previous reports and any additional information reflecting their defence policy, military strategies and doctrines;

6. *Invites* Member States to provide, preferably with their annual report, their national points of contact, on the basis of annex II and paragraph 72 (*e*) of the report of the Group of Governmental Experts;

7. *Encourages* relevant international bodies and regional organizations to promote transparency of military expenditures and to enhance complementarities among reporting systems, taking into account the particular characteristics of each region, and to consider the possibility of an exchange of information with the United Nations;

8. *Takes note* of the annual reports of the Secretary-General;[3]

9. *Requests* the Secretary-General, within available resources:

(*a*) To continue the practice of sending an annual note verbale to Member States requesting the submission of their Report on Military Expenditures;

(*b*) To circulate annually a note verbale to Member States detailing which reports on military expenditures were submitted and are available electronically on the website for military expenditures;[4]

(*c*) To continue consultations with relevant international bodies, with a view to ascertaining requirements for adjusting the present instrument, with a view to encouraging wider participation, and to make recommendations, based on the outcome of those consultations and taking into account the views

---

[3] A/58/202 and Add.1–3, A/59/192 and Add.1, A/60/159 and Add.1–3, A/61/133 and Add.1–3, A/62/158 and Add.1–3, A/63/97 and Add.1 and 2, A/64/113 and Add.1 and 2, A/65/118 and Corr.1 and Add.1 and 2 and A/66/117 and Add.1.

[4] www.un.org/disarmament/convarms/Milex/.

of Member States, on necessary changes to the content and structure of the standardized reporting system;

(*d*) To encourage relevant international bodies and organizations to promote transparency of military expenditures and to consult with those bodies and organizations with emphasis on examining possibilities for enhancing complementarities among international and regional reporting systems and for exchanging related information between those bodies and the United Nations;

(*e*) To continue to foster further cooperation with relevant regional organizations with a view to raising awareness of the Report on Military Expenditures and its role as a confidence-building measure;

(*f*) To encourage the United Nations regional centres for peace and disarmament in Africa, in Asia and the Pacific, and in Latin America and the Caribbean to assist Member States in their regions in enhancing their knowledge of the standardized reporting system;

(*g*) To promote international and regional/subregional symposiums and training seminars to explain the purpose of the standardized reporting system and to give relevant technical instructions;

(*h*) To report on experiences gained during such symposiums and training seminars;

(*i*) To provide, upon request, technical assistance to Member States lacking the capacity to report data, and to encourage Member States to voluntarily provide bilateral assistance to other Member States;

(*j*) To encourage the Office for Disarmament Affairs of the Secretariat, with the financial and technical support of interested States, as appropriate, to continue to improve the existing database on military expenditures with a view to making it more user-friendly and up-to-date technologically and to increasing its functionality;

10. *Encourages* Member States:

(*a*) To inform the Secretary-General about possible problems with the standardized reporting system and their reasons for not submitting the requested data;

(*b*) To continue to provide the Secretary-General with their views and suggestions on ways and means to improve the future functioning of and broaden participation in the standardized reporting system, including necessary changes to its content and structure,

11. *Recommends* the establishment of a process for periodic reviews, in order to ensure the continued relevance and operation of the Report on Military Expenditures and that another review of the continuing relevance and operation of the Report be conducted in five years;

12. *Decides* to include in the provisional agenda of its sixty-eighth session the item entitled "Objective information on military matters, including transparency of military expenditures".

Action by the General Assembly

Date: 2 December 2011   Meeting: 71st plenary meeting
Vote: Adopted without a vote   Report: A/66/401

Sponsors

Albania, Armenia, Australia, Austria, Belgium, Bosnia and Herzegovina, Bulgaria, Canada, Chile, Costa Rica, Croatia, Cyprus, Czech Republic, Denmark, Dominican Republic, Estonia, Finland, France, **Germany**, Greece, Hungary, Ireland, Italy, Japan, Kazakhstan, Latvia, Liechtenstein, Lithuania, Luxembourg, Mali, Malta, Monaco, Montenegro, Netherlands, New Zealand, Norway, Peru, Poland, Portugal, Republic of Korea, Republic of Moldova, Romania, Russian Federation, Senegal, Serbia, Slovakia, Slovenia, Spain, Sweden, Switzerland, Thailand, the former Yugoslav Republic of Macedonia, Ukraine, United Kingdom, United States

Co-sponsors

Argentina, Democratic Republic of the Congo, Georgia, Iceland, Liberia, San Marino

Action by the First Committee

Date: 27 October 2011   Meeting: 22nd meeting
Vote: Adopted without a vote   Draft resolution: A/C.1/66/L.35

Agenda item 88

66/21   Prohibition of the development and manufacture of new types of weapons of mass destruction and new systems of such weapons: report of the Conference on Disarmament

Text

The General Assembly,

Recalling its previous resolutions on the prohibition of the development and manufacture of new types of weapons of mass destruction and new systems of such weapons,

Recalling also its resolutions 51/37 of 10 December 1996, 54/44 of 1 December 1999, 57/50 of 22 November 2002, 60/46 of 8 December 2005 and 63/36 of 2 December 2008 relating to the prohibition of the development and manufacture of new types of weapons of mass destruction and new systems of such weapons,

Recalling further paragraph 77 of the Final Document of the Tenth Special Session of the General Assembly,[1]

Determined to prevent the emergence of new types of weapons of mass destruction that have characteristics comparable in destructive effect to those of weapons of mass destruction identified in the definition of weapons of mass destruction adopted by the United Nations in 1948,[2]

Noting with appreciation the discussions which have been held in the Conference on Disarmament under the item entitled "New types of weapons of mass destruction and new systems of such weapons; radiological weapons",[3]

Noting the desirability of keeping the matter under review, as appropriate,

1.   *Reaffirms* that effective measures should be taken to prevent the emergence of new types of weapons of mass destruction;

2.   *Requests* the Conference on Disarmament, without prejudice to further overview of its agenda, to keep the matter under review, as appropriate, with a view to making, when necessary, recommendations on undertaking specific negotiations on identified types of such weapons;

---

[1] Resolution S-10/2.
[2] The definition was adopted by the Commission for Conventional Armaments (see S/C.3/32/Rev.1).
[3] *Official Records of the General Assembly, Sixty-fourth Session, Supplement No. 27* (A/64/27), chap. III, sect. E; ibid., *Sixty-fifth Session, Supplement No. 27* (A/65/27), chap. III, sect. E; and ibid., *Sixty-sixth Session, Supplement No. 27* (A/66/27), chap. III, sect. E.

3.   *Calls upon* all States, immediately following any recommendations of the Conference on Disarmament, to give favourable consideration to those recommendations;

4.   *Requests* the Secretary-General to transmit to the Conference on Disarmament all documents relating to the consideration of this item by the General Assembly at its sixty-sixth session;

5.   *Requests* the Conference on Disarmament to report the results of any consideration of the matter in its annual reports to the General Assembly;

6.   *Decides* to include in the provisional agenda of its sixty-ninth session the item entitled "Prohibition of the development and manufacture of new types of weapons of mass destruction and new systems of such weapons: report of the Conference on Disarmament".

Action by the General Assembly

Date: 2 December 2011   Meeting: 71st plenary meeting
Vote: 168-1-1   Report: A/66/402

Sponsors

Armenia, Azerbaijan, Bangladesh, **Belarus**, Cuba, Indonesia, Kazakhstan, Kyrgyzstan, Lesotho, Poland, Russian Federation, Tajikistan, Ukraine, Uzbekistan

Co-sponsors

Egypt, Nicaragua, Pakistan, Turkmenistan, Venezuela (Bolivarian Republic of)

*Recorded vote**

In favour:

Afghanistan, Albania, Algeria, Andorra, Angola, Antigua and Barbuda, Argentina, Australia, Austria, Azerbaijan, Bahamas, Bahrain, Bangladesh, Barbados, Belarus, Belgium, Belize, Benin, Bolivia (Plurinational State of), Bosnia and Herzegovina, Brazil, Brunei Darussalam, Bulgaria, Cambodia, Cameroon, Canada, Cape Verde, Chad, Chile, China, Colombia, Comoros, Congo, Costa Rica, Côte d'Ivoire, Croatia, Cuba, Cyprus, Czech Republic, Democratic People's Republic of Korea, Denmark, Djibouti, Dominican Republic, Ecuador, Egypt, El Salvador, Estonia, Ethiopia, Fiji, Finland, France, Georgia, Germany, Ghana, Greece, Guatemala, Guinea, Guinea-Bissau, Guyana, Haiti, Honduras, Hungary, Iceland, India, Indonesia, Iran (Islamic

---

*   Subsequently, the delegations of Armenia, Bhutan, Botswana, Burkina Faso, Switzerland and Timor-Leste advised the Secretariat that they had intended to vote in favour. The voting tally above does not reflect this information.

Republic of), Iraq, Ireland, Italy, Jamaica, Japan, Jordan, Kazakhstan, Kenya, Kuwait, Kyrgyzstan, Lao People's Democratic Republic, Latvia, Lebanon, Lesotho, Liberia, Libyan Arab Jamahiriya, Liechtenstein, Lithuania, Luxembourg, Madagascar, Malawi, Malaysia, Maldives, Mali, Malta, Marshall Islands, Mauritania, Mauritius, Mexico, Micronesia (Federated States of), Monaco, Mongolia, Montenegro, Morocco, Mozambique, Myanmar, Namibia, Nepal, Netherlands, New Zealand, Nicaragua, Niger, Nigeria, Norway, Oman, Pakistan, Palau, Panama, Papua New Guinea, Paraguay, Peru, Philippines, Poland, Portugal, Qatar, Republic of Korea, Republic of Moldova, Romania, Russian Federation, Saint Kitts and Nevis, Saint Lucia, Saint Vincent and the Grenadines, Samoa, San Marino, Sao Tome and Principe, Saudi Arabia, Senegal, Serbia, Seychelles, Sierra Leone, Singapore, Slovakia, Slovenia, Solomon Islands, South Africa, Spain, Sri Lanka, Sudan, Suriname, Swaziland, Sweden, Syrian Arab Republic, Tajikistan, Thailand, the former Yugoslav Republic of Macedonia, Togo, Tonga, Tunisia, Turkey, Turkmenistan, Ukraine, United Arab Emirates, United Kingdom, United Republic of Tanzania, Uruguay, Uzbekistan, Vanuatu, Venezuela (Bolivarian Republic of), Viet Nam, Yemen, Zambia, Zimbabwe

Against:
United States

Abstaining:
Israel

Action by the First Committee

Date: 27 October 2011
Vote: 173-1-1

Meeting: 22nd meeting
Draft resolution: A/C.1/66/L.24

Agenda item 89

66/22   Implementation of the Declaration of the Indian Ocean as a Zone of Peace

Text

The General Assembly,

Recalling the Declaration of the Indian Ocean as a Zone of Peace, contained in its resolution 2832 (XXVI) of 16 December 1971, and recalling also its resolutions 54/47 of 1 December 1999, 56/16 of 29 November 2001, 58/29 of 8 December 2003, 60/48 of 8 December 2005, 62/14 of 5 December 2007 and 64/23 of 2 December 2009 and other relevant resolutions,

Recalling also the report of the Meeting of the Littoral and Hinterland States of the Indian Ocean held in New York from 2 to 13 July 1979,[1]

Recalling further paragraph 102 of the Final Document of the Thirteenth Conference of Heads of State or Government of Non-Aligned Countries, held at Kuala Lumpur in 24 and 25 February 2003,[2] in which it was noted, inter alia, that the Chair of the Ad Hoc Committee on the Indian Ocean would continue his informal consultations on the future work of the Committee,

Emphasizing the need to foster consensual approaches that are conducive to the pursuit of such endeavours,

Noting the initiatives taken by countries of the region to promote cooperation, in particular economic cooperation, in the Indian Ocean area and the possible contribution of such initiatives to overall objectives of a zone of peace,

Convinced that the participation of all permanent members of the Security Council and the major maritime users of the Indian Ocean in the work of the Ad Hoc Committee is important and would assist the progress of a mutually beneficial dialogue to develop conditions of peace, security and stability in the Indian Ocean region,

Considering that greater efforts and more time are required to develop a focused discussion on practical measures to ensure conditions of peace, security and stability in the Indian Ocean region,

Having considered the report of the Ad Hoc Committee on the Indian Ocean,[3]

1.   *Takes note* of the report of the Ad Hoc Committee on the Indian Ocean;[3]

---

[1]   *Official Records of the General Assembly, Thirty-fourth Session, Supplement No. 45* and corrigendum (A/34/45 and Corr.1).

[2]   See A/57/759-S/2003/332, annex I.

[3]   *Official Records of the General Assembly, Sixty-sixth Session, Supplement No 29* (A/66/29).

2.   *Reiterates its conviction* that the participation of all permanent members of the Security Council and the major maritime users of the Indian Ocean in the work of the Ad Hoc Committee is important and would greatly facilitate the development of a mutually beneficial dialogue to advance peace, security and stability in the Indian Ocean region;

3.   *Requests* the Chair of the Ad Hoc Committee to continue his informal consultations with the members of the Committee and to report through the Committee to the General Assembly at its sixty-eighth session;

4.   *Requests* the Secretary-General to continue to render, within existing resources, all necessary assistance to the Ad Hoc Committee, including the provision of summary records;

5.   *Decides* to include in the provisional agenda of its sixty-eighth session the item entitled "Implementation of the Declaration of the Indian Ocean as a Zone of Peace".

Action by the General Assembly

Date:	2 December 2011	Meeting:	71st plenary meeting
Vote:	124-4-46	Report:	A/66/403

Sponsors

Indonesia, on behalf of States Members of the United Nations that are members of the Movement of Non-Aligned Countries

*Recorded vote**

In favour:

Afghanistan, Algeria, Angola, Antigua and Barbuda, Argentina, Armenia, Australia, Azerbaijan, Bahamas, Bahrain, Bangladesh, Barbados, Belarus, Belize, Benin, Bhutan, Bolivia (Plurinational State of), Brazil, Brunei Darussalam, Burkina Faso, Cambodia, Cameroon, Cape Verde, Chad, Chile, China, Colombia, Comoros, Congo, Costa Rica, Côte d'Ivoire, Cuba, Democratic People's Republic of Korea, Djibouti, Dominican Republic, Ecuador, Egypt, Ethiopia, Fiji, Ghana, Guatemala, Guinea, Guinea-Bissau, Guyana, Haiti, Honduras, India, Indonesia, Iran (Islamic Republic of), Iraq, Jamaica, Japan, Jordan, Kazakhstan, Kenya, Kuwait, Kyrgyzstan, Lao People's Democratic Republic, Lebanon, Lesotho, Liberia, Libyan Arab Jamahiriya, Madagascar, Malawi, Malaysia, Maldives, Mali, Mauritania, Mauritius, Mexico, Mongolia, Morocco, Mozambique, Myanmar, Namibia, Nepal, New Zealand, Nicaragua, Niger, Nigeria, Oman, Pakistan, Panama, Papua New

---

* Subsequently, the delegation of Botswana advised the Secretariat that it had intended to vote in favour; the delegation of Switzerland advised the Secretariat that it had intended to abstain. The voting tally above does not reflect this information.

Guinea, Paraguay, Peru, Philippines, Qatar, Republic of Korea, Russian Federation, Saint Kitts and Nevis, Saint Lucia, Saint Vincent and the Grenadines, Samoa, Sao Tome and Principe, Saudi Arabia, Senegal, Seychelles, Sierra Leone, Singapore, Solomon Islands, South Africa, Sri Lanka, Sudan, Suriname, Swaziland, Syrian Arab Republic, Tajikistan, Thailand, Timor-Leste, Togo, Tonga, Tunisia, Turkmenistan, United Arab Emirates, United Republic of Tanzania, Uruguay, Uzbekistan, Vanuatu, Venezuela (Bolivarian Republic of), Viet Nam, Yemen, Zambia, Zimbabwe

Against:
France, Israel, United Kingdom, United States

Abstaining:
Albania, Andorra, Austria, Belgium, Bosnia and Herzegovina, Bulgaria, Canada, Croatia, Cyprus, Czech Republic, Denmark, El Salvador, Estonia, Finland, Georgia, Germany, Greece, Hungary, Iceland, Ireland, Italy, Latvia, Liechtenstein, Lithuania, Luxembourg, Malta, Marshall Islands, Micronesia (Federated States of), Monaco, Montenegro, Netherlands, Norway, Palau, Poland, Portugal, Republic of Moldova, Romania, San Marino, Serbia, Slovakia, Slovenia, Spain, Sweden, the former Yugoslav Republic of Macedonia, Turkey, Ukraine

Action by the First Committee

Date: 26 October 2011	Meeting: 21st meeting
Vote: 124-4-45	Draft resolution: A/C.1/66/L.5

Agenda item 90

66/23   African Nuclear-Weapon-Free Zone Treaty

Text

The General Assembly,

Recalling its resolutions 51/53 of 10 December 1996 and 56/17 of 29 November 2001 and all its other relevant resolutions, as well as those of the Organization of African Unity and of the African Union,

Recalling also the signing of the African Nuclear-Weapon-Free Zone Treaty (Treaty of Pelindaba)[1] in Cairo on 11 April 1996,

Recalling further the Cairo Declaration adopted on that occasion,[2] which emphasized that nuclear-weapon-free zones, especially in regions of tension, such as the Middle East, enhance global and regional peace and security,

Recalling the statement made by the President of the Security Council on behalf of the members of the Council on 12 April 1996,[3] affirming that the signature of the Treaty constituted an important contribution by the African countries to the maintenance of international peace and security,

Considering that the establishment of nuclear-weapon-free zones, especially in the Middle East, would enhance the security of Africa and the viability of the African nuclear-weapon-free zone,

1.   *Recalls with satisfaction* the entry into force of the African Nuclear-Weapon-Free Zone Treaty (Treaty of Pelindaba)[1] on 15 July 2009;

2.   *Calls upon* African States that have not yet done so to sign and ratify the Treaty as soon as possible;

3.   *Expresses its appreciation* to the nuclear-weapon States that have signed the Protocols to the Treaty[1] that concern them, and calls upon those that have not yet ratified the Protocols that concern them to do so as soon as possible;

4.   *Calls upon* the States contemplated in Protocol III to the Treaty that have not yet done so to take all necessary measures to ensure the speedy application of the Treaty to territories for which they are, de jure or de facto, internationally responsible and which lie within the limits of the geographical zone established in the Treaty;

5.   *Calls upon* the African States parties to the Treaty on the Non-Proliferation of Nuclear Weapons[4] that have not yet done so to conclude

---

[1] See A/50/426, annex.
[2] A/51/113-S/1996/276, annex.
[3] S/PRST/1996/17; see *Resolutions and Decisions of the Security Council, 1996.*
[4] United Nations, *Treaty Series*, vol. 729, No. 10485.

comprehensive safeguards agreements with the International Atomic Energy Agency pursuant to the Treaty, thereby satisfying the requirements of article 9 (*b*) of and annex II to the Treaty of Pelindaba, and to conclude additional protocols to their safeguards agreements on the basis of the Model Protocol approved by the Board of Governors of the Agency on 15 May 1997;[5]

6.   *Expresses its gratitude* to the Secretary-General of the United Nations, the Chair of the African Union Commission and the Director General of the International Atomic Energy Agency for the diligence with which they have rendered effective assistance to the signatories to the Treaty;

7.   *Decides* to include in the provisional agenda of its sixty-seventh session the item entitled "African Nuclear-Weapon-Free Zone Treaty".

Action by the General Assembly

Date: 2 December 2011   Meeting: 71st plenary meeting
Vote: Adopted without a vote   Report: A/66/404

Sponsors

Nigeria, on behalf of the States Members of the United Nations that are members of the Group of African States

Co-sponsors

Australia, Chile, Kazakhstan, Mexico, New Zealand, Nicaragua

Action by the First Committee

Date: 27 October 2011   Meeting: 22nd meeting
Vote: Adopted without a vote   Draft resolution: A/C.1/66/L.51

---

[5] Model Protocol Additional to the Agreement(s) between State(s) and the International Atomic Energy Agency for the Application of Safeguards (International Atomic Energy Agency, document INFCIRC/540 (Corrected)).

Agenda item 93

66/24   **Developments in the field of information and telecommunications in the context of international security**

Text

The General Assembly,

Recalling its resolutions 53/70 of 4 December 1998, 54/49 of 1 December 1999, 55/28 of 20 November 2000, 56/19 of 29 November 2001, 57/53 of 22 November 2002, 58/32 of 8 December 2003, 59/61 of 3 December 2004, 60/45 of 8 December 2005, 61/54 of 6 December 2006, 62/17 of 5 December 2007, 63/37 of 2 December 2008, 64/25 of 2 December 2009 and 65/41 of 8 December 2010,

Recalling also its resolutions on the role of science and technology in the context of international security, in which, inter alia, it recognized that scientific and technological developments could have both civilian and military applications and that progress in science and technology for civilian applications needed to be maintained and encouraged,

Noting that considerable progress has been made in developing and applying the latest information technologies and means of telecommunication,

Affirming that it sees in this process the broadest positive opportunities for the further development of civilization, the expansion of opportunities for cooperation for the common good of all States, the enhancement of the creative potential of humankind and additional improvements in the circulation of information in the global community,

Recalling, in this connection, the approaches and principles outlined at the Information Society and Development Conference, held in Midrand, South Africa, from 13 to 15 May 1996,

Bearing in mind the results of the Ministerial Conference on Terrorism, held in Paris on 30 July 1996, and the recommendations that were made,[1]

Bearing in mind also the results of the World Summit on the Information Society, held in Geneva from 10 to 12 December 2003 (first phase) and in Tunis from 16 to 18 November 2005 (second phase),[2]

Noting that the dissemination and use of information technologies and means affect the interests of the entire international community and that optimum effectiveness is enhanced by broad international cooperation,

---

[1] See A/51/261, annex.
[2] See A/C.2/59/3, annex, and A/60/687.

Expressing concern that these technologies and means can potentially be used for purposes that are inconsistent with the objectives of maintaining international stability and security and may adversely affect the integrity of the infrastructure of States to the detriment of their security in both civil and military fields,

Considering that it is necessary to prevent the use of information resources or technologies for criminal or terrorist purposes,

Noting the contribution of those Member States that have submitted their assessments on issues of information security to the Secretary-General pursuant to paragraphs 1 to 3 of resolutions 53/70, 54/49, 55/28, 56/19, 57/53, 58/32, 59/61, 60/45, 61/54, 62/17, 63/37, 64/25 and 65/41,

Taking note of the reports of the Secretary-General containing those assessments,[3]

Welcoming the initiative taken by the Secretariat and the United Nations Institute for Disarmament Research in convening international meetings of experts in Geneva in August 1999 and April 2008 on developments in the field of information and telecommunications in the context of international security, as well as the results of those meetings,

Considering that the assessments of the Member States contained in the reports of the Secretary-General and the international meetings of experts have contributed to a better understanding of the substance of issues of international information security and related notions,

Bearing in mind that the Secretary-General, in fulfilment of resolution 60/45, established in 2009, on the basis of equitable geographical distribution, a group of governmental experts, which, in accordance with its mandate, considered existing and potential threats in the sphere of information security and possible cooperative measures to address them and conducted a study on relevant international concepts aimed at strengthening the security of global information and telecommunications systems,

Welcoming the effective work of the Group of Governmental Experts on Developments in the Field of Information and Telecommunications in the Context of International Security and the relevant report transmitted by the Secretary-General,[4]

Taking note of the assessments and recommendations contained in the report of the Group of Governmental Experts,

1.   *Calls upon* Member States to promote further at multilateral levels the consideration of existing and potential threats in the field of information

---

[3] A/54/213, A/55/140 and Corr.1 and Add.1, A/56/164 and Add.1, A/57/166 and Add.1, A/58/373, A/59/116 and Add.1, A/60/95 and Add.1, A/61/161 and Add.1, A/62/98 and Add.1, A/64/129 and Add.1, A/65/154 and A/66/152 and Add.1.

[4] See A/65/201.

security, as well as possible strategies to address the threats emerging in this field, consistent with the need to preserve the free flow of information;

2. *Considers* that the purpose of such strategies could be served through further examination of relevant international concepts aimed at strengthening the security of global information and telecommunications systems;

3. *Invites* all Member States, taking into account the assessments and recommendations contained in the report of the Group of Governmental Experts on Developments in the Field of Information and Telecommunications in the Context of International Security,[4] to continue to inform the Secretary-General of their views and assessments on the following questions:

(*a*) General appreciation of the issues of information security;

(*b*) Efforts taken at the national level to strengthen information security and promote international cooperation in this field;

(*c*) The content of the concepts mentioned in paragraph 2 above;

(*d*) Possible measures that could be taken by the international community to strengthen information security at the global level;

4. *Requests* the Secretary-General, with the assistance of a group of governmental experts, to be established in 2012 on the basis of equitable geographical distribution, taking into account the assessments and recommendations contained in the above-mentioned report, to continue to study existing and potential threats in the sphere of information security and possible cooperative measures to address them, including norms, rules or principles of responsible behaviour of States and confidence-building measures with regard to information space, as well as the concepts referred to in paragraph 2 above, and to submit to the General Assembly at its sixty-eighth session a report on the results of this study;

5. *Decides* to include in the provisional agenda of its sixty-seventh session the item entitled "Developments in the field of information and telecommunications in the context of international security".

Action by the General Assembly

Date: 2 December 2011   Meeting: 71st plenary meeting
Vote: Adopted without a vote   Report: A/66/407

Sponsors

Armenia, Azerbaijan, Belarus, Brazil, China, Costa Rica, Cuba, India, Indonesia, Kazakhstan, Kyrgyzstan, Mali, Myanmar, Nicaragua, **Russian Federation**, Serbia, Sierra Leone, Syrian Arab Republic, Tajikistan, Turkmenistan, Uganda, Ukraine, Uzbekistan, Viet Nam

Co-sponsors

Argentina, Colombia, Cyprus, Democratic People's Republic of Korea, Democratic Republic of the Congo, El Salvador, Ethiopia, Guatemala, Turkey

Action by the First Committee

Date: 27 October 2011   Meeting: 22nd meeting
Vote: Adopted without a vote   Draft resolution: A/C.1/66/L.30

Agenda item 94

66/25 Establishment of a nuclear-weapon-free zone in the region of the Middle East

Text

The General Assembly,

Recalling its resolutions 3263 (XXIX) of 9 December 1974, 3474 (XXX) of 11 December 1975, 31/71 of 10 December 1976, 32/82 of 12 December 1977, 33/64 of 14 December 1978, 34/77 of 11 December 1979, 35/147 of 12 December 1980, 36/87 A and B of 9 December 1981, 37/75 of 9 December 1982, 38/64 of 15 December 1983, 39/54 of 12 December 1984, 40/82 of 12 December 1985, 41/48 of 3 December 1986, 42/28 of 30 November 1987, 43/65 of 7 December 1988, 44/108 of 15 December 1989, 45/52 of 4 December 1990, 46/30 of 6 December 1991, 47/48 of 9 December 1992, 48/71 of 16 December 1993, 49/71 of 15 December 1994, 50/66 of 12 December 1995, 51/41 of 10 December 1996, 52/34 of 9 December 1997, 53/74 of 4 December 1998, 54/51 of 1 December 1999, 55/30 of 20 November 2000, 56/21 of 29 November 2001, 57/55 of 22 November 2002, 58/34 of 8 December 2003, 59/63 of 3 December 2004, 60/52 of 8 December 2005, 61/56 of 6 December 2006, 62/18 of 5 December 2007, 63/38 of 2 December 2008, 64/26 of 2 December 2009 and 65/42 of 8 December 2010 on the establishment of a nuclear-weapon-free zone in the region of the Middle East,

Recalling also the recommendations for the establishment of a nuclear-weapon-free zone in the region of the Middle East consistent with paragraphs 60 to 63, and in particular paragraph 63 (*d*), of the Final Document of the Tenth Special Session of the General Assembly,[1]

Emphasizing the basic provisions of the above-mentioned resolutions, which call upon all parties directly concerned to consider taking the practical and urgent steps required for the implementation of the proposal to establish a nuclear-weapon-free zone in the region of the Middle East and, pending and during the establishment of such a zone, to declare solemnly that they will refrain, on a reciprocal basis, from producing, acquiring or in any other way possessing nuclear weapons and nuclear explosive devices and from permitting the stationing of nuclear weapons on their territory by any third party, to agree to place their nuclear facilities under International Atomic Energy Agency safeguards and to declare their support for the establishment of the zone and to deposit such declarations with the Security Council for consideration, as appropriate,

Reaffirming the inalienable right of all States to acquire and develop nuclear energy for peaceful purposes,

---

[1] Resolution S-10/2.

Emphasizing the need for appropriate measures on the question of the prohibition of military attacks on nuclear facilities,

Bearing in mind the consensus reached by the General Assembly since its thirty-fifth session that the establishment of a nuclear-weapon-free zone in the region of the Middle East would greatly enhance international peace and security,

Desirous of building on that consensus so that substantial progress can be made towards establishing a nuclear-weapon-free zone in the region of the Middle East,

Welcoming all initiatives leading to general and complete disarmament, including in the region of the Middle East, and in particular on the establishment therein of a zone free of weapons of mass destruction, including nuclear weapons,

Noting the peace negotiations in the Middle East, which should be of a comprehensive nature and represent an appropriate framework for the peaceful settlement of contentious issues in the region,

Recognizing the importance of credible regional security, including the establishment of a mutually verifiable nuclear-weapon-free zone,

Emphasizing the essential role of the United Nations in the establishment of a mutually verifiable nuclear-weapon-free zone,

Having examined the report of the Secretary-General on the implementation of resolution 65/42,[2]

1.   *Urges* all parties directly concerned seriously to consider taking the practical and urgent steps required for the implementation of the proposal to establish a nuclear-weapon-free zone in the region of the Middle East in accordance with the relevant resolutions of the General Assembly, and, as a means of promoting this objective, invites the countries concerned to adhere to the Treaty on the Non-Proliferation of Nuclear Weapons;[3]

2.   *Calls upon* all countries of the region that have not yet done so, pending the establishment of the zone, to agree to place all their nuclear activities under International Atomic Energy Agency safeguards;

3.   *Takes note* of resolution GC(55)/RES/14, adopted on 23 September 2011 by the General Conference of the International Atomic Energy Agency at its fifty-fifth regular session, concerning the application of Agency safeguards in the Middle East;[4]

---

[2] A/66/153 (Part I) and Add.1 and 2.

[3] United Nations, *Treaty Series*, vol. 729, No. 10485.

[4] See International Atomic Energy Agency, *Resolutions and Other Decisions of the General Conference, Fifty-fifth Regular Session, 19–23 September 2011* (GC(55)/RES/ DEC(2011)).

4. *Notes* the importance of the ongoing bilateral Middle East peace negotiations and the activities of the multilateral Working Group on Arms Control and Regional Security in promoting mutual confidence and security in the Middle East, including the establishment of a nuclear-weapon-free zone;

5. *Invites* all countries of the region, pending the establishment of a nuclear-weapon-free zone in the region of the Middle East, to declare their support for establishing such a zone, consistent with paragraph 63 (*d*) of the Final Document of the Tenth Special Session of the General Assembly,[1] and to deposit those declarations with the Security Council;

6. *Also invites* those countries, pending the establishment of the zone, not to develop, produce, test or otherwise acquire nuclear weapons or permit the stationing on their territories, or territories under their control, of nuclear weapons or nuclear explosive devices;

7. *Invites* the nuclear-weapon States and all other States to render their assistance in the establishment of the zone and at the same time to refrain from any action that runs counter to both the letter and the spirit of the present resolution;

8. *Takes note* of the report of the Secretary-General;[2]

9. *Invites* all parties to consider the appropriate means that may contribute towards the goal of general and complete disarmament and the establishment of a zone free of weapons of mass destruction in the region of the Middle East;

10. *Requests* the Secretary-General to continue to pursue consultations with the States of the region and other concerned States, in accordance with paragraph 7 of resolution 46/30 and taking into account the evolving situation in the region, and to seek from those States their views on the measures outlined in chapters III and IV of the study annexed to the report of the Secretary-General of 10 October 1990[5] or other relevant measures, in order to move towards the establishment of a nuclear-weapon-free zone in the region of the Middle East;

11. *Also requests* the Secretary-General to submit to the General Assembly at its sixty-seventh session a report on the implementation of the present resolution;

12. *Decides* to include in the provisional agenda of its sixty-seventh session the item entitled "Establishment of a nuclear-weapon-free zone in the region of the Middle East".

---

[5] A/45/435.

Action by the General Assembly

Date: 2 December 2011   Meeting: 71st plenary meeting
Vote: Adopted without a vote   Report: A/66/408

Sponsors

Egypt

Action by the First Committee

Date: 26 October 2011   Meeting: 21st meeting
Vote: Adopted without a vote   Draft resolution: A/C.1/66/L.1

Agenda item 95

66/26 Conclusion of effective international arrangements to assure non-nuclear-weapon States against the use or threat of use of nuclear weapons

Text

The General Assembly,

Bearing in mind the need to allay the legitimate concern of the States of the world with regard to ensuring lasting security for their peoples,

Convinced that nuclear weapons pose the greatest threat to mankind and to the survival of civilization,

Noting that the renewed interest in nuclear disarmament should be translated into concrete actions for the achievement of general and complete disarmament under effective international control,

Convinced that nuclear disarmament and the complete elimination of nuclear weapons are essential to remove the danger of nuclear war,

Determined to abide strictly by the relevant provisions of the Charter of the United Nations on the non-use of force or threat of force,

Recognizing that the independence, territorial integrity and sovereignty of non-nuclear-weapon States need to be safeguarded against the use or threat of use of force, including the use or threat of use of nuclear weapons,

Considering that, until nuclear disarmament is achieved on a universal basis, it is imperative for the international community to develop effective measures and arrangements to ensure the security of non-nuclear-weapon States against the use or threat of use of nuclear weapons from any quarter,

Recognizing that effective measures and arrangements to assure non-nuclear-weapon States against the use or threat of use of nuclear weapons can contribute positively to the prevention of the spread of nuclear weapons,

Bearing in mind paragraph 59 of the Final Document of the Tenth Special Session of the General Assembly, the first special session devoted to disarmament,[1] in which it urged the nuclear-weapon States to pursue efforts to conclude, as appropriate, effective arrangements to assure non-nuclear-weapon States against the use or threat of use of nuclear weapons, and desirous of promoting the implementation of the relevant provisions of the Final Document,

---

[1] Resolution S-10/2.

Recalling the relevant parts of the special report of the Committee on Disarmament[2] submitted to the General Assembly at its twelfth special session, the second special session devoted to disarmament,[3] and of the special report of the Conference on Disarmament submitted to the Assembly at its fifteenth special session, the third special session devoted to disarmament,[4] as well as the report of the Conference on its 1992 session,[5]

Recalling also paragraph 12 of the Declaration of the 1980s as the Second Disarmament Decade, contained in the annex to its resolution 35/46 of 3 December 1980, which states, inter alia, that all efforts should be exerted by the Committee on Disarmament urgently to negotiate with a view to reaching agreement on effective international arrangements to assure non-nuclear-weapon States against the use or threat of use of nuclear weapons,

Noting the in-depth negotiations undertaken in the Conference on Disarmament and its Ad Hoc Committee on Effective International Arrangements to Assure Non-Nuclear-Weapon States against the Use or Threat of Use of Nuclear Weapons,[6] with a view to reaching agreement on this question,

Taking note of the proposals submitted under the item in the Conference on Disarmament, including the drafts of an international convention,

Taking note also of the relevant decision of the Thirteenth Conference of Heads of State or Government of Non-Aligned Countries, held at Kuala Lumpur on 24 and 25 February 2003,[7] which was reiterated at the Fourteenth and Fifteenth Conferences of Heads of State or Government of Non-Aligned Countries, held at Havana and Sharm el-Sheikh, Egypt, on 15 and 16 September 2006,[8] and 15 and 16 July 2009,[9] respectively, as well as the relevant recommendations of the Organization of Islamic Cooperation,

Taking note further of the unilateral declarations made by all the nuclear-weapon States on their policies of non-use or non-threat of use of nuclear weapons against the non-nuclear-weapon States,

Noting the support expressed in the Conference on Disarmament and in the General Assembly for the elaboration of an international convention to assure non-nuclear-weapon States against the use or threat of use of nuclear

---

[2] The Committee on Disarmament was redesignated the Conference on Disarmament as from 7 February 1984.

[3] *Official Records of the General Assembly, Twelfth Special Session, Supplement No. 2* (A/S-12/2), sect. III.C.

[4] Ibid., *Fifteenth Special Session, Supplement No. 2* (A/S-15/2), sect. III.F.

[5] Ibid., *Forty-seventh Session, Supplement No. 27* (A/47/27), sect. III.F.

[6] Ibid., *Forty-eighth Session, Supplement No. 27* (A/48/27), para. 39.

[7] See A/57/759-S/2003/332, annex I.

[8] See A/61/472-S/2006/780, annex I.

[9] See S/2009/459, annex, para. 118.

weapons, as well as the difficulties pointed out in evolving a common approach acceptable to all,

Taking note of Security Council resolution 984 (1995) of 11 April 1995 and the views expressed on it,

Recalling its relevant resolutions adopted in previous years, in particular resolutions 45/54 of 4 December 1990, 46/32 of 6 December 1991, 47/50 of 9 December 1992, 48/73 of 16 December 1993, 49/73 of 15 December 1994, 50/68 of 12 December 1995, 51/43 of 10 December 1996, 52/36 of 9 December 1997, 53/75 of 4 December 1998, 54/52 of 1 December 1999, 55/31 of 20 November 2000, 56/22 of 29 November 2001, 57/56 of 22 November 2002, 58/35 of 8 December 2003, 59/64 of 3 December 2004, 60/53 of 8 December 2005, 61/57 of 6 December 2006, 62/19 of 5 December 2007, 63/39 of 2 December 2008, 64/27 of 2 December 2009 and 65/43 of 8 December 2010,

1.   *Reaffirms* the urgent need to reach an early agreement on effective international arrangements to assure non-nuclear-weapon States against the use or threat of use of nuclear weapons;

2.   *Notes with satisfaction* that in the Conference on Disarmament there is no objection, in principle, to the idea of an international convention to assure non-nuclear-weapon States against the use or threat of use of nuclear weapons, although the difficulties with regard to evolving a common approach acceptable to all have also been pointed out;

3.   *Appeals* to all States, especially the nuclear-weapon States, to work actively towards an early agreement on a common approach and, in particular, on a common formula that could be included in an international instrument of a legally binding character;

4.   *Recommends* that further intensive efforts be devoted to the search for such a common approach or common formula and that the various alternative approaches, including, in particular, those considered in the Conference on Disarmament, be further explored in order to overcome the difficulties;

5.   *Also recommends* that the Conference on Disarmament actively continue intensive negotiations with a view to reaching early agreement and concluding effective international agreements to assure the non-nuclear-weapon States against the use or threat of use of nuclear weapons, taking into account the widespread support for the conclusion of an international convention and giving consideration to any other proposals designed to secure the same objective;

6.   *Decides* to include in the provisional agenda of its sixty-seventh session the item entitled "Conclusion of effective international arrangements

to assure non-nuclear-weapon States against the use or threat of use of nuclear weapons".

Action by the General Assembly

Date: 2 December 2011
Vote: 120-0-57

Meeting: 71st plenary meeting
Report: A/66/409

Sponsors

Bangladesh, Brunei Darussalam, Cambodia, Cuba, Ecuador, Egypt, El Salvador, Honduras, Indonesia, Iran (Islamic Republic of), Iraq, Kazakhstan, Malaysia, Myanmar, Nicaragua, **Pakistan**, Peru, Philippines, Saudi Arabia, Sierra Leone, Sri Lanka, Syrian Arab Republic, Viet Nam

Co-sponsors

Brazil, Colombia, Congo, Libyan Arab Jamahiriya, Uzbekistan

Recorded vote*

In favour:

Afghanistan, Algeria, Angola, Antigua and Barbuda, Azerbaijan, Bahamas, Bahrain, Bangladesh, Barbados, Belarus, Belize, Benin, Bhutan, Bolivia (Plurinational State of), Botswana, Brazil, Brunei Darussalam, Burkina Faso, Cambodia, Cameroon, Cape Verde, Chad, Chile, China, Colombia, Comoros, Congo, Costa Rica, Côte d'Ivoire, Cuba, Democratic People's Republic of Korea, Djibouti, Dominican Republic, Ecuador, Egypt, El Salvador, Ethiopia, Fiji, Ghana, Guatemala, Guinea, Guinea-Bissau, Guyana, Haiti, Honduras, India, Indonesia, Iran (Islamic Republic of), Iraq, Jamaica, Japan, Jordan, Kazakhstan, Kenya, Kuwait, Kyrgyzstan, Lao People's Democratic Republic, Lebanon, Lesotho, Liberia, Libyan Arab Jamahiriya, Madagascar, Malawi, Malaysia, Maldives, Mali, Mauritania, Mauritius, Mexico, Mongolia, Morocco, Mozambique, Myanmar, Namibia, Nepal, Nicaragua, Niger, Nigeria, Oman, Pakistan, Panama, Papua New Guinea, Paraguay, Peru, Philippines, Qatar, Saint Kitts and Nevis, Saint Lucia, Saint Vincent and the Grenadines, Samoa, Sao Tome and Principe, Saudi Arabia, Senegal, Seychelles, Sierra Leone, Singapore, Solomon Islands, Sri Lanka, Sudan, Suriname, Swaziland, Syrian Arab Republic, Tajikistan, Thailand, Timor-Leste, Togo, Tonga, Tunisia, Turkmenistan, Uganda, United Arab Emirates, United Republic of Tanzania, Uruguay, Uzbekistan, Vanuatu, Venezuela (Bolivarian Republic of), Viet Nam, Yemen, Zambia, Zimbabwe

---

* Subsequently, the delegation of Switzerland advised the Secretariat that it had intended to abstain. The voting tally above does not reflect this information.

Against:
      None.

Abstaining:
      Albania, Andorra, Argentina, Armenia, Australia, Austria, Belgium, Bosnia and Herzegovina, Bulgaria, Canada, Croatia, Cyprus, Czech Republic, Denmark, Estonia, Finland, France, Georgia, Germany, Greece, Hungary, Iceland, Ireland, Israel, Italy, Latvia, Liechtenstein, Lithuania, Luxembourg, Malta, Marshall Islands, Micronesia (Federated States of), Monaco, Montenegro, Netherlands, New Zealand, Norway, Palau, Poland, Portugal, Republic of Korea, Republic of Moldova, Romania, Russian Federation, San Marino, Serbia, Slovakia, Slovenia, South Africa, Spain, Sweden, the former Yugoslav Republic of Macedonia, Turkey, Tuvalu, Ukraine, United Kingdom, United States

Action by the First Committee

Date:	28 October 2011	Meeting:	23rd meeting
Vote:	119-0-56	Draft resolution:	A/C.1/66/L.25

Agenda item 96

66/27 Prevention of an arms race in outer space

Text

The General Assembly,

Recognizing the common interest of all mankind in the exploration and use of outer space for peaceful purposes,

Reaffirming the will of all States that the exploration and use of outer space, including the Moon and other celestial bodies, shall be for peaceful purposes and shall be carried out for the benefit and in the interest of all countries, irrespective of their degree of economic or scientific development,

Reaffirming also the provisions of articles III and IV of the Treaty on Principles Governing the Activities of States in the Exploration and Use of Outer Space, including the Moon and Other Celestial Bodies,[1]

Recalling the obligation of all States to observe the provisions of the Charter of the United Nations regarding the use or threat of use of force in their international relations, including in their space activities,

Reaffirming paragraph 80 of the Final Document of the Tenth Special Session of the General Assembly,[2] in which it is stated that in order to prevent an arms race in outer space, further measures should be taken and appropriate international negotiations held in accordance with the spirit of the Treaty,

Recalling its previous resolutions on this issue, and taking note of the proposals submitted to the General Assembly at its tenth special session and at its regular sessions, and of the recommendations made to the competent organs of the United Nations and to the Conference on Disarmament,

Recognizing that prevention of an arms race in outer space would avert a grave danger for international peace and security,

Emphasizing the paramount importance of strict compliance with existing arms limitation and disarmament agreements relevant to outer space, including bilateral agreements, and with the existing legal regime concerning the use of outer space,

Considering that wide participation in the legal regime applicable to outer space could contribute to enhancing its effectiveness,

Noting that the Ad Hoc Committee on the Prevention of an Arms Race in Outer Space, taking into account its previous efforts since its establishment in 1985 and seeking to enhance its functioning in qualitative terms, continued the examination and identification of various issues, existing agreements and

---

[1] United Nations, *Treaty Series*, vol. 610, No. 8843.
[2] Resolution S-10/2.

existing proposals, as well as future initiatives relevant to the prevention of an arms race in outer space,[3] and that this contributed to a better understanding of a number of problems and to a clearer perception of the various positions,

Noting also that there were no objections in principle in the Conference on Disarmament to the re-establishment of the Ad Hoc Committee, subject to re-examination of the mandate contained in the decision of the Conference on Disarmament of 13 February 1992,[4]

Emphasizing the mutually complementary nature of bilateral and multilateral efforts for the prevention of an arms race in outer space, and hoping that concrete results will emerge from those efforts as soon as possible,

Convinced that further measures should be examined in the search for effective and verifiable bilateral and multilateral agreements in order to prevent an arms race in outer space, including the weaponization of outer space,

Stressing that the growing use of outer space increases the need for greater transparency and better information on the part of the international community,

Recalling, in this context, its previous resolutions, in particular resolutions 45/55 B of 4 December 1990, 47/51 of 9 December 1992 and 48/74 A of 16 December 1993, in which, inter alia, it reaffirmed the importance of confidence-building measures as a means conducive to ensuring the attainment of the objective of the prevention of an arms race in outer space,

Conscious of the benefits of confidence- and security-building measures in the military field,

Recognizing that negotiations for the conclusion of an international agreement or agreements to prevent an arms race in outer space remain a priority task of the Conference on Disarmament and that the concrete proposals on confidence-building measures could form an integral part of such agreements,

Noting with satisfaction the constructive, structured and focused debate on the prevention of an arms race in outer space at the Conference on Disarmament in 2009, 2010 and 2011,

Taking note of the introduction by China and the Russian Federation at the Conference on Disarmament of the draft treaty on the prevention of the placement of weapons in outer space and of the threat or use of force against outer space objects,[5]

---

[3] *Official Records of the General Assembly, Forty-ninth Session, Supplement No. 27* (A/49/27), sect. III.D (para. 5 of the quoted text).

[4] CD/1125.

[5] See CD/1839.

Taking note also of the decision of the Conference on Disarmament to establish for its 2009 session a working group to discuss, substantially, without limitation, all issues related to the prevention of an arms race in outer space,

1. *Reaffirms* the importance and urgency of preventing an arms race in outer space and the readiness of all States to contribute to that common objective, in conformity with the provisions of the Treaty on Principles Governing the Activities of States in the Exploration and Use of Outer Space, including the Moon and Other Celestial Bodies;[1]

2. *Reaffirms its recognition*, as stated in the report of the Ad Hoc Committee on the Prevention of an Arms Race in Outer Space, that the legal regime applicable to outer space does not in and of itself guarantee the prevention of an arms race in outer space, that the regime plays a significant role in the prevention of an arms race in that environment, that there is a need to consolidate and reinforce that regime and enhance its effectiveness and that it is important to comply strictly with existing agreements, both bilateral and multilateral;[6]

3. *Emphasizes* the necessity of further measures with appropriate and effective provisions for verification to prevent an arms race in outer space;

4. *Calls upon* all States, in particular those with major space capabilities, to contribute actively to the objective of the peaceful use of outer space and of the prevention of an arms race in outer space and to refrain from actions contrary to that objective and to the relevant existing treaties in the interest of maintaining international peace and security and promoting international cooperation;

5. *Reiterates* that the Conference on Disarmament, as the sole multilateral disarmament negotiating forum, has the primary role in the negotiation of a multilateral agreement or agreements, as appropriate, on the prevention of an arms race in outer space in all its aspects;

6. *Invites* the Conference on Disarmament to establish a working group under its agenda item entitled "Prevention of an arms race in outer space" as early as possible during its 2012 session;

7. *Recognizes*, in this respect, the growing convergence of views on the elaboration of measures designed to strengthen transparency, confidence and security in the peaceful uses of outer space;

8. *Urges* States conducting activities in outer space, as well as States interested in conducting such activities, to keep the Conference on Disarmament informed of the progress of bilateral and multilateral negotiations on the matter, if any, so as to facilitate its work;

---

[6] See *Official Records of the General Assembly, Forty-fifth Session, Supplement No. 27* (A/45/27), para. 118 (para. 63 of the quoted text).

9.   *Decides* to include in the provisional agenda of its sixty-seventh session the item entitled "Prevention of an arms race in outer space".

Action by the General Assembly

Date: 2 December 2011   Meeting: 71st plenary meeting
Vote: 176-0-2   Report: A/66/410

Sponsors

Sri Lanka

Co-sponsors

Algeria, Armenia, Bangladesh, Bhutan, Brazil, China, Cuba, Democratic Republic of the Congo, Dominican Republic, Egypt, Guatemala, Honduras, India, Indonesia, Iran (Islamic Republic of), Kazakhstan, Libyan Arab Jamahiriya, Malaysia, Mongolia, Myanmar, Nepal, Pakistan, Russian Federation, Syrian Arab Republic, Tajikistan, Trinidad and Tobago

Recorded vote

In favour:

Afghanistan, Albania, Algeria, Andorra, Angola, Antigua and Barbuda, Argentina, Armenia, Australia, Austria, Azerbaijan, Bahamas, Bahrain, Bangladesh, Barbados, Belarus, Belgium, Belize, Benin, Bhutan, Bolivia (Plurinational State of), Bosnia and Herzegovina, Botswana, Brazil, Brunei Darussalam, Bulgaria, Burkina Faso, Cambodia, Cameroon, Canada, Cape Verde, Chad, Chile, China, Colombia, Comoros, Congo, Costa Rica, Côte d'Ivoire, Croatia, Cuba, Cyprus, Czech Republic, Democratic People's Republic of Korea, Denmark, Djibouti, Dominican Republic, Ecuador, Egypt, El Salvador, Estonia, Ethiopia, Fiji, Finland, France, Georgia, Germany, Ghana, Greece, Guatemala, Guinea, Guinea-Bissau, Guyana, Haiti, Honduras, Hungary, Iceland, India, Indonesia, Iran (Islamic Republic of), Iraq, Ireland, Italy, Jamaica, Japan, Jordan, Kazakhstan, Kenya, Kuwait, Kyrgyzstan, Lao People's Democratic Republic, Latvia, Lebanon, Lesotho, Liberia, Libyan Arab Jamahiriya, Liechtenstein, Lithuania, Luxembourg, Madagascar, Malawi, Malaysia, Maldives, Mali, Malta, Marshall Islands, Mauritania, Mauritius, Mexico, Micronesia (Federated States of), Monaco, Mongolia, Montenegro, Morocco, Mozambique, Myanmar, Namibia, Nepal, Netherlands, New Zealand, Nicaragua, Niger, Nigeria, Norway, Oman, Pakistan, Palau, Panama, Papua New Guinea, Paraguay, Peru, Philippines, Poland, Portugal, Qatar, Republic of Korea, Republic of Moldova, Romania, Russian Federation, Saint Kitts and Nevis, Saint Lucia, Saint Vincent and the Grenadines, Samoa, San Marino, Sao Tome and Principe, Saudi Arabia, Senegal, Serbia, Seychelles, Sierra Leone, Singapore, Slovakia,

Slovenia, Solomon Islands, South Africa, Spain, Sri Lanka, Sudan, Suriname, Swaziland, Sweden, Switzerland, Syrian Arab Republic, Tajikistan, Thailand, the former Yugoslav Republic of Macedonia, Timor-Leste, Togo, Tonga, Tunisia, Turkey, Turkmenistan, Tuvalu, Uganda, Ukraine, United Arab Emirates, United Kingdom, United Republic of Tanzania, Uruguay, Uzbekistan, Vanuatu, Venezuela (Bolivarian Republic of), Viet Nam, Yemen, Zambia, Zimbabwe

Against:
None.

Abstaining:
Israel, United States

Action by the First Committee

Date: 26 October 2011   Meeting: 21st meeting
Vote: 171-0-2   Draft resolution: A/C.1/66/L.14

Agenda item 98

66/28   Follow-up to nuclear disarmament obligations agreed to at the 1995, 2000 and 2010 Review Conferences of the Parties to the Treaty on the Non-Proliferation of Nuclear Weapons

Text

The General Assembly,

Recalling its various resolutions in the field of nuclear disarmament, including its recent resolutions 64/31 of 2 December 2009 and 65/56, 65/76 and 65/80 of 8 December 2010,

Bearing in mind its resolution 2373 (XXII) of 12 June 1968, the annex to which contains the Treaty on the Non-Proliferation of Nuclear Weapons,[1]

Noting the provisions of article VIII, paragraph 3, of the Treaty regarding the convening of review conferences at five-year intervals,

Recalling its resolution 50/70 Q of 12 December 1995, in which the General Assembly noted that the States parties to the Treaty affirmed the need to continue to move with determination towards the full realization and effective implementation of the provisions of the Treaty, and accordingly adopted a set of principles and objectives,

Recalling also that, on 11 May 1995, the 1995 Review and Extension Conference of the Parties to the Treaty on the Non-Proliferation of Nuclear Weapons adopted three decisions on, respectively, strengthening the review process for the Treaty, principles and objectives for nuclear non-proliferation and disarmament, and extension of the Treaty,[2]

Reaffirming the resolution on the Middle East adopted on 11 May 1995 by the 1995 Review and Extension Conference,[2] in which the Conference reaffirmed the importance of the early realization of universal adherence to the Treaty and placement of nuclear facilities under full-scope International Atomic Energy Agency safeguards,

Reaffirming also its resolution 55/33 D of 20 November 2000, in which the General Assembly welcomed the adoption by consensus on 19 May 2000 of the Final Document of the 2000 Review Conference of the Parties to the Treaty on the Non-Proliferation of Nuclear Weapons,[3] including, in particular, the documents entitled "Review of the operation of the Treaty, taking into

---

[1] See also United Nations, *Treaty Series*, vol. 729, No. 10485.

[2] See *1995 Review and Extension Conference of the Parties to the Treaty on the Non-Proliferation of Nuclear Weapons, Final Document, Part I* (NPT/CONF.1995/32 (Part I) and Corr.2), annex.

[3] *2000 Review Conference of the Parties to the Treaty on the Non-Proliferation of Nuclear Weapons, Final Document*, vols. I-III (NPT/CONF.2000/28 (Parts I–IV)).

..

account the decisions and the resolution adopted by the 1995 Review and Extension Conference" and "Improving the effectiveness of the strengthened review process for the Treaty",[4]

Taking into consideration the unequivocal undertaking by the nuclear-weapon States, in the Final Document of the 2000 Review Conference, to accomplish the total elimination of their nuclear arsenals leading to nuclear disarmament, to which all States parties to the Treaty are committed under article VI of the Treaty,

Welcoming the adoption by the 2010 Review Conference of the Parties to the Treaty on the Non-Proliferation of Nuclear Weapons of a substantive Final Document containing conclusions and recommendations for follow-on actions relating to nuclear disarmament,[5]

1. *Recalls* that the 2010 Review Conference of the Parties to the Treaty on the Non-Proliferation of Nuclear Weapons reaffirmed the continued validity of the practical steps agreed to in the Final Document of the 2000 Review Conference of the Parties to the Treaty on the Non-Proliferation of Nuclear Weapons;[6]

2. *Determines* to pursue practical steps for systematic and progressive efforts to implement article VI of the Treaty on the Non-Proliferation of Nuclear Weapons[1] and paragraphs 3 and 4 (*c*) of the decision on principles and objectives for nuclear non-proliferation and disarmament of the 1995 Review and Extension Conference of the Parties to the Treaty on the Non-Proliferation of Nuclear Weapons;[2]

3. *Calls for* practical steps, as agreed to at the 2000 Review Conference of the Parties to the Treaty on the Non-Proliferation of Nuclear Weapons, to be taken by all nuclear-weapon States, which would lead to nuclear disarmament in a way that promotes international stability and, based on the principle of undiminished security for all:

(*a*) Further efforts to be made by the nuclear-weapon States to reduce their nuclear arsenals unilaterally;

(*b*) Increased transparency by the nuclear-weapon States with regard to nuclear weapons capabilities and the implementation of agreements pursuant to article VI of the Treaty and as a voluntary confidence-building measure to support further progress in nuclear disarmament;

---

[4] Ibid., vol. I (NPT/CONF.2000/28 (Parts I and II)), part I.

[5] *2010 Review Conference of the Parties to the Treaty on the Non-Proliferation of Nuclear Weapons, Final Document*, vol. I (NPT/CONF.2010/50 (Vol. I)), part I, *Conclusions and recommendations for follow-on actions*, sect. I.

[6] *2000 Review Conference of the Parties to the Treaty on the Non-Proliferation of Nuclear Weapons, Final Document*, vol. I (NPT/CONF.2000/28 (Parts I and II)), part I, section entitled "Article VI and eighth to twelfth preambular paragraphs", para. 15.

(*c*)   The further reduction of non-strategic nuclear weapons, based on unilateral initiatives and as an integral part of the nuclear arms reduction and disarmament process;

(*d*)   Concrete agreed measures to reduce further the operational status of nuclear weapons systems;

(*e*)   A diminishing role for nuclear weapons in security policies so as to minimize the risk that these weapons will ever be used and to facilitate the process of their total elimination;

(*f*)   The engagement, as soon as appropriate, of all the nuclear-weapon States in the process leading to the total elimination of their nuclear weapons;

4.   *Notes* that the 2000 and 2010 Review Conferences agreed that legally binding security assurances by the five nuclear-weapon States to the non-nuclear-weapon States parties to the Treaty strengthen the nuclear non-proliferation regime;

5.   *Urges* the States parties to the Treaty to follow up on the implementation of the nuclear disarmament obligations under the Treaty agreed to at the 1995, 2000 and 2010 Review Conferences within the framework of review conferences and their preparatory committees;

6.   *Decides* to include in the provisional agenda of its sixty-eighth session an item entitled "Follow-up to nuclear disarmament obligations agreed to at the 1995, 2000 and 2010 Review Conferences of the Parties to the Treaty on the Non-Proliferation of Nuclear Weapons".

Action by the General Assembly

Date: 2 December 2011   Meeting: 71st plenary meeting
Vote: 118-52-6   Report: A/66/412
        113-9-48, p.p. 6*
        118-7-43, p.p. 9

Sponsors

Iran (Islamic Republic of)

Co-sponsors

Bangladesh, Sri Lanka

---

* Abbreviations: o.p.= operative paragraph; p.p.= preambular paragraph.

Recorded vote

As a whole

In favour:

Afghanistan, Algeria, Angola, Antigua and Barbuda, Argentina, Azerbaijan, Bahamas, Bahrain, Bangladesh, Barbados, Belarus, Belize, Benin, Bhutan, Bolivia (Plurinational State of), Botswana, Brazil, Brunei Darussalam, Burkina Faso, Cambodia, Cameroon, Cape Verde, Chad, Chile, Colombia, Comoros, Congo, Costa Rica, Côte d'Ivoire, Cuba, Democratic People's Republic of Korea, Djibouti, Dominican Republic, Ecuador, Egypt, El Salvador, Ethiopia, Fiji, Gabon, Ghana, Grenada, Guatemala, Guinea, Guinea-Bissau, Guyana, Haiti, Honduras, Indonesia, Iran (Islamic Republic of), Iraq, Jamaica, Jordan, Kazakhstan, Kenya, Kuwait, Kyrgyzstan, Lao People's Democratic Republic, Lebanon, Lesotho, Liberia, Libyan Arab Jamahiriya, Madagascar, Malawi, Malaysia, Maldives, Mali, Marshall Islands, Mauritania, Mauritius, Mexico, Mongolia, Morocco, Mozambique, Myanmar, Namibia, Nepal, Nicaragua, Niger, Nigeria, Oman, Papua New Guinea, Paraguay, Peru, Philippines, Qatar, Saint Kitts and Nevis, Saint Lucia, Saint Vincent and the Grenadines, Sao Tome and Principe, Saudi Arabia, Senegal, Seychelles, Sierra Leone, Singapore, Solomon Islands, South Africa, Sri Lanka, Sudan, Suriname, Swaziland, Syrian Arab Republic, Tajikistan, Thailand, Togo, Tunisia, Turkmenistan, Uganda, Ukraine, United Arab Emirates, United Republic of Tanzania, Uruguay, Uzbekistan, Vanuatu, Venezuela (Bolivarian Republic of), Viet Nam, Yemen, Zambia, Zimbabwe

Against:

Albania, Andorra, Australia, Austria, Belgium, Bosnia and Herzegovina, Bulgaria, Canada, Croatia, Cyprus, Czech Republic, Denmark, Estonia, Finland, France, Germany, Greece, Hungary, Iceland, Ireland, Israel, Italy, Japan, Latvia, Liechtenstein, Lithuania, Luxembourg, Malta, Micronesia (Federated States of), Monaco, Montenegro, Netherlands, New Zealand, Norway, Palau, Panama, Poland, Portugal, Republic of Korea, Republic of Moldova, Romania, Russian Federation, San Marino, Serbia, Slovakia, Slovenia, Spain, Sweden, Switzerland, the former Yugoslav Republic of Macedonia, United Kingdom, United States

Abstaining:

Armenia, China, India, Pakistan, Samoa, Tonga

Sixth preambular paragraph*

In favour:

Afghanistan, Algeria, Angola, Antigua and Barbuda, Argentina, Azerbaijan, Bahamas, Bahrain, Bangladesh, Barbados, Belarus, Belize, Benin, Bhutan, Bolivia (Plurinational State of), Botswana, Brazil, Brunei Darussalam, Cambodia, Cape Verde, Chile, Colombia, Comoros, Costa Rica, Côte d'Ivoire, Cuba, Democratic People's Republic of Korea, Djibouti, Dominican Republic, Ecuador, Egypt, El Salvador, Ethiopia, Fiji, Ghana, Grenada, Guatemala, Guinea, Guinea-Bissau, Guyana, Haiti, Honduras, Indonesia, Iran (Islamic Republic of), Iraq, Jamaica, Jordan, Kazakhstan, Kenya, Kuwait, Kyrgyzstan, Lao People's Democratic Republic, Lebanon, Lesotho, Liberia, Libyan Arab Jamahiriya, Madagascar, Malawi, Malaysia, Maldives, Mali, Mauritania, Mauritius, Mexico, Mongolia, Morocco, Mozambique, Myanmar, Nepal, New Zealand, Nicaragua, Niger, Nigeria, Oman, Papua New Guinea, Paraguay, Peru, Philippines, Qatar, Russian Federation, Saint Kitts and Nevis, Saint Lucia, Saint Vincent and the Grenadines, Sao Tome and Principe, Saudi Arabia, Senegal, Seychelles, Sierra Leone, Singapore, Solomon Islands, South Africa, Sri Lanka, Sudan, Suriname, Swaziland, Syrian Arab Republic, Tajikistan, Thailand, Togo, Tunisia, Turkmenistan, Uganda, Ukraine, United Arab Emirates, United Republic of Tanzania, Uruguay, Uzbekistan, Vanuatu, Venezuela (Bolivarian Republic of), Viet Nam, Yemen, Zambia, Zimbabwe

Against:

Canada, Israel, Japan, Marshall Islands, Micronesia (Federated States of), Palau, Panama, Republic of Korea, United States

Abstaining:

Albania, Andorra, Armenia, Australia, Austria, Belgium, Bosnia and Herzegovina, Bulgaria, Chad, Croatia, Cyprus, Czech Republic, Denmark, Estonia, Finland, France, Germany, Greece, Hungary, Iceland, India, Ireland, Italy, Latvia, Liechtenstein, Lithuania, Luxembourg, Malta, Monaco, Montenegro, Netherlands, Norway, Pakistan, Poland, Portugal, Republic of Moldova, Romania, Samoa, San Marino, Serbia, Slovakia, Slovenia, Spain, Sweden, Switzerland, the former Yugoslav Republic of Macedonia, Tonga, United Kingdom

---

* Subsequently, the delegations of Liechtenstein and Switzerland advised the Secretariat that they had intended to vote in favour; the delegation of the Republic of Korea advised the Secretariat that it had intended to abstain. The voting tally above does not reflect this information.

*Ninth preambular paragraph***

In favour:

Afghanistan, Algeria, Angola, Antigua and Barbuda, Argentina, Azerbaijan, Bahamas, Bahrain, Bangladesh, Barbados, Belarus, Belize, Bhutan, Bolivia (Plurinational State of), Botswana, Brazil, Brunei Darussalam, Burkina Faso, Cambodia, Cape Verde, Chad, Chile, China, Colombia, Comoros, Congo, Costa Rica, Côte d'Ivoire, Cuba, Democratic People's Republic of Korea, Djibouti, Dominican Republic, Ecuador, Egypt, El Salvador, Ethiopia, Fiji, Ghana, Grenada, Guatemala, Guinea, Guinea-Bissau, Guyana, Haiti, Honduras, Indonesia, Iran (Islamic Republic of), Iraq, Jamaica, Jordan, Kazakhstan, Kenya, Kuwait, Kyrgyzstan, Lao People's Democratic Republic, Lebanon, Lesotho, Liberia, Libyan Arab Jamahiriya, Liechtenstein, Madagascar, Malawi, Malaysia, Maldives, Mali, Mauritania, Mauritius, Mexico, Mongolia, Morocco, Mozambique, Myanmar, Namibia, Nepal, New Zealand, Nicaragua, Niger, Nigeria, Oman, Papua New Guinea, Paraguay, Peru, Philippines, Qatar, Russian Federation, Saint Kitts and Nevis, Saint Lucia, Saint Vincent and the Grenadines, Sao Tome and Principe, Saudi Arabia, Senegal, Seychelles, Sierra Leone, Singapore, Solomon Islands, South Africa, Sri Lanka, Sudan, Suriname, Swaziland, Syrian Arab Republic, Tajikistan, Thailand, Togo, Tunisia, Turkmenistan, Uganda, Ukraine, United Arab Emirates, United Republic of Tanzania, Uruguay, Uzbekistan, Vanuatu, Venezuela (Bolivarian Republic of), Viet Nam, Yemen, Zambia, Zimbabwe

Against:

Canada, France, Israel, Japan, Panama, United Kingdom, United States

Abstaining:

Albania, Andorra, Armenia, Australia, Austria, Belgium, Bosnia and Herzegovina, Bulgaria, Croatia, Cyprus, Czech Republic, Denmark, Estonia, Finland, Germany, Greece, Hungary, Iceland, India, Ireland, Italy, Latvia, Lithuania, Luxembourg, Malta, Monaco, Montenegro, Netherlands, Norway, Pakistan, Poland, Portugal, Republic of Moldova, Romania, San Marino, Serbia, Slovakia, Slovenia, Spain, Sweden, Switzerland, the former Yugoslav Republic of Macedonia, Tonga

Action by the First Committee

Date: 26 October 2011	Meeting: 21st meeting
Vote: 105-52-10	Draft resolution: A/C.1/66/L.3
110-7-47, p.p. 6	
111-7-44, p.p. 9	

** Subsequently, the delegation of Switzerland advised the Secretariat that it had intended to vote in favour. The voting tally above does not reflect this information.

Agenda item 98

66/29 Implementation of the Convention on the Prohibition of the Use, Stockpiling, Production and Transfer of Anti-personnel Mines and on Their Destruction

Text

The General Assembly,

Recalling its resolutions 54/54 B of 1 December 1999, 55/33 V of 20 November 2000, 56/24 M of 29 November 2001, 57/74 of 22 November 2002, 58/53 of 8 December 2003, 59/84 of 3 December 2004, 60/80 of 8 December 2005, 61/84 of 6 December 2006, 62/41 of 5 December 2007, 63/42 of 2 December 2008, 64/56 of 2 December 2009 and 65/48 of 8 December 2010,

Reaffirming its determination to put an end to the suffering and casualties caused by anti-personnel mines, which kill or injure thousands of people — women, girls, boys and men — every year, and which place people living in affected areas at risk and hinder the development of their communities,

Believing it necessary to do the utmost to contribute in an efficient and coordinated manner to facing the challenge of removing anti-personnel mines placed throughout the world and to assure their destruction,

Wishing to do the utmost in ensuring assistance for the care and rehabilitation, including the social and economic reintegration, of mine victims,

Noting with satisfaction the work undertaken to implement the Convention on the Prohibition of the Use, Stockpiling, Production and Transfer of Anti-personnel Mines and on Their Destruction[1] and the substantial progress made towards addressing the global anti-personnel landmine problem,

Recalling the first to tenth meetings of the States parties to the Convention, held in Maputo (1999),[2] Geneva (2000),[3] Managua (2001),[4] Geneva (2002),[5] Bangkok (2003),[6] Zagreb (2005),[7] Geneva (2006),[8] the Dead

---

[1] United Nations, *Treaty Series*, vol. 2056, No. 35597.
[2] See APLC/MSP.1/1999/1.
[3] See APLC/MSP.2/2000/1.
[4] See APLC/MSP.3/2001/1.
[5] See APLC/MSP.4/2002/1.
[6] See APLC/MSP.5/2003/5.
[7] See APLC/MSP.6/2005/5.
[8] See APLC/MSP.7/2006/5.

Sea (2007),[9] Geneva (2008)[10] and Geneva (2010)[11] and the First Review Conference of the States Parties to the Convention, held in Nairobi (2004),[12]

Recalling also the Second Review Conference of the States Parties to the Convention, held in Cartagena, Colombia, from 30 November to 4 December 2009,[13] at which the international community reviewed the implementation of the Convention and the States parties adopted the Cartagena Declaration[14] and the Cartagena Action Plan 2010–2014[15] to support enhanced implementation and promotion of the Convention,

Noting with satisfaction that additional States have ratified or acceded to the Convention, bringing the total number of States that have formally accepted the obligations of the Convention to one hundred and fifty-seven,

Emphasizing the desirability of attracting the adherence of all States to the Convention, and determined to work strenuously towards the promotion of its universalization and norms,

Noting with regret that anti-personnel mines continue to be used in some conflicts around the world, causing human suffering and impeding post-conflict development,

1. *Invites* all States that have not signed the Convention on the Prohibition of the Use, Stockpiling, Production and Transfer of Anti-personnel Mines and on Their Destruction[1] to accede to it without delay;

2. *Urges* all States that have signed but have not ratified the Convention to ratify it without delay;

3. *Stresses* the importance of the full and effective implementation of and compliance with the Convention, including through the continued implementation of the Cartagena Action Plan 2010–2014;[15]

4. *Urges* all States parties to provide the Secretary-General with complete and timely information as required under article 7 of the Convention in order to promote transparency and compliance with the Convention;

5. *Invites* all States that have not ratified the Convention or acceded to it to provide, on a voluntary basis, information to make global mine action efforts more effective;

6. *Renews its call upon* all States and other relevant parties to work together to promote, support and advance the care, rehabilitation and social and economic reintegration of mine victims, mine risk education programmes

---

9   See APLC/MSP.8/2007/6.
10   See APLC/MSP.9/2008/4 and Corr.1 and 2.
11   See APLC/MSP.10/2010/7.
12   See APLC/CONF/2004/5 and Corr.1.
13   See APLC/CONF/2009/9.
14   Ibid., part IV.
15   Ibid., part III.

and the removal and destruction of anti-personnel mines placed or stockpiled throughout the world;

7.   *Urges* all States to remain seized of the issue at the highest political level and, where in a position to do so, to promote adherence to the Convention through bilateral, subregional, regional and multilateral contacts, outreach, seminars and other means;

8.   *Reiterates its invitation and encouragement* to all interested States, the United Nations, other relevant international organizations or institutions, regional organizations, the International Committee of the Red Cross and relevant non-governmental organizations to attend the Eleventh Meeting of the States Parties to the Convention, to be held in Phnom Penh from 28 November to 2 December 2011, and to participate in the future meeting programme of the Convention;

9.   *Requests* the Secretary-General, in accordance with article 11, paragraph 2, of the Convention, to undertake the preparations necessary to convene the Twelfth Meeting of the States Parties to the Convention and, on behalf of the States parties and in accordance with article 11, paragraph 4, of the Convention, to invite States not parties to the Convention, as well as the United Nations, other relevant international organizations or institutions, regional organizations, the International Committee of the Red Cross and relevant non-governmental organizations, to attend the Twelfth Meeting of the States Parties and future meetings as observers;

10.   *Decides* to remain seized of the matter.

Action by the General Assembly

Date: 2 December 2011   Meeting: 71st plenary meeting
Vote: 162-0-18   Report: A/66/412

Sponsors

Albania, Cambodia, Norway

Recorded vote

In favour:

Afghanistan, Albania, Algeria, Andorra, Angola, Antigua and Barbuda, Argentina, Armenia, Australia, Austria, Azerbaijan, Bahamas, Bahrain, Bangladesh, Barbados, Belarus, Belgium, Belize, Benin, Bhutan, Bolivia (Plurinational State of), Bosnia and Herzegovina, Botswana, Brazil, Brunei Darussalam, Bulgaria, Burkina Faso, Cambodia, Cameroon, Canada, Cape Verde, Chad, Chile, China, Colombia, Comoros, Congo, Costa Rica, Côte d'Ivoire, Croatia, Cyprus, Czech Republic, Denmark, Djibouti, Dominican Republic, Ecuador, El Salvador, Estonia, Ethiopia, Fiji, Finland, France, Gabon, Georgia, Germany, Ghana, Greece, Grenada, Guatemala, Guinea, Guinea-Bissau, Guyana, Haiti,

Honduras, Hungary, Iceland, Indonesia, Iraq, Ireland, Italy, Jamaica, Japan, Jordan, Kazakhstan, Kenya, Kuwait, Kyrgyzstan, Lao People's Democratic Republic, Latvia, Lesotho, Liberia, Liechtenstein, Lithuania, Luxembourg, Madagascar, Malawi, Malaysia, Maldives, Mali, Malta, Marshall Islands, Mauritania, Mauritius, Mexico, Micronesia (Federated States of), Monaco, Mongolia, Montenegro, Morocco, Mozambique, Namibia, Netherlands, New Zealand, Nicaragua, Niger, Nigeria, Norway, Oman, Palau, Panama, Papua New Guinea, Paraguay, Peru, Philippines, Poland, Portugal, Qatar, Republic of Moldova, Romania, Saint Kitts and Nevis, Saint Lucia, Saint Vincent and the Grenadines, Samoa, San Marino, Sao Tome and Principe, Senegal, Serbia, Seychelles, Sierra Leone, Singapore, Slovakia, Slovenia, Solomon Islands, South Africa, Spain, Sri Lanka, Sudan, Suriname, Swaziland, Sweden, Switzerland, Tajikistan, Thailand, the former Yugoslav Republic of Macedonia, Timor-Leste, Togo, Tonga, Tunisia, Turkey, Turkmenistan, Tuvalu, Uganda, Ukraine, United Arab Emirates, United Kingdom, United Republic of Tanzania, Uruguay, Vanuatu, Venezuela (Bolivarian Republic of), Yemen, Zambia, Zimbabwe

Against:

None.

Abstaining:

Cuba, Democratic People's Republic of Korea, Egypt, India, Iran (Islamic Republic of), Israel, Lebanon, Libyan Arab Jamahiriya, Myanmar, Nepal, Pakistan, Republic of Korea, Russian Federation, Saudi Arabia, Syrian Arab Republic, United States, Uzbekistan, Viet Nam

Action by the First Committee

Date: 28 October 2011   Meeting: 23rd meeting
Vote: 155-0-17   Draft resolution: A/C.1/66/L.4

Agenda item 98

66/30   Relationship between disarmament and development

Text

The General Assembly,

Recalling that the Charter of the United Nations envisages the establishment and maintenance of international peace and security with the least diversion for armaments of the world's human and economic resources,

Recalling also the provisions of the Final Document of the Tenth Special Session of the General Assembly concerning the relationship between disarmament and development,[1] as well as the adoption on 11 September 1987 of the Final Document of the International Conference on the Relationship between Disarmament and Development,[2]

Recalling further its resolutions 49/75 J of 15 December 1994, 50/70 G of 12 December 1995, 51/45 D of 10 December 1996, 52/38 D of 9 December 1997, 53/77 K of 4 December 1998, 54/54 T of 1 December 1999, 55/33 L of 20 November 2000, 56/24 E of 29 November 2001, 57/65 of 22 November 2002, 59/78 of 3 December 2004, 60/61 of 8 December 2005, 61/64 of 6 December 2006, 62/48 of 5 December 2007, 63/52 of 2 December 2008, 64/32 of 2 December 2009 and 65/52 of 8 December 2010, and its decision 58/520 of 8 December 2003,

Bearing in mind the Final Document of the Twelfth Conference of Heads of State or Government of Non-Aligned Countries, held in Durban, South Africa, from 29 August to 3 September 1998,[3] and the Final Document of the Thirteenth Ministerial Conference of the Movement of Non-Aligned Countries, held in Cartagena, Colombia, on 8 and 9 April 2000,[4] as well as the Final Documents of the Fifteenth Summit Conference of Heads of State and Government of the Movement of Non-Aligned Countries, held in Sharm el-Sheikh, Egypt, from 11 to 16 July 2009,[5] and of the Sixteenth Ministerial Conference and Commemorative Meeting of the Movement of Non-Aligned Countries, held in Bali, Indonesia, from 23 to 27 May 2011,[6]

Mindful of the changes in international relations that have taken place since the adoption on 11 September 1987 of the Final Document of the International Conference on the Relationship between Disarmament and

---

[1] See resolution S-10/2.

[2] See *Report of the International Conference on the Relationship between Disarmament and Development, New York, 24 August 11–September 1987* (A/CONF.130/39).

[3] A/53/667-S/1998/1071, annex I.

[4] A/54/917-S/2000/580, annex.

[5] A/63/965-S/2009/514, annex.

[6] A/65/896-S/2011/407, annex I.

Development, including the development agenda that has emerged over the past decade,

Bearing in mind the new challenges for the international community in the fields of development, poverty eradication and the elimination of the diseases that afflict humanity,

Stressing the importance of the symbiotic relationship between disarmament and development and the important role of security in this connection, and concerned at increasing global military expenditure, which could otherwise be spent on development needs,

Recalling the report of the Group of Governmental Experts on the relationship between disarmament and development[7] and its reappraisal of this significant issue in the current international context,

Bearing in mind the importance of following up on the implementation of the action programme adopted at the 1987 International Conference on the Relationship between Disarmament and Development,[2]

1.   *Stresses* the central role of the United Nations in the disarmament-development relationship, and requests the Secretary-General to strengthen further the role of the Organization in this field, in particular the high-level Steering Group on Disarmament and Development, in order to ensure continued and effective coordination and close cooperation between the relevant United Nations departments, agencies and sub-agencies;

2.   *Requests* the Secretary-General to continue to take action, through appropriate organs and within available resources, for the implementation of the action programme adopted at the 1987 International Conference on the Relationship between Disarmament and Development;[2]

3.   *Urges* the international community to devote part of the resources made available by the implementation of disarmament and arms limitation agreements to economic and social development, with a view to reducing the ever-widening gap between developed and developing countries;

4.   *Encourages* the international community to achieve the Millennium Development Goals and to make reference to the contribution that disarmament could provide in meeting them when it reviews its progress towards this purpose in 2012, as well as to make greater efforts to integrate disarmament, humanitarian and development activities;

5.   *Encourages* the relevant regional and subregional organizations and institutions, non-governmental organizations and research institutes to incorporate issues related to the relationship between disarmament and development into their agendas and, in this regard, to take into account the

---

[7] See A/59/119.

report of the Group of Governmental Experts on the relationship between disarmament and development;[7]

6.   *Reiterates its invitation* to Member States to provide the Secretary-General with information regarding measures and efforts to devote part of the resources made available by the implementation of disarmament and arms limitation agreements to economic and social development, with a view to reducing the ever-widening gap between developed and developing countries;

7.   *Requests* the Secretary-General to report to the General Assembly at its sixty-seventh session on the implementation of the present resolution, including the information provided by Member States pursuant to paragraph 6 above;

8.   *Decides* to include in the provisional agenda of its sixty-seventh session the item entitled "Relationship between disarmament and development".

Action by the General Assembly

Date: 2 December 2011   Meeting: 71st plenary meeting
Vote: Adopted without a vote   Report: A/66/412

Sponsors

Indonesia, on behalf of the States Members of the United Nations that are members of the Movement of Non-Aligned Countries

Co-sponsors

Bangladesh, Congo

Action by the First Committee

Date: 27 October 2011   Meeting: 22nd meeting
Vote: Adopted without a vote   Draft resolution: A/C.1/66/L.6

Agenda item 98

66/31   Observance of environmental norms in the drafting and implementation of agreements on disarmament and arms control

Text

The General Assembly,

Recalling its resolutions 50/70 M of 12 December 1995, 51/45 E of 10 December 1996, 52/38 E of 9 December 1997, 53/77 J of 4 December 1998, 54/54 S of 1 December 1999, 55/33 K of 20 November 2000, 56/24 F of 29 November 2001, 57/64 of 22 November 2002, 58/45 of 8 December 2003, 59/68 of 3 December 2004, 60/60 of 8 December 2005, 61/63 of 6 December 2006, 62/28 of 5 December 2007, 63/51 of 2 December 2008, 64/33 of 2 December 2009 and 65/53 of 8 December 2010,

Emphasizing the importance of the observance of environmental norms in the preparation and implementation of disarmament and arms limitation agreements,

Recognizing that it is necessary to take duly into account the agreements adopted at the United Nations Conference on Environment and Development, as well as prior relevant agreements, in the drafting and implementation of agreements on disarmament and arms limitation,

Taking note of the report of the Secretary-General submitted pursuant to resolution 65/53,[1]

Noting that the Fifteenth Summit Conference of Heads of State and Government of the Movement of Non-Aligned Countries, held in Sharm el-Sheikh, Egypt, from 11 to 16 July 2009, and the Sixteenth Ministerial Conference and Commemorative Meeting of the Movement of Non-Aligned Countries, held in Bali, Indonesia, from 23 to 27 May 2011, welcomed the adoption by the General Assembly, without a vote, of resolutions 63/51 and 65/53, on the observance of environmental norms in the drafting and the implementation of agreements on disarmament and arms control,

Mindful of the detrimental environmental effects of the use of nuclear weapons,

1.   *Reaffirms* that international disarmament forums should take fully into account the relevant environmental norms in negotiating treaties and agreements on disarmament and arms limitation and that all States, through their actions, should contribute fully to ensuring compliance with the aforementioned norms in the implementation of treaties and conventions to which they are parties;

---

[1]   A/66/97 and Add.1.

2.   *Calls upon* States to adopt unilateral, bilateral, regional and multilateral measures so as to contribute to ensuring the application of scientific and technological progress within the framework of international security, disarmament and other related spheres, without detriment to the environment or to its effective contribution to attaining sustainable development;

3.   *Welcomes* the information provided by Member States on the implementation of the measures they have adopted to promote the objectives envisaged in the present resolution;[1]

4.   *Invites* all Member States to communicate to the Secretary-General information on the measures they have adopted to promote the objectives envisaged in the present resolution, and requests the Secretary-General to submit a report containing that information to the General Assembly at its sixty-seventh session;

5.   *Decides* to include in the provisional agenda of its sixty-seventh session the item entitled "Observance of environmental norms in the drafting and implementation of agreements on disarmament and arms control".

Action by the General Assembly

Date: 2 December 2011   Meeting: 71st plenary meeting
Vote: Adopted without a vote   Report: A/66/412

Sponsors

Indonesia, on behalf of the States Members of the United Nations that are members of the Movement of Non-Aligned Countries

Co-sponsors

Bangladesh

Action by the First Committee

Date: 27 October 2011   Meeting: 22nd meeting
Vote: Adopted without a vote   Draft resolution: A/C.1/66/L.7

Agenda item 98

66/32 Promotion of multilateralism in the area of disarmament and non-proliferation

Text

The General Assembly,

Determined to foster strict respect for the purposes and principles enshrined in the Charter of the United Nations,

Recalling its resolution 56/24 T of 29 November 2001 on multilateral cooperation in the area of disarmament and non-proliferation and global efforts against terrorism and other relevant resolutions, as well as its resolutions 57/63 of 22 November 2002, 58/44 of 8 December 2003, 59/69 of 3 December 2004, 60/59 of 8 December 2005, 61/62 of 6 December 2006, 62/27 of 5 December 2007, 63/50 of 2 December 2008, 64/34 of 2 December 2009 and 65/54 of 8 December 2010 on the promotion of multilateralism in the area of disarmament and non-proliferation,

Recalling also the purpose of the United Nations to maintain international peace and security and, to that end, to take effective collective measures for the prevention and removal of threats to the peace and for the suppression of acts of aggression or other breaches of the peace, and to bring about by peaceful means, and in conformity with the principles of justice and international law, adjustment or settlement of international disputes or situations which might lead to a breach of the peace, as enshrined in the Charter,

Recalling further the United Nations Millennium Declaration,[1] which states, inter alia, that the responsibility for managing worldwide economic and social development, as well as threats to international peace and security, must be shared among the nations of the world and should be exercised multilaterally and that, as the most universal and most representative organization in the world, the United Nations must play the central role,

Convinced that, in the globalization era and with the information revolution, arms regulation, non-proliferation and disarmament problems are more than ever the concern of all countries in the world, which are affected in one way or another by these problems and, therefore, should have the possibility to participate in the negotiations that arise to tackle them,

Bearing in mind the existence of a broad structure of disarmament and arms regulation agreements resulting from non-discriminatory and transparent multilateral negotiations with the participation of a large number of countries, regardless of their size and power,

---

[1] See resolution 55/2.

Aware of the need to advance further in the field of arms regulation, non-proliferation and disarmament on the basis of universal, multilateral, non-discriminatory and transparent negotiations with the goal of reaching general and complete disarmament under strict international control,

Recognizing the complementarity of bilateral, plurilateral and multilateral negotiations on disarmament,

Recognizing also that the proliferation and development of weapons of mass destruction, including nuclear weapons, are among the most immediate threats to international peace and security which need to be dealt with, with the highest priority,

Considering that the multilateral disarmament agreements provide the mechanism for States parties to consult one another and to cooperate in solving any problems which may arise in relation to the objective of, or in the application of, the provisions of the agreements and that such consultations and cooperation may also be undertaken through appropriate international procedures within the framework of the United Nations and in accordance with the Charter,

Stressing that international cooperation, the peaceful settlement of disputes, dialogue and confidence-building measures would make an essential contribution to the creation of multilateral and bilateral friendly relations among peoples and nations,

Being concerned at the continuous erosion of multilateralism in the field of arms regulation, non-proliferation and disarmament, and recognizing that a resort to unilateral actions by Member States in resolving their security concerns would jeopardize international peace and security and undermine confidence in the international security system as well as the foundations of the United Nations itself,

Noting that the Fifteenth Summit Conference of Heads of State and Government of the Movement of Non-Aligned Countries, held in Sharm el-Sheikh, Egypt, from 11 to 16 July 2009, and the Sixteenth Ministerial Conference and Commemorative Meeting of the Movement of Non-Aligned Countries, held in Bali, Indonesia, from 23 to 27 May 2011, welcomed the adoption of resolutions 63/50 and 65/54, on the promotion of multilateralism in the area of disarmament and non-proliferation, and underlined the fact that multilateralism and multilaterally agreed solutions, in accordance with the Charter, provide the only sustainable method of addressing disarmament and international security issues,

Reaffirming the absolute validity of multilateral diplomacy in the field of disarmament and non-proliferation, and determined to promote multilateralism as an essential way to develop arms regulation and disarmament negotiations,

1.   *Reaffirms* multilateralism as the core principle in negotiations in the area of disarmament and non-proliferation with a view to maintaining and strengthening universal norms and enlarging their scope;

2.   *Also reaffirms* multilateralism as the core principle in resolving disarmament and non-proliferation concerns;

3.   *Urges* the participation of all interested States in multilateral negotiations on arms regulation, non-proliferation and disarmament in a non-discriminatory and transparent manner;

4.   *Underlines* the importance of preserving the existing agreements on arms regulation and disarmament, which constitute an expression of the results of international cooperation and multilateral negotiations in response to the challenges facing mankind;

5.   *Calls once again upon* all Member States to renew and fulfil their individual and collective commitments to multilateral cooperation as an important means of pursuing and achieving their common objectives in the area of disarmament and non-proliferation;

6.   *Requests* the States parties to the relevant instruments on weapons of mass destruction to consult and cooperate among themselves in resolving their concerns with regard to cases of non-compliance as well as on implementation, in accordance with the procedures defined in those instruments, and to refrain from resorting or threatening to resort to unilateral actions or directing unverified non-compliance accusations against one another to resolve their concerns;

7.   *Takes note* of the report of the Secretary-General containing the replies of Member States on the promotion of multilateralism in the area of disarmament and non-proliferation, submitted pursuant to resolution 65/54;[2]

8.   *Requests* the Secretary-General to seek the views of Member States on the issue of the promotion of multilateralism in the area of disarmament and non-proliferation and to submit a report thereon to the General Assembly at its sixty-seventh session;

9.   *Decides* to include in the provisional agenda of its sixty-seventh session the item entitled "Promotion of multilateralism in the area of disarmament and non-proliferation".

Action by the General Assembly

Date: 2 December 2011   Meeting: 71st plenary meeting
Vote: 125-5-48   Report: A/66/412

---

[2] A/66/111 and Add.1.

Sponsors

Indonesia, on behalf of the States Members of the United Nations that are members of the Movement of Non-Aligned Countries

Co-sponsors

Bangladesh, Brazil, Congo

Recorded vote*

In favour:

Afghanistan, Algeria, Angola, Antigua and Barbuda, Argentina, Azerbaijan, Bahamas, Bahrain, Bangladesh, Barbados, Belarus, Belize, Benin, Bhutan, Bolivia (Plurinational State of), Botswana, Brazil, Brunei Darussalam, Burkina Faso, Cambodia, Cameroon, Cape Verde, Chad, Chile, China, Colombia, Comoros, Congo, Costa Rica, Côte d'Ivoire, Cuba, Democratic People's Republic of Korea, Djibouti, Dominican Republic, Ecuador, Egypt, Ethiopia, Fiji, Gabon, Ghana, Grenada, Guatemala, Guinea, Guinea-Bissau, Guyana, Haiti, Honduras, Hungary, India, Indonesia, Iran (Islamic Republic of), Iraq, Jamaica, Jordan, Kazakhstan, Kenya, Kuwait, Kyrgyzstan, Lao People's Democratic Republic, Lebanon, Lesotho, Liberia, Libyan Arab Jamahiriya, Madagascar, Malawi, Malaysia, Maldives, Mali, Marshall Islands, Mauritania, Mauritius, Mexico, Mongolia, Morocco, Mozambique, Myanmar, Namibia, Nepal, Nicaragua, Niger, Nigeria, Oman, Pakistan, Panama, Papua New Guinea, Paraguay, Peru, Philippines, Qatar, Russian Federation, Saint Kitts and Nevis, Saint Lucia, Saint Vincent and the Grenadines, Sao Tome and Principe, Saudi Arabia, Senegal, Serbia, Seychelles, Sierra Leone, Singapore, Solomon Islands, Sri Lanka, Sudan, Suriname, Swaziland, Syrian Arab Republic, Tajikistan, Thailand, Timor-Leste, Togo, Tunisia, Turkmenistan, Tuvalu, Uganda, Ukraine, United Arab Emirates, United Republic of Tanzania, Uruguay, Uzbekistan, Vanuatu, Venezuela (Bolivarian Republic of), Viet Nam, Yemen, Zambia, Zimbabwe

Against:

Israel, Micronesia (Federated States of), Palau, United Kingdom, United States

---

* Subsequently, the delegation of South Africa advised the Secretariat that it had intended to vote in favour; the delegation of Montenegro advised the Secretariat that it had intended to vote against; and the delegation of Hungary advised the Secretariat that it had intended to abstain. The voting tally above does not reflect this information.

Abstaining:

Albania, Andorra, Armenia, Australia, Austria, Belgium, Bosnia and Herzegovina, Bulgaria, Canada, Croatia, Cyprus, Czech Republic, Denmark, El Salvador, Estonia, Finland, France, Georgia, Germany, Greece, Iceland, Ireland, Italy, Japan, Latvia, Liechtenstein, Lithuania, Luxembourg, Malta, Monaco, Montenegro, Netherlands, New Zealand, Norway, Poland, Portugal, Republic of Korea, Republic of Moldova, Romania, Samoa, San Marino, Slovakia, Slovenia, Spain, Sweden, Switzerland, the former Yugoslav Republic of Macedonia, Turkey

Action by the First Committee

Date: 27 October 2011   Meeting: 22nd meeting
Vote: 120-4-49   Draft resolution: A/C.1/66/L.8

Agenda item 98

66/33   2015 Review Conference of the Parties to the Treaty on the Non-Proliferation of Nuclear Weapons and its Preparatory Committee

Text

The General Assembly,

Recalling its resolution 2373 (XXII) of 12 June 1968, the annex to which contains the Treaty on the Non-Proliferation of Nuclear Weapons,[1]

Noting the provisions of article VIII, paragraph 3, of the Treaty regarding the convening of review conferences at five-year intervals,

Recalling the outcomes of the 1995 Review and Extension Conference of the Parties to the Treaty on the Non-Proliferation of Nuclear Weapons[2] and of the 2000 Review Conference of the Parties to the Treaty,[3]

Recalling also the decision of the 2000 Review Conference of the Parties to the Treaty on improving the effectiveness of the strengthened review process for the Treaty,[4] which reaffirmed the provisions in the decision on strengthening the review process for the Treaty, adopted by the 1995 Review and Extension Conference of the Parties to the Treaty,[5]

Noting the decision on strengthening the review process for the Treaty, in which it was agreed that review conferences should continue to be held every five years, and noting that, accordingly, the next review conference should be held in 2015,

Recalling the decision of the 2000 Review Conference that three sessions of the Preparatory Committee should be held in the years prior to the review conference,[4]

Welcoming the successful outcome of the 2010 Review Conference of the Parties to the Treaty on the Non-Proliferation of Nuclear Weapons, held

---

[1] See also United Nations, *Treaty Series*, vol. 729, No. 10485.

[2] See *1995 Review and Extension Conference of the Parties to the Treaty on the Non-Proliferation of Nuclear Weapons, Final Document, Part I* (NPT/CONF.1995/32 (Part I) and Corr.2).

[3] See *2000 Review Conference of the Parties to the Treaty on the Non-Proliferation of Nuclear Weapons, Final Document*, vols. I–III (NPT/CONF.2000/28 (Parts I–IV)).

[4] Ibid., vol. I (NPT/CONF.2000/28 (Parts I and II)), part I.

[5] *1995 Review and Extension Conference of the Parties to the Treaty on the Non-Proliferation of Nuclear Weapons, Final Document, Part I* (NPT/CONF.1995/32 (Part I) and Corr.2), annex, decision 1.

from 3 to 28 May 2010,[6] and reaffirming the necessity of fully implementing the follow-on actions adopted at the Review Conference,[7]

1. *Takes note* of the decision of the parties to the Treaty on the Non-Proliferation of Nuclear Weapons,[1] following appropriate consultations, to hold the first session of the Preparatory Committee in Vienna from 30 April to 11 May 2012;

2. *Requests* the Secretary-General to render the necessary assistance and to provide such services, including summary records, as may be required for the 2015 Review Conference of the Parties to the Treaty on the Non-Proliferation of Nuclear Weapons and its Preparatory Committee.

Action by the General Assembly

Date: 2 December 2011   Meeting: 71st plenary meeting
Vote: 175-0-3   Report: A/66/412
     174-0-3, p.p. 7

Sponsors

Philippines

Recorded vote

As a whole*

In favour:

Afghanistan, Albania, Algeria, Andorra, Angola, Antigua and Barbuda, Argentina, Armenia, Australia, Austria, Azerbaijan, Bahamas, Bahrain, Bangladesh, Barbados, Belarus, Belgium, Belize, Benin, Bhutan, Bolivia (Plurinational State of), Bosnia and Herzegovina, Botswana, Brazil, Brunei Darussalam, Bulgaria, Burkina Faso, Cambodia, Cameroon, Canada, Cape Verde, Chad, Chile, China, Colombia, Comoros, Congo, Costa Rica, Côte d'Ivoire, Croatia, Cuba, Cyprus, Czech Republic, Denmark, Djibouti, Dominican Republic, Ecuador, Egypt, El Salvador, Estonia, Ethiopia, Fiji, Finland, France, Gabon, Georgia, Germany, Ghana, Greece, Grenada, Guatemala, Guinea, Guinea-Bissau, Guyana, Haiti, Honduras, Hungary, Iceland, Indonesia, Iran (Islamic Republic of), Iraq, Ireland, Italy, Jamaica, Japan, Jordan, Kazakhstan, Kenya, Kuwait, Kyrgyzstan, Lao People's Democratic Republic, Latvia, Lebanon, Lesotho, Liberia, Libyan Arab Jamahiriya, Liechtenstein,

---

[6] *2010 Review Conference of the Parties to the Treaty on the Non-Proliferation of Nuclear Weapons, Final Document*, vols. I–III (NPT/CONF.2010/50 (Vols. I–III)).

[7] Ibid., vol. I (NPT/CONF.2010/50 (Vol. I)), part I, *Conclusions and recommendations for follow-on actions*.

* Subsequently, the delegation of the Democratic People's Republic of Korea advised the Secretariat that it had intended to abstain. The voting tally above does not reflect this information.

Lithuania, Luxembourg, Madagascar, Malawi, Malaysia, Maldives, Mali, Malta, Marshall Islands, Mauritania, Mauritius, Mexico, Micronesia (Federated States of), Monaco, Mongolia, Montenegro, Morocco, Mozambique, Myanmar, Namibia, Nepal, Netherlands, New Zealand, Nicaragua, Niger, Nigeria, Norway, Oman, Palau, Panama, Papua New Guinea, Paraguay, Peru, Philippines, Poland, Portugal, Qatar, Republic of Korea, Republic of Moldova, Romania, Russian Federation, Saint Kitts and Nevis, Saint Lucia, Saint Vincent and the Grenadines, Samoa, San Marino, Sao Tome and Principe, Saudi Arabia, Senegal, Serbia, Seychelles, Sierra Leone, Singapore, Slovakia, Slovenia, Solomon Islands, South Africa, Spain, Sri Lanka, Sudan, Suriname, Swaziland, Sweden, Switzerland, Syrian Arab Republic, Tajikistan, Thailand, the former Yugoslav Republic of Macedonia, Timor-Leste, Togo, Tonga, Tunisia, Turkey, Turkmenistan, Uganda, Ukraine, United Arab Emirates, United Kingdom, United Republic of Tanzania, United States, Uruguay, Uzbekistan, Vanuatu, Venezuela (Bolivarian Republic of), Viet Nam, Yemen, Zambia, Zimbabwe

Against:
None.

Abstaining:
India, Israel, Pakistan

*Seventh preambular paragraph***

In favour:

Afghanistan, Albania, Algeria, Andorra, Angola, Antigua and Barbuda, Argentina, Armenia, Australia, Austria, Azerbaijan, Bahamas, Bahrain, Bangladesh, Barbados, Belarus, Belgium, Belize, Benin, Bhutan, Bolivia (Plurinational State of), Bosnia and Herzegovina, Botswana, Brazil, Brunei Darussalam, Bulgaria, Burkina Faso, Cambodia, Canada, Cape Verde, Chad, Chile, China, Colombia, Comoros, Congo, Costa Rica, Côte d'Ivoire, Croatia, Cuba, Cyprus, Czech Republic, Denmark, Djibouti, Dominican Republic, Ecuador, Egypt, El Salvador, Estonia, Ethiopia, Fiji, Finland, France, Gabon, Georgia, Germany, Ghana, Greece, Grenada, Guatemala, Guinea, Guinea-Bissau, Guyana, Haiti, Honduras, Hungary, Iceland, Indonesia, Iran (Islamic Republic of), Iraq, Ireland, Italy, Jamaica, Japan, Jordan, Kazakhstan, Kenya, Kuwait, Kyrgyzstan, Lao People's Democratic Republic, Latvia, Lebanon, Lesotho, Liberia, Libyan Arab Jamahiriya, Liechtenstein, Lithuania, Luxembourg, Madagascar, Malawi, Malaysia, Maldives, Mali, Malta,

---

** Subsequently, the delegation of the Democratic People's Republic of Korea advised the Secretariat that it had intended to vote against. The voting tally above does not reflect this information.

Marshall Islands, Mauritania, Mauritius, Mexico, Micronesia (Federated States of), Monaco, Mongolia, Montenegro, Morocco, Mozambique, Myanmar, Namibia, Nepal, Netherlands, New Zealand, Nicaragua, Niger, Nigeria, Norway, Oman, Palau, Panama, Papua New Guinea, Paraguay, Peru, Philippines, Poland, Portugal, Qatar, Republic of Korea, Republic of Moldova, Romania, Russian Federation, Saint Kitts and Nevis, Saint Lucia, Saint Vincent and the Grenadines, Samoa, San Marino, Sao Tome and Principe, Saudi Arabia, Senegal, Serbia, Seychelles, Sierra Leone, Singapore, Slovakia, Slovenia, Solomon Islands, South Africa, Spain, Sri Lanka, Sudan, Suriname, Swaziland, Sweden, Switzerland, Syrian Arab Republic, Tajikistan, Thailand, the former Yugoslav Republic of Macedonia, Timor-Leste, Togo, Tonga, Tunisia, Turkey, Turkmenistan, Uganda, Ukraine, United Arab Emirates, United Kingdom, United Republic of Tanzania, United States, Uruguay, Uzbekistan, Vanuatu, Venezuela (Bolivarian Republic of), Viet Nam, Yemen, Zambia, Zimbabwe

Against:
   None.

Abstaining:
   India, Israel, Pakistan

Action by the First Committee

Date: 28 October 2011	Meeting: 23rd meeting
Vote: 169-0-3	Draft resolution: A/C.1/66/L.15
169-0-3, p.p. 7	

Agenda item 98

66/34 Assistance to States for curbing the illicit traffic in small arms and light weapons and collecting them

Text

The General Assembly,

Recalling its resolution 65/50 of 8 December 2010 on assistance to States for curbing the illicit traffic in small arms and light weapons and collecting them,

Deeply concerned by the magnitude of human casualty and suffering, especially among children, caused by the illicit proliferation and use of small arms and light weapons,

Concerned by the negative impact that the illicit proliferation and use of those weapons continue to have on the efforts of States in the Sahelo-Saharan subregion in the areas of poverty eradication, sustainable development and the maintenance of peace, security and stability,

Bearing in mind the Bamako Declaration on an African Common Position on the Illicit Proliferation, Circulation and Trafficking of Small Arms and Light Weapons, adopted at Bamako on 1 December 2000,[1]

Recalling the report of the Secretary-General entitled "In larger freedom: towards development, security and human rights for all",[2] in which he emphasized that States must strive just as hard to eliminate the threat of illicit small arms and light weapons as they do to eliminate the threat of weapons of mass destruction,

Recalling also the International Instrument to Enable States to Identify and Trace, in a Timely and Reliable Manner, Illicit Small Arms and Light Weapons, adopted on 8 December 2005,[3]

Recalling further the expression of support in the 2005 World Summit Outcome for the implementation of the Programme of Action to Prevent, Combat and Eradicate the Illicit Trade in Small Arms and Light Weapons in All Its Aspects,[4]

Recalling the adoption, at the thirtieth ordinary summit of the Economic Community of West African States, held in Abuja in June 2006, of the Convention on Small Arms and Light Weapons, Their Ammunition and Other

---

[1] A/CONF.192/PC/23, annex.
[2] A/59/2005.
[3] A/60/88 and Corr.2, annex; see also decision 60/519.
[4] See resolution 60/1, para. 94.

Related Materials,[5] in replacement of the moratorium on the importation, exportation and manufacture of small arms and light weapons in West Africa,

Recalling also the entry into force of the Convention on Small Arms and Light Weapons, Their Ammunition and Other Related Materials on 29 September 2009,

Recalling further the decision taken by the Economic Community to establish a Small Arms Unit responsible for advocating appropriate policies and developing and implementing programmes, as well as the establishment of the Economic Community's Small Arms Control Programme, launched on 6 June 2006 in Bamako, in replacement of the Programme for Coordination and Assistance for Security and Development,

Taking note of the latest report of the Secretary-General on assistance to States for curbing the illicit traffic in small arms and light weapons and collecting them and the illicit trade in small arms and light weapons in all its aspects,[6]

Recalling, in that regard, the decision of the European Union to significantly support the Economic Community in its efforts to combat the illicit proliferation of small arms and light weapons,

Recognizing the important role that civil society organizations play, by raising public awareness, in efforts to curb the illicit traffic in small arms and light weapons,

Recalling the report of the United Nations Conference to Review Progress Made in the Implementation of the Programme of Action to Prevent, Combat and Eradicate the Illicit Trade in Small Arms and Light Weapons in All Its Aspects, held in New York from 26 June to 7 July 2006,[7]

1.   *Commends* the United Nations and international, regional and other organizations for their assistance to States for curbing the illicit traffic in small arms and light weapons and collecting them;

2.   *Encourages* the Secretary-General to pursue his efforts in the context of the implementation of General Assembly resolution 49/75 G of 15 December 1994 and the recommendations of the United Nations advisory missions aimed at curbing the illicit circulation of small arms and light weapons and collecting them in the affected States that so request, with the support of the United Nations Regional Centre for Peace and Disarmament in Africa and in close cooperation with the African Union;

3.   *Encourages* the international community to support the implementation of the Economic Community of West African States

---

[5] See United Nations Institute for Disarmament Research, *Disarmament Forum*, No. 4, 2008, *The Complex Dynamics of Small Arms in West Africa*. Available from www.unidir.org.

[6] A/66/177.

[7] A/CONF.192/2006/RC/9.

Convention on Small Arms and Light Weapons, Their Ammunition and Other Related Materials;

4.   *Encourages* the countries of the Sahelo-Saharan subregion to facilitate the effective functioning of national commissions to combat the illicit proliferation of small arms and light weapons, and in that regard invites the international community to lend its support wherever possible;

5.   *Encourages* the collaboration of civil society organizations and associations in the efforts of the national commissions to combat the illicit traffic in small arms and light weapons and in the implementation of the Programme of Action to Prevent, Combat and Eradicate the Illicit Trade in Small Arms and Light Weapons in All Its Aspects; [8]

6.   *Encourages* cooperation among State organs, international organizations and civil society in support of programmes and projects aimed at combating the illicit traffic in small arms and light weapons and collecting them;

7.   *Calls upon* the international community to provide technical and financial support to strengthen the capacity of civil society organizations to take action to help to combat the illicit trade in small arms and light weapons;

8.   *Invites* the Secretary-General and those States and organizations that are in a position to do so to continue to provide assistance to States for curbing the illicit traffic in small arms and light weapons and collecting them;

9.   *Requests* the Secretary-General to continue to consider the matter and to report to the General Assembly at its sixty-seventh session on the implementation of the present resolution;

10.   *Decides* to include in the provisional agenda of its sixty-seventh session the item entitled "Assistance to States for curbing the illicit traffic in small arms and light weapons and collecting them".

Action by the General Assembly

Date: 2 December 2011   Meeting: 71st plenary meeting
Vote: Adopted without a vote   Report: A/66/412

---

[8] See *Report of the United Nations Conference on the Illicit Trade in Small Arms and Light Weapons in All Its Aspects, New York, 9–20 July 2001* (A/CONF.192/15), chap. IV, para. 24.

Sponsors

Mali, on behalf of the States Members of the United Nations that are members of the Economic Community of West African States, Australia, Belgium, Bulgaria, Cameroon, Chad, the Dominican Republic, Eritrea, Estonia, Finland, France, Germany, Greece, Honduras, Hungary, Ireland, Italy, Luxembourg, Malta, Montenegro, Morocco, Norway, Poland, Portugal, Romania, Serbia, Slovakia, Slovenia, Spain, Sweden, United Kingdom

Co-sponsors

Albania, Algeria, Andorra, Angola, Austria, Bahamas, Bangladesh, Barbados, Belize, Bosnia and Herzegovina, Botswana, Canada, Colombia, Comoros, Congo, Croatia, Chile, Cyprus, Czech Republic, Democratic Republic of the Congo, Denmark, El Salvador, Ethiopia, Gabon, Georgia, Guatemala, Guyana, Haiti, Iceland, Jamaica, Kenya, Lesotho, Latvia, Liechtenstein, Lithuania, Madagascar, Malawi, Mauritania, Mozambique, Netherlands, Panama, Papua New Guinea, Republic of Moldova, Saint Kitts and Nevis, San Marino, South Africa, South Sudan, Suriname, Switzerland, Thailand, Trinidad and Tobago, Turkey, Uganda, United Republic of Tanzania, Zambia

Action by the First Committee

Date: 27 October 2011   Meeting: 22nd meeting
Vote: Adopted without a vote   Draft resolution: A/C.1/66/L.18

Agenda item 98

66/35 Implementation of the Convention on the Prohibition of the Development, Production, Stockpiling and Use of Chemical Weapons and on Their Destruction

Text

The General Assembly,

Recalling its previous resolutions on the subject of chemical weapons, in particular resolution 65/57 of 8 December 2010, adopted without a vote, in which it noted with appreciation the ongoing work to achieve the objective and purpose of the Convention on the Prohibition of the Development, Production, Stockpiling and Use of Chemical Weapons and on Their Destruction,[1]

Determined to achieve the effective prohibition of the development, production, acquisition, transfer, stockpiling and use of chemical weapons and their destruction,

Noting with satisfaction that, since the adoption of resolution 63/48 of 2 December 2008, four additional States have acceded to the Convention, bringing the total number of States parties to the Convention to one hundred and eighty-eight,

Reaffirming the importance of the outcome of the Second Special Session of the Conference of the States Parties to Review the Operation of the Chemical Weapons Convention (hereinafter "the Second Review Conference"), including the consensus final report,[2] which addressed all aspects of the Convention and made important recommendations on its continued implementation,

Emphasizing that the Second Review Conference welcomed the fact that, eleven years after its entry into force, the Convention remained a unique multilateral agreement banning an entire category of weapons of mass destruction in a non-discriminatory and verifiable manner under strict and effective international control,

1. *Emphasizes* that the universality of the Convention on the Prohibition of the Development, Production, Stockpiling and Use of Chemical Weapons and on Their Destruction[1] is fundamental to the achievement of its objective and purpose, acknowledges progress made in the implementation of the action plan for the universality of the Convention, and calls upon all States that have not yet done so to become parties to the Convention without delay;

---

[1] United Nations, *Treaty Series*, vol. 1974, No. 33757.
[2] See Organization for the Prohibition of Chemical Weapons, document RC-2/4.

2.   *Underlines* the fact that implementation of the Convention makes a major contribution to international peace and security through the elimination of existing stockpiles of chemical weapons and the prohibition of the acquisition or use of chemical weapons, and provides for assistance and protection in the event of use, or threat of use, of chemical weapons and for international cooperation for peaceful purposes in the field of chemical activities;

3.   *Stresses* the importance to the Convention that all possessors of chemical weapons, chemical weapons production facilities or chemical weapons development facilities, including previously declared possessor States, should be among the States parties to the Convention, and welcomes progress to that end;

4.   *Reaffirms* the obligation of the States parties to the Convention to destroy chemical weapons and to destroy or convert chemical weapons production facilities within the time limits provided for by the Convention;

5.   *Stresses* that the full and effective implementation of all provisions of the Convention, including those on national implementation (article VII) and assistance and protection (article X), constitutes an important contribution to the efforts of the United Nations in the global fight against terrorism in all its forms and manifestations;

6.   *Notes* that the effective application of the verification system builds confidence in compliance with the Convention by States parties;

7.   *Stresses* the importance of the Organization for the Prohibition of Chemical Weapons in verifying compliance with the provisions of the Convention as well as in promoting the timely and efficient accomplishment of all its objectives;

8.   *Urges* all States parties to the Convention to meet in full and on time their obligations under the Convention and to support the Organization for the Prohibition of Chemical Weapons in its implementation activities;

9.   *Welcomes* progress made in the national implementation of article VII obligations, commends the States parties and the Technical Secretariat for assisting other States parties, on request, with the implementation of the follow-up to the plan of action regarding article VII obligations, and urges States parties that have not fulfilled their obligations under article VII to do so without further delay, in accordance with their constitutional processes;

10.   *Emphasizes* the continuing relevance and importance of the provisions of article X of the Convention, and welcomes the activities of the Organization for the Prohibition of Chemical Weapons in relation to assistance and protection against chemical weapons;

11. *Reaffirms* that the provisions of the Convention shall be implemented in a manner that avoids hampering the economic or technological development of States parties and international cooperation in the field of chemical activities for purposes not prohibited under the Convention, including the international exchange of scientific and technical information, and chemicals and equipment for the production, processing or use of chemicals for purposes not prohibited under the Convention;

12. *Emphasizes* the importance of article XI provisions relating to the economic and technological development of States parties, recalls that the full, effective and non-discriminatory implementation of those provisions contributes to universality, and also reaffirms the undertaking of the States parties to foster international cooperation for peaceful purposes in the field of chemical activities of the States parties and the importance of that cooperation and its contribution to the promotion of the Convention as a whole;

13. *Notes with appreciation* the ongoing work of the Organization for the Prohibition of Chemical Weapons to achieve the objective and purpose of the Convention, to ensure the full implementation of its provisions, including those for international verification of compliance with it, and to provide a forum for consultation and cooperation among States parties;

14. *Welcomes* the cooperation between the United Nations and the Organization for the Prohibition of Chemical Weapons within the framework of the Relationship Agreement between the United Nations and the Organization, in accordance with the provisions of the Convention;

15. *Decides* to include in the provisional agenda of its sixty-seventh session the item entitled "Implementation of the Convention on the Prohibition of the Development, Production, Stockpiling and Use of Chemical Weapons and on Their Destruction".

Action by the General Assembly

Date: 2 December 2011   Meeting: 71st plenary meeting
Vote: Adopted without a vote   Report: A/66/412

Sponsors

Poland

Action by the First Committee

Date: 26 October 2011   Meeting: 21st meeting
Vote: Adopted without a vote   Draft resolution: A/C.1/66/L.19

Agenda item 98

66/36   Regional disarmament

Text

The General Assembly,

Recalling its resolutions 45/58 P of 4 December 1990, 46/36 I of 6 December 1991, 47/52 J of 9 December 1992, 48/75 I of 16 December 1993, 49/75 N of 15 December 1994, 50/70 K of 12 December 1995, 51/45 K of 10 December 1996, 52/38 P of 9 December 1997, 53/77 O of 4 December 1998, 54/54 N of 1 December 1999, 55/33 O of 20 November 2000, 56/24 H of 29 November 2001, 57/76 of 22 November 2002, 58/38 of 8 December 2003, 59/89 of 3 December 2004, 60/63 of 8 December 2005, 61/80 of 6 December 2006, 62/38 of 5 December 2007, 63/43 of 2 December 2008, 64/41 of 2 December 2009 and 65/45 of 8 December 2010 on regional disarmament,

Believing that the efforts of the international community to move towards the ideal of general and complete disarmament are guided by the inherent human desire for genuine peace and security, the elimination of the danger of war and the release of economic, intellectual and other resources for peaceful pursuits,

Affirming the abiding commitment of all States to the purposes and principles enshrined in the Charter of the United Nations in the conduct of their international relations,

Noting that essential guidelines for progress towards general and complete disarmament were adopted at the tenth special session of the General Assembly,[1]

Taking note of the guidelines and recommendations for regional approaches to disarmament within the context of global security adopted by the Disarmament Commission at its 1993 substantive session,[2]

Welcoming the prospects of genuine progress in the field of disarmament engendered in recent years as a result of negotiations between the two super-Powers,

Taking note of the recent proposals for disarmament at the regional and subregional levels,

Recognizing the importance of confidence-building measures for regional and international peace and security,

---

[1] See resolution S-10/2.
[2] *Official Records of the General Assembly, Forty-eighth Session, Supplement No. 42* (A/48/42), annex II.

Convinced that endeavours by countries to promote regional disarmament, taking into account the specific characteristics of each region and in accordance with the principle of undiminished security at the lowest level of armaments, would enhance the security of all States and would thus contribute to international peace and security by reducing the risk of regional conflicts,

1. *Stresses* that sustained efforts are needed, within the framework of the Conference on Disarmament and under the umbrella of the United Nations, to make progress on the entire range of disarmament issues;

2. *Affirms* that global and regional approaches to disarmament complement each other and should therefore be pursued simultaneously to promote regional and international peace and security;

3. *Calls upon* States to conclude agreements, wherever possible, for nuclear non-proliferation, disarmament and confidence-building measures at the regional and subregional levels;

4. *Welcomes* the initiatives towards disarmament, nuclear non-proliferation and security undertaken by some countries at the regional and subregional levels;

5. *Supports and encourages* efforts aimed at promoting confidence-building measures at the regional and subregional levels to ease regional tensions and to further disarmament and nuclear non-proliferation measures at the regional and subregional levels;

6. *Decides* to include in the provisional agenda of its sixty-seventh session the item entitled "Regional disarmament".

Action by the General Assembly

Date: 2 December 2011   Meeting: 71st plenary meeting
Vote: Adopted without a vote   Report: A/66/412

Sponsors

Egypt, Indonesia, Jordan, Malaysia, Nepal, **Pakistan**, Peru, Saudi Arabia, Sri Lanka, Turkey

Co-sponsors

Bangladesh, Congo, Democratic Republic of the Congo, Kuwait

Action by the First Committee

Date: 26 October 2011   Meeting: 21st meeting
Vote: Adopted without a vote   Draft resolution: A/C.1/66/L.26

Agenda item 98

66/37   Conventional arms control at the regional and subregional levels

Text

The General Assembly,

Recalling its resolutions 48/75 J of 16 December 1993, 49/75 O of 15 December 1994, 50/70 L of 12 December 1995, 51/45 Q of 10 December 1996, 52/38 Q of 9 December 1997, 53/77 P of 4 December 1998, 54/54 M of 1 December 1999, 55/33 P of 20 November 2000, 56/24 I of 29 November 2001, 57/77 of 22 November 2002, 58/39 of 8 December 2003, 59/88 of 3 December 2004, 60/75 of 8 December 2005, 61/82 of 6 December 2006, 62/44 of 5 December 2007, 63/44 of 2 December 2008, 64/42 of 2 December 2009 and 65/46 of 8 December 2010,

Recognizing the crucial role of conventional arms control in promoting regional and international peace and security,

Convinced that conventional arms control needs to be pursued primarily in the regional and subregional contexts since most threats to peace and security in the post-cold-war era arise mainly among States located in the same region or subregion,

Aware that the preservation of a balance in the defence capabilities of States at the lowest level of armaments would contribute to peace and stability and should be a prime objective of conventional arms control,

Desirous of promoting agreements to strengthen regional peace and security at the lowest possible level of armaments and military forces,

Noting with particular interest the initiatives taken in this regard in different regions of the world, in particular the commencement of consultations among a number of Latin American countries and the proposals for conventional arms control made in the context of South Asia, and recognizing, in the context of this subject, the relevance and value of the Treaty on Conventional Armed Forces in Europe,[1] which is a cornerstone of European security,

Believing that militarily significant States and States with larger military capabilities have a special responsibility in promoting such agreements for regional security,

Believing also that an important objective of conventional arms control in regions of tension should be to prevent the possibility of military attack launched by surprise and to avoid aggression,

---

[1] United Nations, *Treaty Series*, vol. 2441, No. 44001.

1. *Decides* to give urgent consideration to the issues involved in conventional arms control at the regional and subregional levels;

2. *Requests* the Conference on Disarmament to consider the formulation of principles that can serve as a framework for regional agreements on conventional arms control, and looks forward to a report of the Conference on this subject;

3. *Requests* the Secretary-General, in the meantime, to seek the views of Member States on the subject and to submit a report to the General Assembly at its sixty-seventh session;

4. *Decides* to include in the provisional agenda of its sixty-seventh session the item entitled "Conventional arms control at the regional and subregional levels".

Action by the General Assembly

Date: 2 December 2011   Meeting: 71st plenary meeting
Vote: 175-1-2   Report: A/66/412
       141-1-31, o.p. 2

Sponsors

Belarus, Egypt, Italy, Malaysia, **Pakistan**, Peru, Syrian Arab Republic, Ukraine

Co-sponsors

Bangladesh, Democratic Republic of the Congo

Recorded vote

As a whole*

In favour:

Afghanistan, Albania, Algeria, Andorra, Angola, Antigua and Barbuda, Argentina, Armenia, Australia, Austria, Azerbaijan, Bahamas, Bahrain, Bangladesh, Barbados, Belarus, Belgium, Belize, Benin, Bolivia (Plurinational State of), Bosnia and Herzegovina, Botswana, Brazil, Brunei Darussalam, Bulgaria, Burkina Faso, Cambodia, Cameroon, Canada, Cape Verde, Chad, Chile, China, Colombia, Comoros, Congo, Costa Rica, Côte d'Ivoire, Croatia, Cyprus, Czech Republic, Democratic People's Republic of Korea, Denmark, Djibouti, Dominican Republic, Ecuador, Egypt, El Salvador, Estonia, Ethiopia, Fiji, Finland, France, Gabon, Georgia, Germany, Ghana, Greece, Grenada, Guatemala, Guinea, Guinea-Bissau, Guyana, Haiti, Honduras, Hungary, Iceland, Indonesia, Iran (Islamic Republic of), Iraq, Ireland, Israel, Italy, Jamaica, Japan,

---

* Subsequently, the delegations of Kuwait and Turkey advised the Secretariat that they had intended to vote in favour. The voting tally above does not reflect this information.

Jordan, Kazakhstan, Kenya, Kyrgyzstan, Lao People's Democratic Republic, Latvia, Lebanon, Lesotho, Liberia, Libyan Arab Jamahiriya, Liechtenstein, Lithuania, Luxembourg, Madagascar, Malawi, Malaysia, Maldives, Mali, Malta, Marshall Islands, Mauritania, Mauritius, Mexico, Micronesia (Federated States of), Monaco, Mongolia, Montenegro, Morocco, Mozambique, Myanmar, Namibia, Nepal, Netherlands, New Zealand, Nicaragua, Niger, Nigeria, Norway, Oman, Pakistan, Palau, Panama, Papua New Guinea, Paraguay, Peru, Philippines, Poland, Portugal, Qatar, Republic of Korea, Republic of Moldova, Romania, Saint Kitts and Nevis, Saint Lucia, Saint Vincent and the Grenadines, Samoa, San Marino, Sao Tome and Principe, Saudi Arabia, Senegal, Serbia, Seychelles, Sierra Leone, Singapore, Slovakia, Slovenia, Solomon Islands, South Africa, Spain, Sri Lanka, Suriname, Swaziland, Sweden, Switzerland, Syrian Arab Republic, Tajikistan, Thailand, the former Yugoslav Republic of Macedonia, Timor-Leste, Togo, Tonga, Trinidad and Tobago, Tunisia, Turkey, Turkmenistan, Tuvalu, Uganda, Ukraine, United Arab Emirates, United Kingdom, United Republic of Tanzania, United States, Uruguay, Uzbekistan, Vanuatu, Venezuela (Bolivarian Republic of), Viet Nam, Yemen, Zambia, Zimbabwe

Against:
India

Abstaining:
Bhutan, Russian Federation

Operative paragraph two**

In favour:
Afghanistan, Algeria, Angola, Antigua and Barbuda, Argentina, Armenia, Australia, Azerbaijan, Bahamas, Bahrain, Bangladesh, Barbados, Belarus, Belgium, Belize, Benin, Bolivia (Plurinational State of), Botswana, Brazil, Brunei Darussalam, Bulgaria, Burkina Faso, Cambodia, Cameroon, Canada, Cape Verde, Chad, Chile, China, Colombia, Comoros, Congo, Costa Rica, Côte d'Ivoire, Democratic People's Republic of Korea, Denmark, Djibouti, Dominican Republic, Ecuador, Egypt, El Salvador, Ethiopia, Fiji, Gabon, Ghana, Grenada, Guatemala, Guinea, Guinea-Bissau, Guyana, Haiti, Honduras, Indonesia, Iran (Islamic Republic of), Iraq, Italy, Jamaica, Japan, Jordan, Kazakhstan, Kenya, Kuwait, Kyrgyzstan, Lebanon, Lesotho, Liberia, Libyan Arab Jamahiriya, Liechtenstein, Luxembourg, Madagascar, Malawi, Malaysia, Maldives, Mali, Mauritania, Mauritius, Mongolia, Montenegro, Morocco, Mozambique, Namibia, Nepal, Nicaragua, Niger, Nigeria, Oman, Pakistan, Palau, Panama, Papua New Guinea, Paraguay,

---

** Subsequently, the delegation of Switzerland advised the Secretariat that it had intended to abstain. The voting tally above does not reflect this information.

Peru, Philippines, Portugal, Qatar, Republic of Korea, Republic of Moldova, Romania, Russian Federation, Saint Kitts and Nevis, Saint Lucia, Saint Vincent and the Grenadines, Samoa, Sao Tome and Principe, Saudi Arabia, Senegal, Serbia, Seychelles, Sierra Leone, Singapore, Slovakia, Slovenia, Solomon Islands, South Africa, Sri Lanka, Sudan, Suriname, Swaziland, Syrian Arab Republic, Tajikistan, Thailand, the former Yugoslav Republic of Macedonia, Timor-Leste, Togo, Tonga, Tunisia, Turkmenistan, Tuvalu, Uganda, Ukraine, United Arab Emirates, United Republic of Tanzania, United States, Uruguay, Uzbekistan, Vanuatu, Venezuela (Bolivarian Republic of), Viet Nam, Yemen, Zambia, Zimbabwe

Against:
India

Abstaining:
Albania, Andorra, Austria, Bhutan, Bosnia and Herzegovina, Croatia, Cyprus, Czech Republic, Estonia, Finland, France, Georgia, Germany, Greece, Hungary, Ireland, Israel, Latvia, Lithuania, Malta, Mexico, Monaco, Netherlands, New Zealand, Norway, Poland, San Marino, Spain, Sweden, Turkey, United Kingdom

Action by the First Committee

Date: 26 October 2011 Meeting: 21st meeting
Vote: 165-1-3 Draft resolution: A/C.1/66/L.27
133-1-31, o.p. 2

Agenda item 98

66/38 Confidence-building measures in the regional and subregional context

Text

The General Assembly,

Guided by the purposes and principles enshrined in the Charter of the United Nations,

Recalling its resolutions 58/43 of 8 December 2003, 59/87 of 3 December 2004, 60/64 of 8 December 2005, 61/81 of 6 December 2006, 62/45 of 5 December 2007, 63/45 of 2 December 2008, 64/43 of 2 December 2009 and 65/47 of 8 December 2010,

Recalling also its resolution 57/337 of 3 July 2003 entitled "Prevention of armed conflict", in which it calls upon Member States to settle their disputes by peaceful means, as set out in Chapter VI of the Charter, inter alia, by any procedures adopted by the parties,

Recalling further the resolutions and guidelines adopted by consensus by the General Assembly and the Disarmament Commission relating to confidence-building measures and their implementation at the global, regional and subregional levels,

Considering the importance and effectiveness of confidence-building measures taken at the initiative and with the agreement of all States concerned, and taking into account the specific characteristics of each region, since such measures can contribute to regional stability,

Convinced that resources released by disarmament, including regional disarmament, can be devoted to economic and social development and to the protection of the environment for the benefit of all peoples, in particular those of the developing countries,

Recognizing the need for meaningful dialogue among States concerned to avert conflict,

Welcoming the peace processes already initiated by States concerned to resolve their disputes through peaceful means bilaterally or through mediation, inter alia, by third parties, regional organizations or the United Nations,

Recognizing that States in some regions have already taken steps towards confidence-building measures at the bilateral, subregional and regional levels in the political and military fields, including arms control and disarmament, and noting that such confidence-building measures have improved peace and security in those regions and contributed to progress in the socio-economic conditions of their people,

Concerned that the continuation of disputes among States, particularly in the absence of an effective mechanism to resolve them through peaceful means, may contribute to the arms race and endanger the maintenance of international peace and security and the efforts of the international community to promote arms control and disarmament,

1.   *Calls upon* Member States to refrain from the use or threat of use of force in accordance with the purposes and principles of the Charter of the United Nations;

2.   *Reaffirms its commitment* to the peaceful settlement of disputes under Chapter VI of the Charter, in particular Article 33, which provides for a solution by negotiation, enquiry, mediation, conciliation, arbitration, judicial settlement, resort to regional agencies or arrangements or other peaceful means chosen by the parties;

3.   *Reaffirms* the ways and means regarding confidence- and security-building measures set out in the report of the Disarmament Commission on its 1993 session;[1]

4.   *Calls upon* Member States to pursue these ways and means through sustained consultations and dialogue, while at the same time avoiding actions that may hinder or impair such a dialogue;

5.   *Urges* States to comply strictly with all bilateral, regional and international agreements, including arms control and disarmament agreements, to which they are party;

6.   *Emphasizes* that the objective of confidence-building measures should be to help to strengthen international peace and security and to be consistent with the principle of undiminished security at the lowest level of armaments;

7.   *Encourages* the promotion of bilateral and regional confidence-building measures, with the consent and participation of the parties concerned, to avoid conflict and prevent the unintended and accidental outbreak of hostilities;

8.   *Requests* the Secretary-General to submit a report to the General Assembly at its sixty-seventh session containing the views of Member States on confidence-building measures in the regional and subregional context;

9.   *Decides* to include in the provisional agenda of its sixty-seventh session the item entitled "Confidence-building measures in the regional and subregional context".

---

[1] *Official Records of the General Assembly, Forty-eighth Session, Supplement No. 42* (A/48/42), annex II, sect. III.A.

Action by the General Assembly

    Date: 2 December 2011   Meeting: 71st plenary meeting
    Vote: Adopted without a vote   Report: A/66/412

Sponsors

Ecuador, Egypt, Kazakhstan, Malaysia, **Pakistan**, Philippines, Sierra Leone, the Syrian Arab Republic, Ukraine, Uruguay

Co-sponsors

Bangladesh, Kuwait

Action by the First Committee

    Date: 26 October 2011   Meeting: 21st meeting
    Vote: Adopted without a vote   Draft resolution: A/C.1/66/L.28

Agenda Item 98

66/39   Transparency in armaments

Text

The General Assembly,

Recalling its resolutions 46/36 L of 9 December 1991, 47/52 L of 15 December 1992, 48/75 E of 16 December 1993, 49/75 C of 15 December 1994, 50/70 D of 12 December 1995, 51/45 H of 10 December 1996, 52/38 R of 9 December 1997, 53/77 V of 4 December 1998, 54/54 O of 1 December 1999, 55/33 U of 20 November 2000, 56/24 Q of 29 November 2001, 57/75 of 22 November 2002, 58/54 of 8 December 2003, 60/226 of 23 December 2005, 61/77 of 6 December 2006, 63/69 of 2 December 2008 and 64/54 of 2 December 2009, entitled "Transparency in armaments",

Continuing to take the view that an enhanced level of transparency in armaments contributes greatly to confidence-building and security among States and that the establishment of the United Nations Register of Conventional Arms[1] constitutes an important step forward in the promotion of transparency in military matters,

Welcoming the consolidated reports of the Secretary-General on the Register, which include the returns of Member States for 2009[2] and 2010,[3]

Welcoming also the response of Member States to the request contained in paragraphs 9 and 10 of resolution 46/36 L to provide data on their imports and exports of arms, as well as available background information regarding their military holdings, procurement through national production and relevant policies,

Welcoming further the inclusion by some Member States of their transfers of small arms and light weapons in their annual report to the Register as part of their additional background information,

Noting the focused discussions on transparency in armaments that took place in the Conference on Disarmament in 2010 and 2011,

Expressing its concern with respect to the reduction in reporting to the Register in the last two years,

Stressing that the continuing operation of the Register and its further development should be reviewed in order to secure a Register that is capable of attracting the widest possible participation,

---

[1] See resolution 46/36 L.
[2] A/65/133 and Add.1–5.
[3] A/66/127.

1. *Reaffirms its determination* to ensure the effective operation of the United Nations Register of Conventional Arms,[1] as provided for in paragraphs 7 to 10 of resolution 46/36 L;

2. *Calls upon* Member States, with a view to achieving universal participation, to provide the Secretary-General, by 31 May annually, with the requested data and information for the Register, including nil reports if appropriate, on the basis of resolutions 46/36 L and 47/52 L, the recommendations contained in paragraph 64 of the 1997 report of the Secretary-General on the continuing operation of the Register and its further development,[4] the recommendations contained in paragraph 94 of the 2000 report of the Secretary-General and the appendices and annexes thereto,[5] the recommendations contained in paragraphs 112 to 114 of the 2003 report of the Secretary-General,[6] the recommendations contained in paragraphs 123 to 127 of the 2006 report of the Secretary-General[7] and the recommendations contained in paragraphs 71 to 75 of the 2009 report of the Secretary-General;[8]

3. *Invites* Member States in a position to do so, pending further development of the Register, to provide additional information on procurement through national production and military holdings and to make use of the "Remarks" column in the standardized reporting form to provide additional information such as types or models;

4. *Also invites* Member States in a position to do so to provide additional information on transfers of small arms and light weapons on the basis of the optional standardized reporting form, as adopted by the 2006 group of governmental experts,[9] or by any other methods they deem appropriate;

5. *Reaffirms* its decision, with a view to further development of the Register, to keep the scope of and participation in the Register under review and, to that end:

(*a*) Recalls its request to Member States to provide the Secretary-General with their views on the continuing operation of the Register and its further development and on transparency measures related to weapons of mass destruction;

(*b*) Requests the Secretary-General, with the assistance of a group of governmental experts to be convened in 2012, within available resources, on the basis of equitable geographical representation, to prepare a report on the continuing operation of the Register and its further development, taking into

---

[4] A/52/316 and Corr.2.
[5] A/55/281.
[6] A/58/274.
[7] See A/61/261.
[8] See A/64/296.
[9] A/61/261, annex I.

account the work of the Conference on Disarmament, relevant deliberations within the United Nations, the views expressed by Member States and the reports of the Secretary-General on the continuing operation of the Register and its further development, with a view to taking a decision at its sixty-eighth session;

(*c*) Requests the Secretary-General to continue to assist Member States to build capacity to submit meaningful reports, including capacity to report on small arms and light weapons;

6. *Requests* the Secretary-General to implement the recommendations contained in his 2000, 2003, 2006 and 2009 reports on the continuing operation of the Register and its further development and to ensure that sufficient resources are made available for the Secretariat to operate and maintain the Register;

7. *Invites* the Conference on Disarmament to consider continuing its work undertaken in the field of transparency in armaments;

8. *Reiterates its call upon* all Member States to cooperate at the regional and subregional levels, taking fully into account the specific conditions prevailing in the region or subregion, with a view to enhancing and coordinating international efforts aimed at increased openness and transparency in armaments;

9. *Requests* the Secretary-General to report to the General Assembly at its sixty-eighth session on progress made in implementing the present resolution;

10. *Decides* to include in the provisional agenda of its sixty-eighth session the item entitled "Transparency in armaments".

Action by the General Assembly

Date:	2 December 2011	Meeting: 71st plenary meeting
Vote:	156-0-23	Report: A/66/412
	154-0-22, o.p. 2	
	154-0-20, o.p. 3	
	156-0-19, o.p. 4	
	157-0-21, o.p. 5 (b)	
	154-0-24, o.p. 5	
	156-0-22, o.p. 7	

Sponsors

Argentina, Armenia, Australia, Austria, Bangladesh, Belgium, Belize, Brazil, Bulgaria, Burkina Faso, Cameroon, Chad, Chile, Costa Rica, Côte d'Ivoire, Croatia, Cyprus, Czech Republic, Democratic Republic of the Congo, Denmark, Estonia, Finland, France, Germany, Greece, Hungary, Ireland, Italy, Japan, Kazakhstan, Latvia, Lesotho, Liechtenstein,

Lithuania, Luxembourg, Mali, Malta, Micronesia (Federated States of), Montenegro, Nepal, **Netherlands**, New Zealand, Niger, Nigeria, Norway, Panama, Peru, Philippines, Poland, Portugal, Republic of Korea, Republic of Moldova, Romania, Saint Kitts and Nevis, Senegal, Serbia, Sierra Leone, Singapore, Slovakia, Slovenia, Spain, Swaziland, Sweden, Switzerland, the former Yugoslav Republic of Macedonia, Turkey, Ukraine, United Kingdom, United States, Uruguay, Zambia

Co-sponsors

Albania, Andorra, Bosnia and Herzegovina, Canada, Ecuador, El Salvador, Georgia, Ghana, Guatemala, Guinea, Guyana, Haiti, Honduras, Iceland, Israel, Jamaica, Malaysia, Monaco, Mongolia, Paraguay, Samoa, San Marino, South Africa, Suriname, Trinidad and Tobago

Recorded vote

As a whole

In favour:

Afghanistan, Albania, Andorra, Angola, Antigua and Barbuda, Argentina, Armenia, Australia, Austria, Azerbaijan, Bahamas, Bangladesh, Barbados, Belarus, Belgium, Belize, Benin, Bhutan, Bolivia (Plurinational State of), Bosnia and Herzegovina, Botswana, Brazil, Brunei Darussalam, Bulgaria, Burkina Faso, Cambodia, Cameroon, Canada, Cape Verde, Chad, Chile, China, Colombia, Congo, Costa Rica, Côte d'Ivoire, Croatia, Cyprus, Czech Republic, Denmark, Dominican Republic, Ecuador, El Salvador, Eritrea, Estonia, Ethiopia, Fiji, Finland, France, Gabon, Georgia, Germany, Ghana, Greece, Grenada, Guatemala, Guinea, Guinea-Bissau, Guyana, Haiti, Honduras, Hungary, Iceland, India, Indonesia, Ireland, Israel, Italy, Jamaica, Japan, Kazakhstan, Kenya, Kyrgyzstan, Lao People's Democratic Republic, Latvia, Lesotho, Liberia, Liechtenstein, Lithuania, Luxembourg, Madagascar, Malawi, Malaysia, Maldives, Mali, Malta, Marshall Islands, Mauritania, Mauritius, Mexico, Micronesia (Federated States of), Monaco, Mongolia, Montenegro, Mozambique, Namibia, Nepal, Netherlands, New Zealand, Nicaragua, Niger, Nigeria, Norway, Pakistan, Palau, Panama, Papua New Guinea, Paraguay, Peru, Philippines, Poland, Portugal, Republic of Korea, Republic of Moldova, Romania, Russian Federation, Saint Kitts and Nevis, Saint Lucia, Saint Vincent and the Grenadines, Samoa, San Marino, Sao Tome and Principe, Senegal, Serbia, Seychelles, Sierra Leone, Singapore, Slovakia, Slovenia, Solomon Islands, South Africa, Spain, Sri Lanka, Suriname, Swaziland, Sweden, Switzerland, Tajikistan, Thailand, the former Yugoslav Republic of Macedonia, Timor-Leste, Togo, Tonga, Trinidad and Tobago, Turkey, Turkmenistan, Tuvalu,

Ukraine, United Kingdom, United States, Uruguay, Uzbekistan, Vanuatu, Venezuela (Bolivarian Republic of), Zambia, Zimbabwe

Against:
None.

Abstaining:
Algeria, Bahrain, Comoros, Cuba, Djibouti, Egypt, Iran (Islamic Republic of), Iraq, Jordan, Kuwait, Lebanon, Libya, Morocco, Myanmar, Oman, Qatar, Saudi Arabia, Sudan, Syrian Arab Republic, Tunisia, United Arab Emirates, United Republic of Tanzania, Yemen

Operative paragraph two*

In favour:
Afghanistan, Albania, Andorra, Angola, Antigua and Barbuda, Argentina, Armenia, Australia, Austria, Azerbaijan, Bahamas, Bangladesh, Barbados, Belarus, Belgium, Belize, Benin, Bhutan, Bolivia (Plurinational State of), Bosnia and Herzegovina, Botswana, Brazil, Brunei Darussalam, Bulgaria, Burkina Faso, Cambodia, Cameroon, Canada, Cape Verde, Chile, China, Colombia, Congo, Costa Rica, Côte d'Ivoire, Croatia, Cyprus, Czech Republic, Denmark, Dominican Republic, Ecuador, El Salvador, Estonia, Ethiopia, Fiji, Finland, France, Gabon, Georgia, Germany, Ghana, Greece, Grenada, Guatemala, Guinea, Guinea-Bissau, Guyana, Haiti, Honduras, Hungary, Iceland, India, Indonesia, Ireland, Israel, Italy, Jamaica, Japan, Kazakhstan, Kenya, Kyrgyzstan, Latvia, Lesotho, Liberia, Liechtenstein, Lithuania, Luxembourg, Madagascar, Malawi, Malaysia, Maldives, Mali, Malta, Marshall Islands, Mauritania, Mauritius, Mexico, Micronesia (Federated States of), Monaco, Mongolia, Montenegro, Mozambique, Namibia, Nepal, Netherlands, New Zealand, Niger, Nigeria, Norway, Pakistan, Palau, Panama, Papua New Guinea, Paraguay, Peru, Philippines, Poland, Portugal, Qatar, Republic of Korea, Republic of Moldova, Romania, Russian Federation, Saint Kitts and Nevis, Saint Lucia, Saint Vincent and the Grenadines, Samoa, San Marino, Sao Tome and Principe, Senegal, Serbia, Seychelles, Sierra Leone, Singapore, Slovakia, Slovenia, Solomon Islands, South Africa, Spain, Sri Lanka, Suriname, Swaziland, Sweden, Switzerland, Tajikistan, Thailand, the former Yugoslav Republic of Macedonia, Timor-Leste, Togo, Tonga, Trinidad and Tobago, Turkey, Turkmenistan, Tuvalu, Ukraine, United Kingdom, United Republic of Tanzania, United States, Uruguay, Vanuatu, Venezuela (Bolivarian Republic of), Yemen, Zambia, Zimbabwe

---

* Subsequently, the delegation of Yemen advised the Secretariat that it had intended to abstain. The voting tally above does not reflect this information.

Against:
    None.

Abstaining:
    Algeria, Bahrain, Chad, Comoros, Cuba, Djibouti, Egypt, Iran (Islamic Republic of), Iraq, Jordan, Kuwait, Lebanon, Libya, Morocco, Myanmar, Nicaragua, Oman, Saudi Arabia, Sudan, Syrian Arab Republic, Tunisia, United Arab Emirates

Operative paragraph three

In favour:
    Afghanistan, Albania, Andorra, Angola, Antigua and Barbuda, Argentina, Armenia, Australia, Austria, Azerbaijan, Bahamas, Bangladesh, Barbados, Belarus, Belgium, Belize, Benin, Bhutan, Bolivia (Plurinational State of), Bosnia and Herzegovina, Botswana, Brazil, Brunei Darussalam, Bulgaria, Cambodia, Cameroon, Canada, Cape Verde, Chad, Chile, China, Colombia, Costa Rica, Côte d'Ivoire, Croatia, Cuba, Cyprus, Czech Republic, Denmark, Dominican Republic, Ecuador, El Salvador, Eritrea, Estonia, Ethiopia, Fiji, Finland, France, Gabon, Georgia, Germany, Ghana, Greece, Grenada, Guatemala, Guinea, Guinea-Bissau, Guyana, Haiti, Honduras, Hungary, Iceland, India, Indonesia, Ireland, Israel, Italy, Jamaica, Japan, Kazakhstan, Kenya, Kyrgyzstan, Latvia, Lesotho, Liberia, Liechtenstein, Lithuania, Luxembourg, Madagascar, Malawi, Malaysia, Maldives, Mali, Malta, Marshall Islands, Mauritius, Mexico, Micronesia (Federated States of), Monaco, Mongolia, Montenegro, Mozambique, Namibia, Nepal, Netherlands, New Zealand, Nicaragua, Nigeria, Norway, Pakistan, Palau, Panama, Papua New Guinea, Paraguay, Peru, Philippines, Poland, Portugal, Qatar, Republic of Korea, Republic of Moldova, Romania, Russian Federation, Saint Kitts and Nevis, Saint Lucia, Saint Vincent and the Grenadines, Samoa, San Marino, Sao Tome and Principe, Senegal, Serbia, Seychelles, Sierra Leone, Singapore, Slovakia, Slovenia, Solomon Islands, South Africa, Spain, Sri Lanka, Suriname, Swaziland, Sweden, Switzerland, Tajikistan, Thailand, the former Yugoslav Republic of Macedonia, Timor-Leste, Togo, Tonga, Trinidad and Tobago, Turkey, Turkmenistan, Tuvalu, Ukraine, United Kingdom, United Republic of Tanzania, United States, Uruguay, Uzbekistan, Vanuatu, Venezuela (Bolivarian Republic of), Zambia, Zimbabwe

Against:
    None.

Abstaining:
    Algeria, Bahrain, Comoros, Djibouti, Egypt, Iran (Islamic Republic of), Iraq, Jordan, Kuwait, Lebanon, Libya, Morocco, Myanmar, Oman, Saudi Arabia, Sudan, Syrian Arab Republic, Tunisia, United Arab Emirates, Yemen

Operative paragraph four**

In favour:

Afghanistan, Albania, Andorra, Angola, Antigua and Barbuda, Argentina, Armenia, Australia, Austria, Azerbaijan, Bahamas, Bangladesh, Barbados, Belarus, Belgium, Belize, Benin, Bhutan, Bolivia (Plurinational State of), Bosnia and Herzegovina, Botswana, Brazil, Brunei Darussalam, Bulgaria, Burkina Faso, Cambodia, Cameroon, Canada, Cape Verde, Chad, Chile, China, Colombia, Costa Rica, Côte d'Ivoire, Croatia, Cuba, Cyprus, Czech Republic, Denmark, Dominican Republic, Ecuador, El Salvador, Eritrea, Estonia, Ethiopia, Fiji, Finland, France, Gabon, Georgia, Germany, Ghana, Greece, Grenada, Guatemala, Guinea, Guinea-Bissau, Guyana, Haiti, Honduras, Hungary, Iceland, India, Indonesia, Ireland, Israel, Italy, Jamaica, Japan, Kazakhstan, Kenya, Kyrgyzstan, Latvia, Lesotho, Liberia, Liechtenstein, Lithuania, Luxembourg, Madagascar, Malawi, Malaysia, Maldives, Mali, Malta, Marshall Islands, Mauritania, Mauritius, Mexico, Micronesia (Federated States of), Monaco, Mongolia, Montenegro, Mozambique, Namibia, Nepal, Netherlands, New Zealand, Nicaragua, Niger, Norway, Pakistan, Palau, Panama, Papua New Guinea, Paraguay, Peru, Philippines, Poland, Portugal, Qatar, Republic of Korea, Republic of Moldova, Romania, Russian Federation, Saint Kitts and Nevis, Saint Lucia, Saint Vincent and the Grenadines, Samoa, San Marino, Sao Tome and Principe, Senegal, Serbia, Seychelles, Sierra Leone, Singapore, Slovakia, Slovenia, Solomon Islands, South Africa, Spain, Sri Lanka, Suriname, Swaziland, Sweden, Switzerland, Tajikistan, Thailand, the former Yugoslav Republic of Macedonia, Timor-Leste, Togo, Tonga, Trinidad and Tobago, Turkey, Turkmenistan, Tuvalu, Ukraine, United Kingdom, United Republic of Tanzania, United States, Uruguay, Uzbekistan, Vanuatu, Venezuela (Bolivarian Republic of), Zambia, Zimbabwe

Against:

None.

Abstaining:

Algeria, Bahrain, Comoros, Djibouti, Egypt, Iran (Islamic Republic of), Iraq, Jordan, Kuwait, Lebanon, Libya, Morocco, Myanmar, Oman, Saudi Arabia, Sudan, Syrian Arab Republic, Tunisia, Yemen

Operative paragraph five (b)

In favour:

Afghanistan, Albania, Andorra, Angola, Antigua and Barbuda, Argentina, Armenia, Australia, Austria, Azerbaijan, Bahamas,

---

** Subsequently, the delegation of the United Arab Emirates advised the Secretariat that it had intended to abstain. The voting tally above does not reflect this information.

Bangladesh, Barbados, Belarus, Belgium, Belize, Benin, Bhutan, Bolivia (Plurinational State of), Bosnia and Herzegovina, Botswana, Brazil, Brunei Darussalam, Bulgaria, Burkina Faso, Cambodia, Cameroon, Canada, Cape Verde, Chad, Chile, China, Colombia, Congo, Costa Rica, Côte d'Ivoire, Croatia, Cuba, Cyprus, Czech Republic, Denmark, Dominican Republic, Ecuador, El Salvador, Eritrea, Estonia, Ethiopia, Fiji, Finland, France, Gabon, Georgia, Germany, Ghana, Greece, Grenada, Guatemala, Guinea, Guinea-Bissau, Guyana, Haiti, Honduras, Hungary, Iceland, India, Indonesia, Ireland, Israel, Italy, Jamaica, Japan, Kazakhstan, Kenya, Kyrgyzstan, Latvia, Lesotho, Liberia, Liechtenstein, Lithuania, Luxembourg, Madagascar, Malawi, Malaysia, Maldives, Mali, Malta, Marshall Islands, Mauritania, Mauritius, Mexico, Micronesia (Federated States of), Monaco, Mongolia, Montenegro, Mozambique, Namibia, Nepal, Netherlands, New Zealand, Nicaragua, Niger, Nigeria, Norway, Pakistan, Palau, Panama, Papua New Guinea, Paraguay, Peru, Philippines, Poland, Portugal, Republic of Korea, Republic of Moldova, Romania, Russian Federation, Saint Kitts and Nevis, Saint Lucia, Saint Vincent and the Grenadines, Samoa, San Marino, Sao Tome and Principe, Senegal, Serbia, Seychelles, Sierra Leone, Singapore, Slovakia, Slovenia, Solomon Islands, South Africa, Spain, Sri Lanka, Suriname, Swaziland, Sweden, Switzerland, Tajikistan, Thailand, the former Yugoslav Republic of Macedonia, Timor-Leste, Togo, Tonga, Trinidad and Tobago, Turkey, Turkmenistan, Tuvalu, Ukraine, United Kingdom, United Republic of Tanzania, United States, Uruguay, Uzbekistan, Vanuatu, Venezuela (Bolivarian Republic of), Zambia, Zimbabwe

Against:
None.

Abstaining:
Algeria, Bahrain, Comoros, Djibouti, Egypt, Iran (Islamic Republic of), Iraq, Jordan, Kuwait, Lebanon, Libya, Morocco, Myanmar, Oman, Qatar, Saudi Arabia, Sudan, Syrian Arab Republic, Tunisia, United Arab Emirates, Yemen

Operative paragraph five

In favour:
Afghanistan, Albania, Andorra, Angola, Antigua and Barbuda, Argentina, Armenia, Australia, Austria, Azerbaijan, Bahamas, Bangladesh, Barbados, Belarus, Belgium, Belize, Benin, Bhutan, Bolivia (Plurinational State of), Bosnia and Herzegovina, Botswana, Brazil, Brunei Darussalam, Bulgaria, Burkina Faso, Cambodia, Cameroon, Canada, Cape Verde, Chad, Chile, China, Colombia, Congo, Costa Rica, Côte d'Ivoire, Croatia, Cyprus, Czech Republic, Denmark, Dominican Republic, Ecuador, El Salvador, Eritrea, Estonia, Ethiopia, Fiji, Finland,

France, Gabon, Georgia, Germany, Ghana, Greece, Grenada, Guatemala, Guinea, Guinea-Bissau, Guyana, Haiti, Honduras, Hungary, Iceland, India, Indonesia, Ireland, Israel, Italy, Jamaica, Japan, Kazakhstan, Kenya, Kyrgyzstan, Latvia, Lesotho, Liberia, Liechtenstein, Lithuania, Luxembourg, Madagascar, Malawi, Malaysia, Maldives, Mali, Malta, Marshall Islands, Mauritius, Mexico, Micronesia (Federated States of), Monaco, Mongolia, Montenegro, Mozambique, Namibia, Nepal, Netherlands, New Zealand, Niger, Nigeria, Norway, Pakistan, Palau, Panama, Papua New Guinea, Paraguay, Peru, Philippines, Poland, Portugal, Republic of Korea, Republic of Moldova, Romania, Russian Federation, Saint Kitts and Nevis, Saint Lucia, Saint Vincent and the Grenadines, Samoa, San Marino, Sao Tome and Principe, Senegal, Serbia, Seychelles, Sierra Leone, Singapore, Slovakia, Slovenia, Solomon Islands, South Africa, Spain, Sri Lanka, Suriname, Swaziland, Sweden, Switzerland, Tajikistan, Thailand, the former Yugoslav Republic of Macedonia, Timor-Leste, Togo, Tonga, Trinidad and Tobago, Turkey, Turkmenistan, Tuvalu, Ukraine, United Kingdom, United Republic of Tanzania, United States, Uruguay, Uzbekistan, Vanuatu, Venezuela (Bolivarian Republic of), Zambia, Zimbabwe

Against:
None.

Abstaining:
Algeria, Bahrain, Comoros, Cuba, Djibouti, Egypt, Iran (Islamic Republic of), Iraq, Jordan, Kuwait, Lebanon, Libya, Mauritania, Morocco, Myanmar, Nicaragua, Oman, Qatar, Saudi Arabia, Sudan, Syrian Arab Republic, Tunisia, United Arab Emirates, Yemen

Operative paragraph seven

In favour:
Afghanistan, Albania, Andorra, Angola, Antigua and Barbuda, Argentina, Armenia, Australia, Austria, Azerbaijan, Bahamas, Bangladesh, Barbados, Belarus, Belgium, Belize, Benin, Bhutan, Bolivia (Plurinational State of), Bosnia and Herzegovina, Botswana, Brazil, Brunei Darussalam, Bulgaria, Burkina Faso, Cambodia, Cameroon, Canada, Cape Verde, Chad, Chile, China, Colombia, Congo, Costa Rica, Côte d'Ivoire, Croatia, Cuba, Cyprus, Czech Republic, Denmark, Dominican Republic, Ecuador, El Salvador, Eritrea, Estonia, Ethiopia, Fiji, Finland, France, Gabon, Georgia, Germany, Ghana, Greece, Grenada, Guatemala, Guinea, Guinea-Bissau, Guyana, Haiti, Honduras, Hungary, Iceland, India, Indonesia, Ireland, Israel, Italy, Jamaica, Japan, Kazakhstan, Kenya, Kyrgyzstan, Latvia, Lesotho, Liberia, Liechtenstein, Lithuania, Luxembourg, Madagascar, Malawi, Malaysia, Maldives, Mali, Malta, Marshall Islands, Mauritius, Mexico, Micronesia

(Federated States of), Monaco, Mongolia, Montenegro, Mozambique, Namibia, Nepal, Netherlands, New Zealand, Nicaragua, Niger, Nigeria, Norway, Pakistan, Palau, Panama, Papua New Guinea, Paraguay, Peru, Philippines, Poland, Portugal, Republic of Korea, Republic of Moldova, Romania, Russian Federation, Saint Kitts and Nevis, Saint Lucia, Saint Vincent and the Grenadines, Samoa, San Marino, Sao Tome and Principe, Senegal, Serbia, Seychelles, Sierra Leone, Singapore, Slovakia, Slovenia, Solomon Islands, South Africa, Spain, Sri Lanka, Suriname, Swaziland, Sweden, Switzerland, Tajikistan, Thailand, the former Yugoslav Republic of Macedonia, Timor-Leste, Togo, Tonga, Trinidad and Tobago, Turkey, Turkmenistan, Tuvalu, Ukraine, United Kingdom, United Republic of Tanzania, United States, Uruguay, Uzbekistan, Vanuatu, Venezuela (Bolivarian Republic of), Zambia, Zimbabwe

Against:
None.

Abstaining:
Algeria, Bahrain, Comoros, Djibouti, Egypt, Iran (Islamic Republic of), Iraq, Jordan, Kuwait, Lebanon, Libya, Mauritania, Morocco, Myanmar, Oman, Qatar, Saudi Arabia, Sudan, Syrian Arab Republic, Tunisia, United Arab Emirates, Yemen

Action by the First Committee

Date:	27 October 2011	Meeting:	22nd meeting
Vote:	149-0-25	Draft resolution:	A/C.1/66/L.29
	150-0-24, o.p. 2		
	150-0-23, o.p. 3		
	151-0-23, o.p. 4		
	150-0-23, o.p. 5 (b)		
	149-0-25, o.p. 5		
	150-0-23, o.p. 7		

Agenda item 98

66/40 Towards a nuclear-weapon-free world: accelerating the implementation of nuclear disarmament commitments

Text

The General Assembly,

Recalling its resolution 65/59 of 8 December 2010,

Reiterating its grave concern at the danger to humanity posed by the possibility that nuclear weapons could be used, and recalling the expression of deep concern by the 2010 Review Conference of the Parties to the Treaty on the Non-Proliferation of Nuclear Weapons at the catastrophic humanitarian consequences of any use of nuclear weapons,[1]

Reaffirming that nuclear disarmament and nuclear non-proliferation are mutually reinforcing processes requiring urgent irreversible progress on both fronts,

Recalling the decisions entitled "Strengthening the review process for the Treaty", "Principles and objectives for nuclear non-proliferation and disarmament" and "Extension of the Treaty on the Non-Proliferation of Nuclear Weapons" and the resolution on the Middle East, all of which were adopted at the 1995 Review and Extension Conference of the Parties to the Treaty on the Non-Proliferation of Nuclear Weapons,[2] and the Final Document of the 2000[3] and the 2010[4] Review Conference of the Parties to the Treaty on the Non-Proliferation of Nuclear Weapons,

Recalling in particular the unequivocal undertaking by the nuclear-weapon States to accomplish the total elimination of their nuclear arsenals, leading to nuclear disarmament, in accordance with commitments made under article VI of the Treaty on the Non-Proliferation of Nuclear Weapons,[5] and reaffirmed by the 2010 Review Conference,

Reaffirming the commitment of all States parties to the Treaty on the Non-Proliferation of Nuclear Weapons to apply the principles of irreversibility,

---

[1] See *2010 Review Conference of the Parties to the Treaty on the Non-Proliferation of Nuclear Weapons, Final Document*, vol. I (NPT/CONF.2010/50 (Vol. I)), part I, *Conclusions and recommendations for follow-on actions*.

[2] See *1995 Review and Extension Conference of the Parties to the Treaty on the Non-Proliferation of Nuclear Weapons, Final Document, Part I* (NPT/CONF.1995/32 (Part I) and Corr.2), annex.

[3] *2000 Review Conference of the Parties to the Treaty on the Non-Proliferation of Nuclear Weapons, Final Document*, vols. I–III (NPT/CONF.2000/28 (Parts I–IV)).

[4] *2010 Review Conference of the Parties to the Treaty on the Non-Proliferation of Nuclear Weapons, Final Document*, vols. I–III (NPT/CONF.2010/50 (Vols. I–III)).

[5] United Nations, *Treaty Series*, vol. 729, No. 10485.

verifiability and transparency in relation to the implementation of their treaty obligations,

Recognizing the continued vital importance of the entry into force of the Comprehensive Nuclear-Test-Ban Treaty[6] to the advancement of nuclear disarmament and nuclear non-proliferation objectives, and welcoming the recent ratifications of the Treaty by Ghana and Guinea,

Reaffirming the conviction that the establishment of nuclear-weapon-free zones enhances global and regional peace and security, strengthens the nuclear non-proliferation regime and contributes towards realizing the objectives of nuclear disarmament,

Recalling that the 2010 Review Conference encouraged the establishment of further nuclear-weapon-free zones, on the basis of arrangements freely arrived at among the States of the region concerned, and expressing the hope that this will be followed by concerted international efforts to create such zones in areas where they do not currently exist, especially in the Middle East,

Noting with satisfaction the agreement at the 2010 Review Conference on practical steps to fully implement the 1995 resolution on the Middle East,

Recognizing positive developments in the context of nuclear-weapon-free zones, notably the ratification by the Russian Federation of Protocols I and II to the Treaty of Pelindaba,[7] the submission by the United States of America to the United States Senate for advice and consent of the Protocols to the Treaty of Pelindaba and the Treaty of Rarotonga,[8] the consultations between the Association of Southeast Asian Nations and nuclear-weapon States on the Protocol to the Treaty of Bangkok,[9] and the holding of the second Conference of States Parties and Signatories to Treaties that Establish Nuclear-Weapon-Free Zones and Mongolia, in New York on 30 April 2010,

Welcoming the entry into force of the Treaty between the Russian Federation and the United States of America on Measures for the Further Reduction and Limitation of Strategic Offensive Arms, while recalling the encouragement of the 2010 Review Conference to both States to continue discussions on follow-on measures in order to achieve deeper reductions in their nuclear arsenals,

Recalling that the 2010 Review Conference reaffirmed and recognized that the total elimination of nuclear weapons is the only absolute guarantee against the use or threat of use of nuclear weapons and the legitimate interest of non-nuclear-weapon States in receiving unequivocal and legally binding security assurances from nuclear-weapon States,

---

[6] See resolution 50/245.
[7] See A/50/426, annex.
[8] See *The United Nations Disarmament Yearbook*, vol. 10: 1985 (United Nations publication, Sales No. E.86.IX.7), appendix VII.
[9] United Nations, *Treaty Series*, vol. 1981, No. 33873.

Deeply disappointed at the absence of progress towards multilateral negotiations on nuclear disarmament issues, including in the Conference on Disarmament, and underlining the importance of multilateralism in relation to nuclear disarmament, while recognizing the value also of bilateral and regional initiatives,

Mindful that the first meeting of the preparatory process for the 2015 Review Conference of the Parties to the Treaty on the Non-Proliferation of Nuclear Weapons, to take place in May 2012, will begin to lay the groundwork for monitoring the fulfilment by all States parties of their commitments in the 2010 Review Conference action plan,[1] including those by the nuclear-weapon States to accelerate concrete progress on the steps leading to nuclear disarmament,

1.   *Reiterates* that each article of the Treaty on the Non-Proliferation of Nuclear Weapons[5] is binding on the States parties at all times and in all circumstances and that all States parties should be held fully accountable with respect to strict compliance with their obligations under the Treaty, and calls upon all States to comply fully with all decisions, resolutions and other commitments made at Review Conferences;

2.   *Welcomes* the adoption by the 2010 Review Conference of the Parties to the Treaty on the Non-Proliferation of Nuclear Weapons of a substantive final document containing conclusions and recommendations for follow-on actions relating to nuclear disarmament, including concrete steps for the total elimination of nuclear weapons, nuclear non-proliferation, peaceful uses of nuclear energy and the Middle East, particularly implementation of the 1995 resolution on the Middle East;[4]

3.   *Also welcomes*, in particular, the resolve of the 2010 Review Conference to seek a safer world for all and to achieve the peace and security of a world without nuclear weapons, in accordance with the objectives of the Treaty on the Non-Proliferation of Nuclear Weapons;

4.   *Further welcomes* the expression by the 2010 Review Conference of deep concern at the catastrophic humanitarian consequences of any use of nuclear weapons, and its reaffirmation of the need for all States at all times to comply with applicable international law, including international humanitarian law;

5.   *Welcomes* the reaffirmation of the continued validity of the practical steps agreed to in the Final Document of the 2000 Review Conference of the Parties to the Treaty on the Non-Proliferation of Nuclear Weapons,[10] including the specific reaffirmation of the unequivocal undertaking of the nuclear-weapon States to accomplish the total elimination of their nuclear arsenals

---

[10] See *2000 Review Conference of the Parties to the Treaty on the Non-Proliferation of Nuclear Weapons, Final Document*, vol. I (NPT/CONF.2000/28 (Parts I and II)), part I, section entitled "Article VI and eighth to twelfth preambular paragraphs", para. 15.

leading to nuclear disarmament, to which all States parties are committed under article VI of the Treaty;

6.   *Recalls* the commitment by the nuclear-weapon States to undertake further efforts to reduce and ultimately eliminate all types of nuclear weapons, deployed and non-deployed, including through unilateral, bilateral, regional and multilateral measures, underlines the recognition by the 2010 Review Conference of the legitimate interests of non-nuclear-weapon States in nuclear-weapon States constraining their development and qualitative improvement of nuclear weapons and ending their development of advanced new types of nuclear weapons, and calls upon the nuclear-weapon States to take steps in this regard;

7.   *Encourages* further steps by all nuclear-weapon States, in accordance with the action plan on nuclear disarmament of the Final Document of the 2010 Review Conference,[1] to ensure the irreversible removal of all fissile material designated by each nuclear-weapon State as no longer required for military purposes and to support the development of appropriate verification capabilities related to nuclear disarmament;

8.   *Calls upon* all States parties to the Treaty on the Non-Proliferation of Nuclear Weapons to work towards the full implementation of the resolution on the Middle East adopted at the 1995 Review and Extension Conference of the Parties to the Treaty on the Non-Proliferation of Nuclear Weapons,[2] recognizes the endorsement by the 2010 Review Conference of practical steps in a process leading to the full implementation of the 1995 resolution, including the convening of a conference in 2012, to be attended by all States of the region, on the establishment of a Middle East zone free of nuclear weapons and all other weapons of mass destruction, calls upon the Secretary-General and the co-sponsors of the 1995 resolution, in close consultation and cooperation with the States of the region, to undertake all necessary preparations for the convening of the 2012 conference, and in this regard welcomes the recent appointment of a facilitator and designation of a host Government;

9.   *Continues to emphasize* the fundamental role of the Treaty on the Non-Proliferation of Nuclear Weapons in achieving nuclear disarmament and nuclear non-proliferation and calls upon all States parties to spare no effort to achieve the universality of the Treaty, and in this regard urges India, Israel and Pakistan to accede to the Treaty as non-nuclear-weapon States promptly and without conditions;

10. *Urges* the Democratic People's Republic of Korea to fulfil the commitments under the Six-Party Talks, including those in the September 2005 joint statement, to abandon all nuclear weapons and existing nuclear programmes and to return, at an early date, to the Treaty on the Non-Proliferation of Nuclear Weapons and to its adherence to the International

Atomic Energy Agency safeguards agreement, with a view to achieving the denuclearization of the Korean Peninsula in a peaceful manner, and reaffirms its firm support for the Six-Party Talks;

11. *Encourages* all States to work together to overcome obstacles within the international disarmament machinery, including in the Conference on Disarmament, that are inhibiting efforts to advance the cause of nuclear disarmament in a multilateral context;

12. *Stresses*, while noting that the nuclear-weapon States met in Paris on 30 June and 1 July 2011 to consider progress on the commitments they made at the 2010 Review Conference, the importance of the fulfilment of the commitments made by the nuclear-weapon States at the 2010 Review Conference to accelerate concrete progress on the steps leading to nuclear disarmament contained in the Final Document of the 2000 Review Conference and of their prompt engagement to ensure substantial progress in advance of the 2015 Review Conference of the Parties to the Treaty on the Non-Proliferation of Nuclear Weapons;

13. *Recalls* that the commitment of the nuclear-weapon States to accelerate concrete progress on the steps leading to nuclear disarmament as envisaged in action 5 of the 2010 Review Conference action plan is:

(*a*) To rapidly move towards an overall reduction in the global stockpile of all types of nuclear weapons, as identified in action 3 of the action plan;

(*b*) To address the question of all nuclear weapons regardless of their type or their location as an integral part of the general nuclear disarmament process;

(*c*) To further diminish the role and significance of nuclear weapons in all military and security concepts, doctrines and policies;

(*d*) To discuss policies that could prevent the use of nuclear weapons and eventually lead to their elimination, lessen the danger of nuclear war and contribute to the non-proliferation and disarmament of nuclear weapons;

(*e*) To consider the legitimate interest of non-nuclear-weapon States in further reducing the operational status of nuclear-weapons systems in ways that promote international stability and security;

(*f*) To reduce the risk of accidental use of nuclear weapons;

(*g*) To further enhance transparency and mutual confidence;

14. *Calls upon* the nuclear-weapon States to implement these commitments in a manner that enables the States parties to monitor them regularly during each review cycle, and in this regard urges those States to report regularly on the implementation of the commitments;

15. *Welcomes* the announcements made by some nuclear-weapon States providing information about their nuclear arsenals, policies and disarmament efforts, urges those nuclear-weapon States that have not yet done so also to provide this information, and encourages the nuclear-weapon States to agree as soon as possible on a standard reporting format to facilitate this reporting;

16. *Calls upon* the nuclear-weapon States, in this regard and in reference to the outcome of the 2010 Review Conference, to regularly report on their efforts, including as part of any review of nuclear policies, to diminish the role and significance of nuclear weapons in all military and security concepts;

17. *Calls upon* all States parties to the Treaty on the Non-Proliferation of Nuclear Weapons to implement all elements of the 2010 Review Conference action plan in a faithful and timely manner so that progress across all of the pillars of the Treaty can be realized;

18. *Decides* to include in the provisional agenda of its sixty-seventh session the item entitled "Towards a nuclear-weapon-free world: accelerating the implementation of nuclear disarmament commitments" and to review the implementation of the present resolution at that session.

Action by the General Assembly

Date: 2 December 2011   Meeting: 71st plenary meeting
Vote: 169-6-6   Report: A/66/412
    170-1-7, o.p. 1
    168-4-3, o.p. 9

Sponsors

New Zealand, on behalf of the New Agenda Coalition

Co-sponsors

Austria

Recorded vote

As a whole

In favour:

Afghanistan, Albania, Algeria, Andorra, Angola, Antigua and Barbuda, Argentina, Armenia, Australia, Austria, Azerbaijan, Bahamas, Bahrain, Bangladesh, Barbados, Belarus, Belgium, Belize, Benin, Bolivia (Plurinational State of), Bosnia and Herzegovina, Botswana, Brazil, Brunei Darussalam, Bulgaria, Burkina Faso, Cambodia, Cameroon, Canada, Cape Verde, Chad, Chile, Colombia, Comoros, Congo, Costa Rica, Côte d'Ivoire, Croatia, Cuba, Cyprus, Czech Republic, Denmark, Djibouti, Dominican Republic, Ecuador, Egypt, El Salvador, Eritrea,

Estonia, Ethiopia, Fiji, Finland, Gabon, Georgia, Germany, Ghana, Greece, Grenada, Guatemala, Guinea, Guinea-Bissau, Guyana, Haiti, Honduras, Hungary, Iceland, Indonesia, Iran (Islamic Republic of), Iraq, Ireland, Italy, Jamaica, Japan, Jordan, Kazakhstan, Kenya, Kuwait, Kyrgyzstan, Lao People's Democratic Republic, Latvia, Lebanon, Lesotho, Liberia, Libyan Arab Jamahiriya, Liechtenstein, Lithuania, Luxembourg, Madagascar, Malawi, Malaysia, Maldives, Mali, Malta, Marshall Islands, Mauritania, Mauritius, Mexico, Mongolia, Montenegro, Morocco, Mozambique, Myanmar, Namibia, Nepal, Netherlands, New Zealand, Nicaragua, Niger, Nigeria, Norway, Oman, Panama, Papua New Guinea, Paraguay, Peru, Philippines, Poland, Portugal, Qatar, Republic of Korea, Republic of Moldova, Romania, Saint Kitts and Nevis, Saint Lucia, Saint Vincent and the Grenadines, Samoa, San Marino, Sao Tome and Principe, Saudi Arabia, Senegal, Serbia, Seychelles, Sierra Leone, Singapore, Slovakia, Slovenia, Solomon Islands, South Africa, Spain, Sri Lanka, Sudan, Suriname, Swaziland, Sweden, Switzerland, Syrian Arab Republic, Tajikistan, Thailand, the former Yugoslav Republic of Macedonia, Timor-Leste, Togo, Tonga, Trinidad and Tobago, Tunisia, Turkey, Turkmenistan, Tuvalu, Uganda, Ukraine, United Arab Emirates, United Republic of Tanzania, Uruguay, Uzbekistan, Vanuatu, Venezuela (Bolivarian Republic of), Viet Nam, Yemen, Zambia, Zimbabwe

Against:

Democratic People's Republic of Korea, France, India, Israel, United Kingdom, United States

Abstaining:

Bhutan, China, Micronesia (Federated States of), Pakistan, Palau, Russian Federation

Operative paragraph one

In favour:

Afghanistan, Albania, Algeria, Andorra, Angola, Antigua and Barbuda, Argentina, Armenia, Australia, Austria, Azerbaijan, Bahamas, Bahrain, Bangladesh, Barbados, Belarus, Belgium, Belize, Benin, Bhutan, Bolivia (Plurinational State of), Bosnia and Herzegovina, Botswana, Brazil, Brunei Darussalam, Bulgaria, Burkina Faso, Cambodia, Cameroon, Canada, Cape Verde, Chad, Chile, Colombia, Comoros, Congo, Costa Rica, Côte d'Ivoire, Croatia, Cuba, Cyprus, Czech Republic, Denmark, Djibouti, Dominican Republic, Ecuador, Egypt, El Salvador, Eritrea, Estonia, Ethiopia, Fiji, Finland, Gabon, Georgia, Germany, Ghana, Greece, Grenada, Guatemala, Guinea, Guinea-Bissau, Guyana, Haiti, Honduras, Hungary, Iceland, Indonesia, Iran (Islamic Republic of), Iraq, Ireland, Italy, Jamaica, Japan, Jordan, Kazakhstan, Kenya, Kuwait, Kyrgyzstan, Lao People's Democratic Republic, Latvia, Lebanon,

Lesotho, Liberia, Libyan Arab Jamahiriya, Liechtenstein, Lithuania, Luxembourg, Madagascar, Malawi, Malaysia, Maldives, Mali, Malta, Mauritania, Mauritius, Mexico, Mongolia, Montenegro, Morocco, Mozambique, Myanmar, Namibia, Nepal, Netherlands, New Zealand, Nicaragua, Niger, Nigeria, Norway, Oman, Panama, Papua New Guinea, Paraguay, Peru, Philippines, Poland, Portugal, Qatar, Republic of Korea, Republic of Moldova, Romania, Russian Federation, Saint Kitts and Nevis, Saint Lucia, Saint Vincent and the Grenadines, Samoa, San Marino, Sao Tome and Principe, Saudi Arabia, Senegal, Serbia, Seychelles, Sierra Leone, Singapore, Slovakia, Slovenia, Solomon Islands, South Africa, Spain, Sri Lanka, Sudan, Suriname, Swaziland, Sweden, Switzerland, Syrian Arab Republic, Tajikistan, Thailand, the former Yugoslav Republic of Macedonia, Timor-Leste, Togo, Tonga, Trinidad and Tobago, Tunisia, Turkey, Turkmenistan, Tuvalu, Uganda, Ukraine, United Arab Emirates, United Republic of Tanzania, Uruguay, Uzbekistan, Vanuatu, Venezuela (Bolivarian Republic of), Viet Nam, Yemen, Zambia, Zimbabwe

Against:
Democratic People's Republic of Korea

Abstaining:
China, France, India, Israel, Pakistan, United Kingdom, United States

Operative paragraph nine

In favour:
Afghanistan, Albania, Algeria, Andorra, Angola, Antigua and Barbuda, Argentina, Armenia, Australia, Austria, Azerbaijan, Bahamas, Bahrain, Bangladesh, Barbados, Belarus, Belgium, Belize, Benin, Bolivia (Plurinational State of), Bosnia and Herzegovina, Botswana, Brazil, Brunei Darussalam, Bulgaria, Burkina Faso, Cambodia, Cameroon, Canada, Chad, Chile, China, Colombia, Comoros, Congo, Costa Rica, Côte d'Ivoire, Croatia, Cuba, Cyprus, Czech Republic, Denmark, Djibouti, Dominican Republic, Ecuador, Egypt, El Salvador, Eritrea, Estonia, Ethiopia, Fiji, Finland, Gabon, Georgia, Germany, Ghana, Greece, Grenada, Guatemala, Guinea, Guinea-Bissau, Guyana, Haiti, Honduras, Hungary, Iceland, Indonesia, Iran (Islamic Republic of), Iraq, Ireland, Italy, Jamaica, Japan, Jordan, Kazakhstan, Kenya, Kuwait, Kyrgyzstan, Lao People's Democratic Republic, Latvia, Lebanon, Lesotho, Liberia, Libyan Arab Jamahiriya, Liechtenstein, Lithuania, Luxembourg, Madagascar, Malawi, Malaysia, Maldives, Mali, Malta, Mauritania, Mexico, Mongolia, Montenegro, Morocco, Mozambique, Myanmar, Namibia, Nepal, Netherlands, New Zealand, Nicaragua, Niger, Nigeria, Norway, Oman, Panama, Papua New Guinea, Paraguay, Peru, Philippines, Poland, Portugal, Qatar, Republic of Korea, Republic

of Moldova, Romania, Russian Federation, Saint Kitts and Nevis, Saint Lucia, Saint Vincent and the Grenadines, Samoa, San Marino, Sao Tome and Principe, Saudi Arabia, Senegal, Serbia, Seychelles, Sierra Leone, Singapore, Slovakia, Slovenia, Solomon Islands, South Africa, Spain, Sri Lanka, Sudan, Suriname, Swaziland, Sweden, Switzerland, Syrian Arab Republic, Tajikistan, Thailand, the former Yugoslav Republic of Macedonia, Timor-Leste, Togo, Tonga, Trinidad and Tobago, Tunisia, Turkey, Turkmenistan, Tuvalu, Uganda, Ukraine, United Arab Emirates, United Republic of Tanzania, Uruguay, Uzbekistan, Vanuatu, Venezuela (Bolivarian Republic of), Viet Nam, Yemen, Zambia, Zimbabwe

Against:

India, Israel, Pakistan, United States

Abstaining:

Bhutan, France, United Kingdom

Action by the First Committee

Date:	28 October 2011	Meeting:	23rd meeting
Vote:	160-6-4	Draft resolution:	A/C.1/66/L.31/Rev.1
	163-1-8, o.p. 1		
	160-5-3, o.p. 9		

Agenda item 98

66/41 National legislation on transfer of arms, military equipment and dual-use goods and technology

Text

The General Assembly,

Recognizing that disarmament, arms control and non-proliferation are essential for the maintenance of international peace and security,

Recalling that effective national control of the transfer of arms, military equipment and dual-use goods and technology, including those transfers that could contribute to proliferation activities, is an important tool for achieving those objectives,

Recalling also that the States parties to the international disarmament and non-proliferation treaties have undertaken to facilitate the fullest possible exchange of materials, equipment and technological information for peaceful purposes, in accordance with the provisions of those treaties,

Considering that the exchange of national legislation, regulations and procedures on the transfer of arms, military equipment and dual-use goods and technology contributes to mutual understanding and confidence among Member States,

Convinced that such an exchange would be beneficial to Member States that are in the process of developing such legislation,

Welcoming the electronic database established by the Office for Disarmament Affairs of the Secretariat,[1] in which all information exchanged pursuant to General Assembly resolutions 57/66 of 22 November 2002, 58/42 of 8 December 2003, 59/66 of 3 December 2004, 60/69 of 8 December 2005, 62/26 of 5 December 2007 and 64/40 of 2 December 2009, entitled "National legislation on transfer of arms, military equipment and dual-use goods and technology", can be consulted,

Reaffirming the inherent right of individual or collective self-defence in accordance with Article 51 of the Charter of the United Nations,

1. *Invites* Member States that are in a position to do so, without prejudice to the provisions contained in Security Council resolution 1540 (2004) of 28 April 2004 and subsequent relevant Council resolutions, to enact or improve national legislation, regulations and procedures to exercise effective control over the transfer of arms, military equipment and dual-use goods and technology, while ensuring that such legislation, regulations

---

[1] Available from www.un.org/disarmament/convarms/NLDU/.

and procedures are consistent with the obligations of States parties under international treaties;

2.   *Encourages* Member States to provide, on a voluntary basis, information to the Secretary-General on their national legislation, regulations and procedures on the transfer of arms, military equipment and dual-use goods and technology, as well as the changes therein, and requests the Secretary-General to make that information accessible to Member States;

3.   *Decides* to remain attentive to the matter.

Action by the General Assembly

Date: 2 December 2011   Meeting: 71st plenary meeting
Vote: Adopted without a vote   Report: A/66/412

Sponsors

Netherlands

Action by the First Committee

Date: 27 October 2011   Meeting: 22nd meeting
Vote: Adopted without a vote   Draft resolution: A/C.1/66/L.33

Agenda item 98

66/42   Problems arising from the accumulation of conventional ammunition stockpiles in surplus

Text

The General Assembly,

Mindful of contributing to the process initiated within the framework of the United Nations reform to make the Organization more effective in maintaining peace and security by giving it the resources and tools it needs for conflict prevention, peaceful resolution of disputes, peacekeeping, post-conflict peacebuilding and reconstruction,

Underlining the importance of a comprehensive and integrated approach to disarmament through the development of practical measures,

Taking note of the report of the Group of Experts on the problem of ammunition and explosives,[1]

Recalling the recommendation contained in paragraph 27 of the report of the Open-ended Working Group to Negotiate an International Instrument to Enable States to Identify and Trace, in a Timely and Reliable Manner, Illicit Small Arms and Light Weapons, namely, to address the issue of small arms and light weapons ammunition in a comprehensive manner as part of a separate process conducted within the framework of the United Nations,[2]

Noting with satisfaction the work and measures pursued at the regional and subregional levels with regard to the issue of conventional ammunition,

Recalling its decision 59/515 of 3 December 2004 and its resolutions 60/74 of 8 December 2005 and 61/72 of 6 December 2006, its resolution 63/61 of 2 December 2008, by which it welcomed the report of the Group of Governmental Experts established pursuant to resolution 61/72 to consider further steps to enhance cooperation with regard to the issue of conventional ammunition stockpiles in surplus,[3] and its resolution 64/51 of 2 December 2009,

Taking note of the recommendations of the Group of Governmental Experts on developing technical guidelines for the stockpile management of conventional ammunition, which would be available for States on a voluntary basis, and on improving knowledge resource management on technical ammunition issues within the United Nations system,[4] and taking note also

---

[1]   See A/54/155.
[2]   A/60/88 and Corr.2.
[3]   See A/63/182.
[4]   Ibid., paras. 72 and 73.

of the subsequent establishment, within the Secretariat, of the "Saf*er*Guard" knowledge resource management programme,

1.   *Encourages* all interested States to assess, on a voluntary basis, whether, in conformity with their legitimate security needs, parts of their stockpiles of conventional ammunition should be considered to be in surplus, and recognizes that the security of such stockpiles must be taken into consideration and that appropriate controls with regard to the security and safety of stockpiles of conventional ammunition are indispensable at the national level in order to eliminate the risk of explosion, pollution or diversion;

2.   *Appeals* to all interested States to determine the size and nature of their surplus stockpiles of conventional ammunition, whether they represent a security risk, their means of destruction, if appropriate, and whether external assistance is needed to eliminate this risk;

3.   *Encourages* States in a position to do so to assist interested States within a bilateral framework or through international or regional organizations, on a voluntary and transparent basis, in elaborating and implementing programmes to eliminate surplus stockpiles or to improve their management;

4.   *Encourages* all Member States to examine the possibility of developing and implementing, within a national, regional or subregional framework, measures to address accordingly the illicit trafficking related to the accumulation of such stockpiles;

5.   *Takes note* of the replies submitted by Member States in response to the request of the Secretary-General for views regarding the risks arising from the accumulation of conventional ammunition stockpiles in surplus and regarding national ways of strengthening controls on conventional ammunition;[5]

6.   *Continues to encourage* States to implement the recommendations of the report of the Group of Governmental Experts established pursuant to resolution 61/72 to consider further steps to enhance cooperation with regard to the issue of conventional ammunition stockpiles in surplus;[3]

7.   *Welcomes* the completion of the International Ammunition Technical Guidelines[6] and the establishment of the "Saf*er*Guard" knowledge resource management programme for the stockpile management of conventional ammunition, developed by the Office for Disarmament Affairs of the Secretariat, with the full involvement of the Mine Action Service of the Department of Peacekeeping Operations of the Secretariat, in accordance with

---

[5] A/61/118 and Add.1 and A/62/166 and Add.1.

[6] Available from www.un.org/disarmament/convarms/Ammunition/IATG/.

the recommendations of the report of the Group of Governmental Experts established pursuant to resolution 61/72;[3]

8.　*Encourages* States wishing to improve their national stockpile management capacity, prevent the growth of conventional ammunition surpluses and address wider risk mitigation to contact the "Saf*er*Guard" programme, as well as potential national donors and regional organizations, as appropriate, with a view to developing cooperation, including, where relevant, technical expertise;

9.　*Reiterates its decision* to address the issue of conventional ammunition stockpiles in surplus in a comprehensive manner;

10.　*Decides* to include in the provisional agenda of its sixty-eighth session the item entitled "Problems arising from the accumulation of conventional ammunition stockpiles in surplus".

Action by the General Assembly

Date: 2 December 2011　　　Meeting: 71st plenary meeting
Vote: Adopted without a vote　Report: A/66/412

Sponsors

Andorra, Australia, Austria, Belgium, Bulgaria, Bosnia and Herzegovina, Cameroon, Canada, Chad, Chile, Côte d'Ivoire, Croatia, Cyprus, the Czech Republic, Denmark, Ecuador, Estonia, Finland, France, **Germany**, Ghana, Greece, Hungary, Ireland, Italy, Japan, Latvia, Lesotho, Liechtenstein, Lithuania, Luxembourg, Malta, Montenegro, the Netherlands, Norway, Poland, Portugal, Republic of Moldova, Romania, Senegal, Serbia, Slovakia, Slovenia, Spain, Sweden, Switzerland, the former Yugoslav Republic of Macedonia, Trinidad and Tobago, Ukraine, United Kingdom, United States, Zambia

Co-sponsors

Albania, Benin, Democratic Republic of the Congo, El Salvador, Georgia, Iceland, Paraguay, Peru

Action by the First Committee

Date: 26 October 2011　　　Meeting:　　　21st meeting
Vote: Adopted without a vote　Draft resolution: A/C.1/66/L.36

Agenda item 98

66/43 Treaty on the South-East Asia Nuclear-Weapon-Free Zone (Bangkok Treaty)

Text

The General Assembly,

Recalling its resolution 64/39 of 2 December 2009, entitled "Treaty on the South-East Asia Nuclear-Weapon-Free Zone (Bangkok Treaty)",

Welcoming the desire of the South-East Asian States to maintain peace and stability in the region in the spirit of peaceful coexistence and mutual understanding and cooperation,

Noting the entry into force of the Charter of the Association of Southeast Asian Nations on 15 December 2008, which states, inter alia, that one of the purposes of the Association is to preserve South-East Asia as a nuclear-weapon-free zone, free of all other weapons of mass destruction,

Noting also the convening of the second Conference of States Parties and Signatories of Treaties that Establish Nuclear-Weapon-Free Zones and Mongolia,

Reaffirming its conviction of the important role of nuclear-weapon-free zones, established, where appropriate, on the basis of arrangements freely arrived at among States of the region concerned and in accordance with the 1999 guidelines of the Disarmament Commission,[1] in strengthening the nuclear non-proliferation regime, in contributing towards realizing the objectives of nuclear disarmament and in extending the areas of the world that are free of nuclear weapons, and, with particular reference to the responsibilities of the nuclear-weapon States, calling upon all States to seek a safer world for all and to achieve peace and security in a world without nuclear weapons in a way that promotes international stability and based on the principle of undiminished security for all,

Convinced that the establishment of a South-East Asia Nuclear-Weapon-Free Zone, as an essential component of the Declaration on the Zone of Peace, Freedom and Neutrality, signed in Kuala Lumpur on 27 November 1971, will contribute towards strengthening the security of States within the Zone and towards enhancing international peace and security as a whole,

Noting the entry into force of the Treaty on the South-East Asia Nuclear-Weapon-Free Zone on 27 March 1997[2] and the tenth anniversary of its entry into force in 2007,

---

[1] See *Official Records of the General Assembly, Fifty-fourth Session, Supplement No. 42* (A/54/42).

[2] United Nations, *Treaty Series*, vol. 1981, No. 33873.

Welcoming the reaffirmation of South-East Asian States that the South-East Asia Nuclear-Weapon-Free Zone shall continue to play a pivotal role in the area of confidence-building measures, preventive diplomacy and the approaches to conflict resolution as enshrined in the Declaration of the Association of Southeast Asian Nations Concord II (Bali Concord II),[3]

Reaffirming the inalienable right of all the parties to the Treaty on the South East Asia Nuclear-Weapon-Free Zone to develop research, production and use of nuclear energy for peaceful purposes without discrimination and in conformity with the Treaty on the Non-Proliferation of Nuclear Weapons,[4]

Recognizing that by signing and ratifying the relevant protocols to the treaties establishing nuclear-weapon-free zones, nuclear-weapon States would undertake individual legally binding commitments to respect the status of such zones and not to use or threaten to use nuclear weapons against States parties to such treaties,

Recalling the applicable principles and rules of international law relating to the freedom of the high seas and the rights of innocent passage, archipelagic sea lanes passage or transit passage of ships and aircraft, particularly those of the United Nations Convention on the Law of the Sea,[5]

1.   *Welcomes* the commitment and efforts of the Commission for the Treaty on the South-East Asia Nuclear-Weapon-Free Zone to further enhance and strengthen the implementation of the Bangkok Treaty[2] by implementing the Plan of Action for the period 2007–2012, adopted in Manila on 29 July 2007, and the recent decision of the Association of Southeast Asian Nations Political-Security Community Council, established under the Charter of the Association, to give priority to the implementation of the Plan of Action;

2.   *Also welcomes* the resumption of direct consultations between the States parties to the Treaty on the South-East Asia Nuclear-Weapon-Free Zone and the five nuclear-weapon States, and encourages States parties to the Treaty to continue direct consultations with the five nuclear-weapon States to resolve comprehensively, in accordance with the objectives and principles of the Treaty, existing outstanding issues on a number of provisions of the Treaty and the Protocol thereto;

3.   *Encourages* nuclear-weapon States and States parties to the Treaty on the South-East Asia Nuclear-Weapon-Free Zone to work constructively with a view to ensuring the early accession of the nuclear weapon States to the Protocol to the Treaty;

---

[3]   A/58/548, annex I.
[4]   United Nations, *Treaty Series*, vol. 729, No. 10485.
[5]   Ibid., vol. 1833, No. 31363.

4. *Underlines* the value of enhancing and implementing further ways and means of cooperation among the States parties to nuclear-weapon-free zone treaties and the protocols thereto;

5. *Decides* to include in the provisional agenda of its sixty-eighth session the item entitled "Treaty on the South-East Asia Nuclear-Weapon-Free Zone (Bangkok Treaty)".

Action by the General Assembly

Date: 2 December 2011   Meeting: 71st plenary meeting
Vote: Adopted without a vote   Report: A/66/412

Sponsors

Indonesia, on behalf of the States Members of the United Nations that are members of the Association of Southeast Asian Nations and the States parties to the Treaty on the South-East Asia Nuclear-Weapon-Free Zone (Bangkok Treaty)

Co-sponsors

Australia, Bangladesh, Burkina Faso, Chile, China, Colombia, Comoros, Democratic People's Republic of Korea, France, Jamaica, Japan, Kazakhstan, Kyrgyzstan, Mexico, Mongolia, Nepal, New Zealand, Norway, Russian Federation, Timor-Leste, United Kingdom, United States

Action by the First Committee

Date: 28 October 2011   Meeting: 23rd meeting
Vote: Adopted without a vote   Draft resolution: A/C.1/66/L.38

Agenda item 98

66/44 Treaty banning the production of fissile material for nuclear weapons or other nuclear explosive devices

Text

The General Assembly,

Recalling its resolutions 48/75 L of 16 December 1993, 53/77 I of 4 December 1998, 55/33 Y of 20 November 2000, 56/24 J of 29 November 2001, 57/80 of 22 November 2002, 58/57 of 8 December 2003, 59/81 of 3 December 2004, 64/29 of 2 December 2009 and 65/65 of 8 December 2010 on the subject of banning the production of fissile material for nuclear weapons or other nuclear explosive devices,

Recalling also document CD/1299 of 24 March 1995, in which all members of the Conference on Disarmament agreed on the mandate to negotiate a treaty banning the production of fissile material for nuclear weapons or other nuclear explosive devices and which would not preclude any delegation from raising for consideration, in negotiations, any issue noted therein,

Recalling further the support for the Conference on Disarmament expressed by the Security Council summit on nuclear disarmament and nuclear non-proliferation, held on 24 September 2009,

Convinced that a non-discriminatory, multilateral and internationally and effectively verifiable treaty banning the production of fissile material for nuclear weapons or other nuclear explosive devices would be a significant contribution to nuclear disarmament and non-proliferation,

Recognizing the importance of advancing all issues identified in decision CD/1864, adopted by consensus by the Conference on Disarmament on 29 May 2009,

Noting the determination of China, France, the Russian Federation, United Kingdom of Great Britain and Northern Ireland and the United States of America at the meeting held in Paris on 30 June and 1 July 2011 to renew their efforts, with relevant parties, to achieve a treaty banning the production of fissile materials for nuclear weapons and other nuclear explosive devices at the earliest possible date in the Conference on Disarmament,

Expressing frustration with the years of stalemate in the Conference on Disarmament, which has prevented it from fulfilling its mandate as the world's single multilateral disarmament negotiating forum,

1. *Urges* the Conference on Disarmament to agree on and implement early in 2012 a comprehensive programme of work that includes the immediate commencement of negotiations on a treaty banning the production

of fissile material for nuclear weapons or other nuclear explosive devices on the basis of document CD/1299 and the mandate contained therein;

2.   *Resolves* to consider options for the negotiation of a treaty banning the production of fissile material for nuclear weapons or other nuclear explosive devices at its sixty-seventh session should the Conference on Disarmament fail to agree on and implement a comprehensive programme of work by the end of its 2012 session;

3.   *Encourages* interested Member States, without prejudice to their national positions during future negotiations on such a treaty, to continue efforts, including within and on the margins of the Conference on Disarmament, in support of the commencement of negotiations, including through meetings involving scientific experts on various technical aspects of the treaty, drawing on available expertise from the International Atomic Energy Agency and other relevant bodies, as appropriate;

4.   *Decides* to include in the provisional agenda of its sixty-seventh session the item entitled "Treaty banning the production of fissile material for nuclear weapons or other nuclear explosive devices".

Action by the General Assembly

Date: 2 December 2011   Meeting: 71st plenary meeting
Vote: 158-2-21   Report: A/66/412
        157-2-17, o.p. 2
        160-2-16, o.p. 3

Sponsors

Canada

Recorded vote

As a whole

In favour:

Afghanistan, Albania, Andorra, Angola, Antigua and Barbuda, Argentina, Armenia, Australia, Austria, Azerbaijan, Bahamas, Bangladesh, Barbados, Belarus, Belgium, Belize, Benin, Bhutan, Bolivia (Plurinational State of), Bosnia and Herzegovina, Botswana, Brazil, Brunei Darussalam, Bulgaria, Burkina Faso, Cambodia, Cameroon, Canada, Cape Verde, Chad, Chile, China, Colombia, Congo, Costa Rica, Côte d'Ivoire, Croatia, Cuba, Cyprus, Czech Republic, Denmark, Dominican Republic, El Salvador, Eritrea, Estonia, Ethiopia, Fiji, Finland, France, Georgia, Germany, Ghana, Greece, Grenada, Guatemala, Guinea, Guinea-Bissau, Guyana, Haiti, Honduras, Hungary, Iceland, India, Ireland, Italy, Jamaica, Japan, Kazakhstan, Kenya, Kyrgyzstan, Lao People's Democratic Republic, Latvia, Lesotho, Liberia,

Liechtenstein, Lithuania, Luxembourg, Madagascar, Malawi, Malaysia, Maldives, Mali, Malta, Marshall Islands, Mauritania, Mauritius, Mexico, Micronesia (Federated States of), Monaco, Mongolia, Montenegro, Morocco, Mozambique, Myanmar, Namibia, Nepal, Netherlands, New Zealand, Nicaragua, Niger, Nigeria, Norway, Palau, Panama, Papua New Guinea, Paraguay, Peru, Philippines, Poland, Portugal, Republic of Korea, Republic of Moldova, Romania, Russian Federation, Saint Kitts and Nevis, Saint Lucia, Saint Vincent and the Grenadines, Samoa, San Marino, Sao Tome and Principe, Senegal, Serbia, Seychelles, Sierra Leone, Singapore, Slovakia, Slovenia, Solomon Islands, South Africa, Spain, Sri Lanka, Suriname, Swaziland, Sweden, Switzerland, Tajikistan, Thailand, the former Yugoslav Republic of Macedonia, Timor-Leste, Togo, Tonga, Trinidad and Tobago, Turkey, Turkmenistan, Tuvalu, Uganda, Ukraine, United Arab Emirates, United Kingdom, United Republic of Tanzania, United States, Uruguay, Uzbekistan, Vanuatu, Venezuela (Bolivarian Republic of), Viet Nam, Zambia, Zimbabwe

Against:
Democratic People's Republic of Korea, Pakistan

Abstaining:
Algeria, Bahrain, Comoros, Djibouti, Ecuador, Egypt, Indonesia, Iran (Islamic Republic of), Iraq, Israel, Jordan, Kuwait, Lebanon, Libyan Arab Jamahiriya, Oman, Qatar, Saudi Arabia, Sudan, Syrian Arab Republic, Tunisia, Yemen

Operative paragraph two*

In favour:
Afghanistan, Albania, Andorra, Angola, Antigua and Barbuda, Argentina, Armenia, Australia, Austria, Azerbaijan, Bahamas, Bahrain, Bangladesh, Barbados, Belarus, Belgium, Belize, Benin, Bhutan, Bolivia (Plurinational State of), Bosnia and Herzegovina, Botswana, Brazil, Brunei Darussalam, Bulgaria, Burkina Faso, Cameroon, Canada, Cape Verde, Chad, Chile, Colombia, Comoros, Congo, Costa Rica, Côte d'Ivoire, Croatia, Cyprus, Czech Republic, Denmark, Djibouti, Dominican Republic, El Salvador, Eritrea, Estonia, Ethiopia, Fiji, Finland, France, Gabon, Georgia, Germany, Ghana, Greece, Grenada, Guatemala, Guinea, Guinea-Bissau, Guyana, Haiti, Honduras, Hungary, Iceland, India, Iraq, Ireland, Italy, Jamaica, Japan, Kazakhstan, Kenya, Kyrgyzstan, Latvia, Lesotho, Liberia, Liechtenstein, Lithuania, Luxembourg, Madagascar, Malawi, Malaysia, Maldives, Mali, Malta, Marshall Islands, Mauritius, Mexico, Micronesia (Federated States of), Monaco, Mongolia, Montenegro, Mozambique, Nepal, Netherlands,

---

* Subsequently, the delegations of Niger and Oman advised the Secretariat that they had intended to vote in favour. The voting tally above does not reflect this information.

New Zealand, Nicaragua, Nigeria, Norway, Palau, Panama, Papua New Guinea, Paraguay, Peru, Philippines, Poland, Portugal, Qatar, Republic of Korea, Republic of Moldova, Romania, Russian Federation, Saint Kitts and Nevis, Saint Lucia, Saint Vincent and the Grenadines, Samoa, San Marino, Sao Tome and Principe, Saudi Arabia, Serbia, Seychelles, Sierra Leone, Singapore, Slovakia, Slovenia, Solomon Islands, South Africa, Spain, Sri Lanka, Sudan, Suriname, Swaziland, Sweden, Switzerland, Tajikistan, Thailand, the former Yugoslav Republic of Macedonia, Timor-Leste, Togo, Tonga, Trinidad and Tobago, Tunisia, Turkey, Turkmenistan, Tuvalu, Uganda, Ukraine, United Arab Emirates, United Kingdom, United Republic of Tanzania, United States, Uruguay, Uzbekistan, Vanuatu, Venezuela (Bolivarian Republic of), Viet Nam, Zambia, Zimbabwe

Against:

Iran (Islamic Republic of), Pakistan

Abstaining:

Algeria, China, Cuba, Ecuador, Egypt, Indonesia, Israel, Jordan, Kuwait, Lebanon, Mauritania, Morocco, Myanmar, Niger, Oman, Syrian Arab Republic, Yemen

Operative paragraph three

In favour:

Afghanistan, Albania, Andorra, Angola, Antigua and Barbuda, Argentina, Armenia, Australia, Austria, Azerbaijan, Bahamas, Bahrain, Bangladesh, Barbados, Belarus, Belgium, Belize, Benin, Bhutan, Bolivia (Plurinational State of), Bosnia and Herzegovina, Botswana, Brazil, Brunei Darussalam, Bulgaria, Burkina Faso, Cameroon, Canada, Cape Verde, Chad, Chile, Colombia, Comoros, Congo, Costa Rica, Côte d'Ivoire, Croatia, Cyprus, Czech Republic, Denmark, Djibouti, Dominican Republic, El Salvador, Eritrea, Estonia, Ethiopia, Fiji, Finland, France, Gabon, Georgia, Germany, Ghana, Greece, Grenada, Guatemala, Guinea, Guinea-Bissau, Guyana, Haiti, Honduras, Hungary, Iceland, India, Iraq, Ireland, Italy, Jamaica, Japan, Kazakhstan, Kenya, Kyrgyzstan, Latvia, Lesotho, Liberia, Liechtenstein, Lithuania, Luxembourg, Madagascar, Malawi, Malaysia, Maldives, Mali, Malta, Marshall Islands, Mauritania, Mauritius, Mexico, Micronesia (Federated States of), Monaco, Mongolia, Montenegro, Morocco, Mozambique, Namibia, Nepal, Netherlands, New Zealand, Nicaragua, Niger, Nigeria, Norway, Palau, Panama, Papua New Guinea, Paraguay, Peru, Philippines, Poland, Portugal, Qatar, Republic of Korea, Republic of Moldova, Romania, Russian Federation, Saint Kitts and Nevis, Saint Lucia, Saint Vincent and the Grenadines, Samoa, San Marino, Sao Tome and Principe, Saudi Arabia, Serbia, Seychelles, Sierra Leone, Singapore,

Slovakia, Slovenia, Solomon Islands, South Africa, Spain, Sri Lanka, Sudan, Suriname, Swaziland, Sweden, Switzerland, Tajikistan, Thailand, the former Yugoslav Republic of Macedonia, Timor-Leste, Togo, Tonga, Trinidad and Tobago, Turkey, Turkmenistan, Tuvalu, Uganda, Ukraine, United Arab Emirates, United Kingdom, United Republic of Tanzania, United States, Uruguay, Uzbekistan, Vanuatu, Venezuela (Bolivarian Republic of), Viet Nam, Zambia, Zimbabwe

Against:

Democratic People's Republic of Korea, Pakistan

Abstaining:

Algeria, China, Cuba, Ecuador, Egypt, Indonesia, Iran (Islamic Republic of), Israel, Jordan, Kuwait, Lebanon, Myanmar, Oman, Syrian Arab Republic, Tunisia, Yemen

Action by the First Committee

Date: 28 October 2011   Meeting: 23rd meeting
Vote: 151-2-23   Draft resolution: A/C.1/66/L.40/Rev.1
      149-3-16, o.p. 2
      148-2-19, o.p. 3

Agenda item 98

66/45   United action towards the total elimination of nuclear weapons

Text

The General Assembly,

Recalling the need for all States to take further practical steps and effective measures towards the total elimination of nuclear weapons, with a view to achieving a peaceful and secure world free of nuclear weapons, and in this regard confirming the determination of Member States to take united action,

Noting that the ultimate objective of the efforts of States in the disarmament process is general and complete disarmament under strict and effective international control,

Recalling its resolution 65/72 of 8 December 2010,

Expressing deep concern at the catastrophic humanitarian consequences of any use of nuclear weapons, and reaffirming the need for all States at all times to comply with applicable international law, including international humanitarian law, while convinced that every effort should be made to avoid nuclear war and nuclear terrorism,

Reaffirming that the enhancement of international peace and security and the promotion of nuclear disarmament are mutually reinforcing,

Reaffirming also that further advancement in nuclear disarmament will contribute to consolidating the international regime for nuclear non-proliferation, which is, inter alia, essential to international peace and security,

Reaffirming further the crucial importance of the Treaty on the Non-Proliferation of Nuclear Weapons[1] as the cornerstone of the international nuclear non-proliferation regime and an essential foundation for the pursuit of the Treaty's three pillars, namely nuclear disarmament, nuclear non-proliferation and the peaceful uses of nuclear energy,

Recalling the decisions and the resolution of the 1995 Review and Extension Conference of the Parties to the Treaty on the Non-Proliferation of Nuclear Weapons[2] and the Final Document of the 2000[3] and 2010[4] Review

---

[1]   United Nations, *Treaty Series*, vol. 729, No. 10485.

[2]   See *1995 Review and Extension Conference of the Parties to the Treaty on the Non-Proliferation of Nuclear Weapons, Final Document, Part I* (NPT/CONF.1995/32 (Part I) and Corr.2), annex.

[3]   *2000 Review Conference of the Parties to the Treaty on the Non-Proliferation of Nuclear Weapons, Final Document*, vols. I–III (NPT/CONF.2000/28 (Parts I–IV)).

[4]   *2010 Review Conference of the Parties to the Treaty on the Non-Proliferation of Nuclear Weapons, Final Document*, vols. I–III (NPT/CONF.2010/50 (Vols. I–III)).

Conferences of the Parties to the Treaty on the Non-Proliferation of Nuclear Weapons,

Welcoming the successful outcome of the 2010 Review Conference of the Parties to the Treaty on the Non-Proliferation of Nuclear Weapons, held from 3 to 28 May 2010, in the year of the sixty-fifth anniversary of the atomic bombings in Hiroshima and Nagasaki, Japan, and reaffirming the necessity of fully implementing the action plan adopted at the Review Conference,[5]

Noting the high-level meeting on revitalizing the work of the Conference on Disarmament and taking forward multilateral disarmament negotiations, convened by the Secretary-General on 24 September 2010, and the plenary meeting of the General Assembly to follow up on the high-level meeting, held from 27 to 29 July 2011,

Welcoming the entry into force on 5 February 2011 of the Treaty between the Russian Federation and the United States of America on Measures for the Further Reduction and Limitation of Strategic Offensive Arms,

Welcoming also the recent announcements on overall stockpiles of nuclear warheads by France, the United Kingdom of Great Britain and Northern Ireland and the United States of America, as well as the update of the Russian Federation on its nuclear arsenals, which further enhance transparency and increase mutual confidence,

Expressing deep concern regarding the growing dangers posed by the proliferation of weapons of mass destruction, inter alia, nuclear weapons, including that caused by proliferation networks,

Recognizing the importance of the objective of nuclear security, along with the shared goals of Member States of nuclear disarmament, nuclear non-proliferation and peaceful uses of nuclear energy, welcoming the Nuclear Security Summit, held on 12 and 13 April 2010, and looking forward to the Nuclear Security Summit to be held in Seoul in 2012,

Recognizing also the importance of the implementation of Security Council resolutions 1718 (2006) of 14 October 2006 and 1874 (2009) of 12 June 2009 urging the Democratic People's Republic of Korea to abandon all its nuclear weapons and existing nuclear programmes and immediately cease all related activities, expressing concern regarding the Democratic People's Republic of Korea's claimed uranium enrichment programme and light water reactor construction, and declaring that the Democratic People's Republic of Korea cannot have the status of a nuclear-weapon State under the Treaty on the Non-Proliferation of Nuclear Weapons under any circumstances,

1.   *Reaffirms* the importance of all States parties to the Treaty on the Non-Proliferation of Nuclear Weapons[1] complying with their obligations under all the articles of the Treaty;

---

[5] Ibid., vol. I, part I.

2.   *Also reaffirms* the vital importance of the universality of the Treaty on the Non-Proliferation of Nuclear Weapons, and calls upon all States not parties to the Treaty to accede as non-nuclear-weapon States to the Treaty promptly and without any conditions and, pending their accession to the Treaty, to adhere to its terms and take practical steps in support of the Treaty;

3.   *Further reaffirms* the unequivocal undertaking by the nuclear-weapon States to accomplish the total elimination of their nuclear arsenals, leading to nuclear disarmament, to which all States parties to the Treaty on the Non-Proliferation of Nuclear Weapons are committed under article VI thereof;

4.   *Calls upon* nuclear-weapon States to undertake further efforts to reduce and ultimately eliminate all types of nuclear weapons, deployed and non-deployed, including through unilateral, bilateral, regional and multilateral measures;

5.   *Emphasizes* the importance of applying the principles of irreversibility, verifiability and transparency in relation to the process of nuclear disarmament and non-proliferation;

6.   *Recognizes* that nuclear disarmament and achieving the peace and security of a world without nuclear weapons require openness and cooperation, affirms the importance of enhanced confidence through increased transparency and effective verification, emphasizes the importance of the commitment by the nuclear-weapon States at the 2010 Review Conference of the Parties to the Treaty on the Non-Proliferation of Nuclear Weapons to accelerate concrete progress on the steps leading to nuclear disarmament contained in the Final Document of the 2000 Review Conference of the Parties to the Treaty on the Non-Proliferation of Nuclear Weapons in a way that promotes international stability, peace and undiminished and increased security, and the call upon the nuclear-weapon States to report their undertakings in 2014 to the Preparatory Committee for the 2015 Review Conference of the Parties to the Treaty on the Non-Proliferation of Nuclear Weapons,[5] and welcomes in this regard the convening in Paris on 30 June and 1 July 2011 of the first follow-up meeting to the 2010 Review Conference of the five nuclear-weapon States as a transparency and confidence-building measure among them;

7.   *Welcomes* the ongoing implementation by the Russian Federation and the United States of America of the Treaty on Measures for the Further Reduction and Limitation of Strategic Offensive Arms, and encourages them to continue discussions on follow-on measures in order to achieve deeper reductions in their nuclear arsenals;

8.   *Urges* all States that have not yet done so to sign and ratify the Comprehensive Nuclear-Test-Ban Treaty[6] at the earliest opportunity, with a

---

[6] See resolution 50/245.

view to its early entry into force and universalization, stresses the importance of maintaining existing moratoriums on nuclear-weapon test explosions or any other nuclear explosions pending the entry into force of the Treaty, and reaffirms the importance of the continued development of the Treaty verification regime, which will be a significant contribution to providing assurance of compliance with the Treaty;

9. *Reiterates its call for* the immediate commencement of negotiations on a fissile material cut-off treaty and its early conclusion, regrets that negotiations have not yet started, and calls upon all nuclear-weapon States and States not parties to the Treaty on the Non-Proliferation of Nuclear Weapons to declare and maintain moratoriums on the production of fissile material for any nuclear weapons or other nuclear explosive devices pending the entry into force of the treaty;

10. *Calls upon* the nuclear-weapon States to take measures to further reduce the risk of an accidental or unauthorized launch of nuclear weapons in ways that promote international stability and security, while welcoming the measures already taken by several nuclear-weapon States in this regard;

11. *Also calls upon* the nuclear-weapon States to promptly engage with a view to further diminishing the role and significance of nuclear weapons in all military and security concepts, doctrines and policies;

12. *Recognizes* the legitimate interest of non-nuclear-weapon States in receiving unequivocal and legally binding security assurances from nuclear-weapon States which could strengthen the nuclear non-proliferation regime, recalls Security Council resolution 984 (1995) of 11 April 1995, noting the unilateral statements by each of the nuclear-weapon States, and calls upon all nuclear-weapon States to fully respect their existing commitments with regard to security assurances;

13. *Encourages* the establishment of further nuclear-weapon-free zones, where appropriate, on the basis of arrangements freely arrived at among States of the region concerned and in accordance with the 1999 guidelines of the Disarmament Commission,[7] and recognizes that, by signing and ratifying relevant protocols that contain negative security assurances, nuclear-weapon States would undertake individual legally binding commitments with respect to the status of such zones and not to use or threaten to use nuclear weapons against States parties to such treaties;

14. *Calls upon* all States to redouble their efforts to prevent and curb the proliferation of nuclear weapons and their means of delivery and to fully respect and comply with obligations undertaken to forswear nuclear weapons;

15. *Stresses* the importance of the universalization of the comprehensive safeguards agreements of the International Atomic Energy

---

[7] See *Official Records of the General Assembly, Fifty-fourth Session, Supplement No. 42* (A/54/42).

Agency to include States which have not yet adopted and implemented such an agreement, while also strongly reaffirming the follow-on action of the 2010 Review Conference encouraging all States which have not done so to conclude and bring into force as soon as possible the Model Protocol Additional to the Agreement(s) between State(s) and the International Atomic Energy Agency for the Application of Safeguards approved by the Board of Governors of the Agency on 15 May 1997,[8] and the full implementation of relevant Security Council resolutions, including resolution 1540 (2004) of 28 April 2004;

16. *Encourages* every effort to secure all vulnerable nuclear and radiological material, and calls upon all States to work cooperatively as an international community to advance nuclear security, while requesting and providing assistance, including in the field of capacity-building, as necessary;

17. *Encourages* all States to implement the recommendations contained in the report of the Secretary-General on the United Nations study on disarmament and non-proliferation education,[9] in support of achieving a world without nuclear weapons, and to voluntarily share information on efforts they have been undertaking to that end;

18. *Commends and further encourages* the constructive role played by civil society in promoting nuclear non-proliferation and nuclear disarmament, and encourages all States to promote, in cooperation with civil society, disarmament and non-proliferation education which, inter alia, contributes to raising public awareness of the tragic consequences of the use of nuclear weapons and strengthens the momentum of international efforts to promote nuclear disarmament and non-proliferation;

19. *Decides* to include in the provisional agenda of its sixty-seventh session the item entitled "United action towards the total elimination of nuclear weapons".

Action by the General Assembly

Date: 2 December 2011
Vote: 169-1-11
    175-1-4, p.p. 9
    174-3-2, o.p. 2
    177-1-3, o.p. 8
    169-3-6, o.p. 9
    172-1-5, o.p. 15

Meeting: 71st plenary meeting
Report: A/66/412

Sponsors

Afghanistan, Albania, Andorra, Australia, Austria, Bangladesh, Belgium, Benin, Bosnia and Herzegovina, Bulgaria, Burkina Faso, Cambodia, Canada, Chile, Comoros, Costa Rica, Côte d'Ivoire, Croatia, Cyprus,

---

[8] International Atomic Energy Agency, document INFCIRC/540 (Corrected).
[9] See A/57/124.

Czech Republic, Democratic Republic of the Congo, Denmark, El Salvador, Estonia, Finland, Germany, Greece, Haiti, Hungary, Iraq, Italy, **Japan**, Kazakhstan, Kenya, Latvia, Lesotho, Liechtenstein, Lithuania, Luxembourg, Malawi, Mali, Mexico, Micronesia (Federated States of), Montenegro, Nepal, Netherlands, Philippines, Poland, Portugal, Republic of Korea, Romania, Senegal, Slovakia, Slovenia, Spain, Swaziland, Switzerland, Thailand, the former Yugoslav Republic of Macedonia, Tonga, Ukraine, United States, Zambia

Co-sponsors

Antigua and Barbuda, Belize, Burundi, Cameroon, Colombia, Congo, Djibouti, Dominican Republic, Eritrea, Gabon, Georgia, Guatemala, Guinea, Honduras, Iceland, Jordan, Kyrgyzstan, Mozambique, Nigeria, Norway, Palau, Papua New Guinea, Paraguay, Republic of Moldova, Saint Kitts and Nevis, Saint Lucia, Samoa, San Marino, Serbia, Tajikistan, Trinidad and Tobago, Turkey, Uganda, Uruguay, Uzbekistan, Vanuatu

Recorded vote

As a whole

In favour:

Afghanistan, Albania, Algeria, Andorra, Angola, Antigua and Barbuda, Argentina, Armenia, Australia, Austria, Azerbaijan, Bahamas, Bahrain, Bangladesh, Barbados, Belarus, Belgium, Belize, Benin, Bhutan, Bolivia (Plurinational State of), Bosnia and Herzegovina, Botswana, Brunei Darussalam, Bulgaria, Burkina Faso, Cambodia, Cameroon, Canada, Cape Verde, Chad, Chile, Colombia, Comoros, Congo, Costa Rica, Côte d'Ivoire, Croatia, Cyprus, Czech Republic, Denmark, Djibouti, Dominican Republic, Egypt, El Salvador, Eritrea, Estonia, Ethiopia, Fiji, Finland, France, Gabon, Georgia, Germany, Ghana, Greece, Grenada, Guatemala, Guinea, Guinea-Bissau, Guyana, Haiti, Honduras, Hungary, Iceland, Indonesia, Iraq, Ireland, Italy, Jamaica, Japan, Jordan, Kazakhstan, Kenya, Kuwait, Kyrgyzstan, Lao People's Democratic Republic, Latvia, Lebanon, Lesotho, Liberia, Libyan Arab Jamahiriya, Liechtenstein, Lithuania, Luxembourg, Madagascar, Malawi, Malaysia, Maldives, Mali, Malta, Marshall Islands, Mauritania, Mexico, Micronesia (Federated States of), Monaco, Mongolia, Montenegro, Morocco, Mozambique, Namibia, Nepal, Netherlands, New Zealand, Nicaragua, Niger, Nigeria, Norway, Oman, Palau, Panama, Papua New Guinea, Paraguay, Peru, Philippines, Poland, Portugal, Qatar, Republic of Korea, Republic of Moldova, Romania, Russian Federation, Saint Kitts and Nevis, Saint Lucia, Saint Vincent and the Grenadines, Samoa, San Marino, Sao Tome and Principe, Saudi Arabia, Senegal, Serbia, Seychelles, Sierra Leone, Singapore, Slovakia, Slovenia, Solomon Islands, Spain, Sri Lanka, Sudan, Suriname, Swaziland, Sweden, Switzerland, Tajikistan, Thailand, the former Yugoslav Republic of

Macedonia, Timor-Leste, Togo, Tonga, Trinidad and Tobago, Tunisia, Turkey, Turkmenistan, Tuvalu, Uganda, Ukraine, United Arab Emirates, United Kingdom, United Republic of Tanzania, United States, Uruguay, Uzbekistan, Vanuatu, Venezuela (Bolivarian Republic of), Viet Nam, Yemen, Zambia, Zimbabwe

Against:

Democratic People's Republic of Korea

Abstaining:

Brazil, China, Cuba, Ecuador, India, Iran (Islamic Republic of), Israel, Mauritius, Myanmar, Pakistan, Syrian Arab Republic

Ninth preambular paragraph

In favour:

Afghanistan, Albania, Algeria, Andorra, Angola, Antigua and Barbuda, Argentina, Armenia, Australia, Austria, Azerbaijan, Bahamas, Bahrain, Bangladesh, Barbados, Belarus, Belgium, Belize, Benin, Bhutan, Bolivia (Plurinational State of), Bosnia and Herzegovina, Botswana, Brazil, Brunei Darussalam, Bulgaria, Burkina Faso, Cambodia, Cameroon, Canada, Cape Verde, Chad, Chile, Colombia, Comoros, Congo, Costa Rica, Côte d'Ivoire, Croatia, Cuba, Cyprus, Czech Republic, Denmark, Djibouti, Dominican Republic, Ecuador, Egypt, El Salvador, Eritrea, Estonia, Ethiopia, Fiji, Finland, France, Gabon, Georgia, Germany, Ghana, Greece, Grenada, Guatemala, Guinea, Guinea-Bissau, Guyana, Haiti, Honduras, Hungary, Iceland, Indonesia, Iran (Islamic Republic of), Iraq, Ireland, Italy, Jamaica, Japan, Jordan, Kazakhstan, Kenya, Kuwait, Kyrgyzstan, Lao People's Democratic Republic, Latvia, Lebanon, Lesotho, Liberia, Libyan Arab Jamahiriya, Liechtenstein, Lithuania, Luxembourg, Madagascar, Malawi, Malaysia, Maldives, Mali, Malta, Marshall Islands, Mauritania, Mauritius, Mexico, Micronesia (Federated States of), Monaco, Mongolia, Montenegro, Morocco, Mozambique, Myanmar, Namibia, Nepal, Netherlands, New Zealand, Nicaragua, Niger, Nigeria, Norway, Oman, Palau, Panama, Papua New Guinea, Paraguay, Peru, Philippines, Poland, Portugal, Qatar, Republic of Korea, Republic of Moldova, Romania, Russian Federation, Saint Kitts and Nevis, Saint Lucia, Saint Vincent and the Grenadines, Samoa, San Marino, Sao Tome and Principe, Saudi Arabia, Senegal, Serbia, Seychelles, Sierra Leone, Singapore, Slovakia, Slovenia, Solomon Islands, Spain, Sri Lanka, Sudan, Suriname, Swaziland, Sweden, Switzerland, Tajikistan, Thailand, the former Yugoslav Republic of Macedonia, Timor-Leste, Togo, Tonga, Trinidad and Tobago, Tunisia, Turkey, Turkmenistan, Tuvalu, Uganda, Ukraine, United Arab Emirates, United Kingdom, United Republic of Tanzania, United States, Uruguay, Uzbekistan, Vanuatu, Venezuela (Bolivarian Republic of), Viet Nam, Yemen, Zambia, Zimbabwe

Against:

Democratic People's Republic of Korea

Abstaining:

India, Israel, Pakistan, South Africa

Operative paragraph two

In favour:

Afghanistan, Albania, Algeria, Andorra, Angola, Antigua and Barbuda, Argentina, Armenia, Australia, Austria, Azerbaijan, Bahamas, Bahrain, Bangladesh, Barbados, Belarus, Belgium, Belize, Benin, Bolivia (Plurinational State of), Bosnia and Herzegovina, Botswana, Brazil, Brunei Darussalam, Bulgaria, Burkina Faso, Cambodia, Cameroon, Canada, Cape Verde, Chad, Chile, China, Colombia, Comoros, Congo, Costa Rica, Côte d'Ivoire, Croatia, Cuba, Cyprus, Czech Republic, Denmark, Djibouti, Dominican Republic, Ecuador, Egypt, El Salvador, Eritrea, Estonia, Ethiopia, Fiji, Finland, France, Gabon, Georgia, Germany, Ghana, Greece, Grenada, Guatemala, Guinea, Guinea-Bissau, Guyana, Haiti, Honduras, Hungary, Iceland, Indonesia, Iraq, Ireland, Italy, Jamaica, Japan, Jordan, Kazakhstan, Kenya, Kuwait, Kyrgyzstan, Lao People's Democratic Republic, Latvia, Lebanon, Lesotho, Liberia, Libyan Arab Jamahiriya, Liechtenstein, Lithuania, Luxembourg, Madagascar, Malawi, Malaysia, Maldives, Mali, Malta, Marshall Islands, Mauritania, Mexico, Micronesia (Federated States of), Monaco, Mongolia, Montenegro, Morocco, Mozambique, Myanmar, Namibia, Nepal, Netherlands, New Zealand, Nicaragua, Niger, Nigeria, Norway, Oman, Palau, Panama, Papua New Guinea, Paraguay, Peru, Philippines, Poland, Portugal, Qatar, Republic of Korea, Republic of Moldova, Romania, Russian Federation, Saint Kitts and Nevis, Saint Lucia, Saint Vincent and the Grenadines, Samoa, San Marino, Sao Tome and Principe, Saudi Arabia, Senegal, Serbia, Seychelles, Sierra Leone, Singapore, Slovakia, Slovenia, Solomon Islands, South Africa, Spain, Sri Lanka, Sudan, Suriname, Swaziland, Sweden, Switzerland, Tajikistan, Thailand, the former Yugoslav Republic of Macedonia, Timor-Leste, Togo, Tonga, Trinidad and Tobago, Tunisia, Turkey, Turkmenistan, Tuvalu, Uganda, Ukraine, United Arab Emirates, United Kingdom, United Republic of Tanzania, United States, Uruguay, Uzbekistan, Vanuatu, Venezuela (Bolivarian Republic of), Viet Nam, Yemen, Zambia, Zimbabwe

Against:

Democratic People's Republic of Korea, India, Israel

Abstaining:

Bhutan, Pakistan

Operative paragraph eight

In favour:

Afghanistan, Albania, Algeria, Andorra, Angola, Antigua and Barbuda, Argentina, Armenia, Australia, Austria, Azerbaijan, Bahamas, Bahrain, Bangladesh, Barbados, Belarus, Belgium, Belize, Benin, Bhutan, Bolivia (Plurinational State of), Bosnia and Herzegovina, Botswana, Brazil, Brunei Darussalam, Bulgaria, Burkina Faso, Cambodia, Cameroon, Canada, Cape Verde, Chad, Chile, China, Colombia, Comoros, Congo, Costa Rica, Côte d'Ivoire, Croatia, Cuba, Cyprus, Czech Republic, Denmark, Djibouti, Dominican Republic, Ecuador, Egypt, El Salvador, Eritrea, Estonia, Ethiopia, Fiji, Finland, France, Gabon, Georgia, Germany, Ghana, Greece, Grenada, Guatemala, Guinea, Guinea-Bissau, Guyana, Haiti, Honduras, Hungary, Iceland, Indonesia, Iraq, Ireland, Israel, Italy, Jamaica, Japan, Jordan, Kazakhstan, Kenya, Kuwait, Kyrgyzstan, Lao People's Democratic Republic, Latvia, Lebanon, Lesotho, Liberia, Libyan Arab Jamahiriya, Liechtenstein, Lithuania, Luxembourg, Madagascar, Malawi, Malaysia, Maldives, Mali, Malta, Marshall Islands, Mauritania, Mexico, Micronesia (Federated States of), Monaco, Mongolia, Montenegro, Morocco, Mozambique, Myanmar, Namibia, Nepal, Netherlands, New Zealand, Nicaragua, Niger, Nigeria, Norway, Oman, Pakistan, Palau, Panama, Papua New Guinea, Paraguay, Peru, Philippines, Poland, Portugal, Qatar, Republic of Korea, Republic of Moldova, Romania, Russian Federation, Saint Kitts and Nevis, Saint Lucia, Saint Vincent and the Grenadines, Samoa, San Marino, Sao Tome and Principe, Saudi Arabia, Senegal, Serbia, Seychelles, Sierra Leone, Singapore, Slovakia, Slovenia, Solomon Islands, South Africa, Spain, Sri Lanka, Sudan, Suriname, Swaziland, Sweden, Switzerland, Tajikistan, Thailand, the former Yugoslav Republic of Macedonia, Timor-Leste, Togo, Tonga, Trinidad and Tobago, Tunisia, Turkey, Turkmenistan, Tuvalu, Uganda, Ukraine, United Arab Emirates, United Kingdom, United Republic of Tanzania, United States, Uruguay, Uzbekistan, Vanuatu, Venezuela (Bolivarian Republic of), Viet Nam, Yemen, Zambia, Zimbabwe

Against:

Democratic People's Republic of Korea

Abstaining:

India, Mauritius, Syrian Arab Republic

Operative paragraph nine

In favour:

Afghanistan, Albania, Algeria, Andorra, Angola, Antigua and Barbuda, Argentina, Armenia, Australia, Austria, Azerbaijan, Bahamas, Bahrain, Bangladesh, Barbados, Belarus, Belgium, Belize, Benin, Bhutan, Bolivia (Plurinational State of), Bosnia and Herzegovina, Botswana, Brunei Darussalam, Bulgaria, Burkina Faso, Cambodia, Cameroon, Canada,

Cape Verde, Chad, Chile, Colombia, Comoros, Congo, Costa Rica, Côte d'Ivoire, Croatia, Cuba, Cyprus, Czech Republic, Denmark, Djibouti, Dominican Republic, Egypt, El Salvador, Eritrea, Estonia, Ethiopia, Fiji, Finland, France, Gabon, Georgia, Germany, Ghana, Greece, Grenada, Guatemala, Guinea, Guinea-Bissau, Guyana, Haiti, Honduras, Hungary, Iceland, Indonesia, Iraq, Ireland, Italy, Jamaica, Japan, Jordan, Kazakhstan, Kenya, Kuwait, Kyrgyzstan, Lao People's Democratic Republic, Latvia, Lebanon, Lesotho, Liberia, Libyan Arab Jamahiriya, Liechtenstein, Lithuania, Luxembourg, Madagascar, Malawi, Malaysia, Maldives, Mali, Malta, Marshall Islands, Mauritania, Mauritius, Mexico, Micronesia (Federated States of), Monaco, Mongolia, Montenegro, Morocco, Mozambique, Myanmar, Namibia, Nepal, Netherlands, New Zealand, Nicaragua, Niger, Nigeria, Norway, Oman, Palau, Panama, Papua New Guinea, Paraguay, Peru, Philippines, Poland, Portugal, Qatar, Republic of Korea, Republic of Moldova, Romania, Saint Kitts and Nevis, Saint Lucia, Saint Vincent and the Grenadines, Samoa, San Marino, Sao Tome and Principe, Saudi Arabia, Senegal, Serbia, Seychelles, Sierra Leone, Singapore, Slovakia, Slovenia, Solomon Islands, South Africa, Spain, Sudan, Suriname, Swaziland, Sweden, Switzerland, Tajikistan, Thailand, the former Yugoslav Republic of Macedonia, Timor-Leste, Togo, Tonga, Tunisia, Turkey, Turkmenistan, Tuvalu, Uganda, Ukraine, United Arab Emirates, United Kingdom, United Republic of Tanzania, United States, Uruguay, Uzbekistan, Vanuatu, Viet Nam, Yemen, Zambia, Zimbabwe

Against:

China, Democratic People's Republic of Korea, Pakistan

Abstaining:

Brazil, Ecuador, India, Israel, Russian Federation, Venezuela (Bolivarian Republic of)

Operative paragraph fifteen

In favour:

Afghanistan, Albania, Algeria, Andorra, Angola, Antigua and Barbuda, Armenia, Australia, Austria, Azerbaijan, Bahamas, Bahrain, Bangladesh, Barbados, Belarus, Belgium, Belize, Benin, Bhutan, Bolivia (Plurinational State of), Bosnia and Herzegovina, Botswana, Brunei Darussalam, Bulgaria, Burkina Faso, Cambodia, Cameroon, Canada, Cape Verde, Chad, Chile, China, Colombia, Comoros, Congo, Costa Rica, Côte d'Ivoire, Croatia, Cuba, Cyprus, Czech Republic, Denmark, Djibouti, Dominican Republic, Ecuador, Egypt, El Salvador, Eritrea, Estonia, Ethiopia, Fiji, Finland, France, Gabon, Georgia, Germany, Ghana, Greece, Grenada, Guatemala, Guinea, Guinea-Bissau, Guyana, Haiti, Honduras, Hungary, Iceland, Indonesia, Iraq, Ireland, Italy, Jamaica, Japan, Jordan, Kazakhstan, Kenya, Kuwait, Kyrgyzstan, Lao People's Democratic Republic, Latvia, Lebanon,

Lesotho, Liberia, Libyan Arab Jamahiriya, Liechtenstein, Lithuania, Luxembourg, Madagascar, Malawi, Malaysia, Maldives, Mali, Malta, Marshall Islands, Mauritania, Mauritius, Mexico, Monaco, Mongolia, Montenegro, Morocco, Mozambique, Myanmar, Namibia, Nepal, Netherlands, New Zealand, Nicaragua, Niger, Nigeria, Norway, Oman, Palau, Panama, Papua New Guinea, Paraguay, Peru, Philippines, Poland, Portugal, Qatar, Republic of Korea, Republic of Moldova, Romania, Russian Federation, Saint Kitts and Nevis, Saint Lucia, Saint Vincent and the Grenadines, Samoa, San Marino, Sao Tome and Principe, Saudi Arabia, Senegal, Serbia, Seychelles, Sierra Leone, Singapore, Slovakia, Slovenia, Solomon Islands, South Africa, Spain, Sri Lanka, Suriname, Swaziland, Sweden, Switzerland, Tajikistan, Thailand, the former Yugoslav Republic of Macedonia, Timor-Leste, Togo, Tonga, Trinidad and Tobago, Tunisia, Turkey, Turkmenistan, Tuvalu, Uganda, Ukraine, United Arab Emirates, United Kingdom, United Republic of Tanzania, United States, Uruguay, Uzbekistan, Vanuatu, Venezuela (Bolivarian Republic of), Viet Nam, Yemen, Zambia, Zimbabwe

Against:
Democratic People's Republic of Korea

Abstaining:
Argentina, Brazil, India, Israel, Pakistan

Action by the First Committee

Date: 26 October 2011   Meeting: 21st meeting
Vote: 156-1-15   Draft resolution: A/C.1/66/L.41
      165-1-3, p.p. 9
      166-3-2, o.p. 2
      167-1-3, o.p. 8
      161-3-7, o.p. 9
      164-1-5, o.p. 15

Agenda item 98

66/46 Follow-up to the advisory opinion of the International Court of Justice on the *Legality of the Threat or Use of Nuclear Weapons*

Text

> *The General Assembly*,

> *Recalling* its resolutions 49/75 K of 15 December 1994, 51/45 M of 10 December 1996, 52/38 O of 9 December 1997, 53/77 W of 4 December 1998, 54/54 Q of 1 December 1999, 55/33 X of 20 November 2000, 56/24 S of 29 November 2001, 57/85 of 22 November 2002, 58/46 of 8 December 2003, 59/83 of 3 December 2004, 60/76 of 8 December 2005, 61/83 of 6 December 2006, 62/39 of 5 December 2007, 63/49 of 2 December 2008, 64/55 of 2 December 2009 and 65/76 of 8 December 2010,

> *Convinced* that the continuing existence of nuclear weapons poses a threat to humanity and all life on Earth, and recognizing that the only defence against a nuclear catastrophe is the total elimination of nuclear weapons and the certainty that they will never be produced again,

> *Reaffirming* the commitment of the international community to the realization of the goal of a nuclear-weapon-free world through the total elimination of nuclear weapons,

> *Mindful* of the solemn obligations of States parties, undertaken in article VI of the Treaty on the Non-Proliferation of Nuclear Weapons,[1] particularly to pursue negotiations in good faith on effective measures relating to cessation of the nuclear arms race at an early date and to nuclear disarmament,

> *Recalling* the principles and objectives for nuclear non-proliferation and disarmament adopted at the 1995 Review and Extension Conference of the Parties to the Treaty on the Non-Proliferation of Nuclear Weapons,[2] the unequivocal commitment of nuclear-weapon States to accomplish the total elimination of their nuclear arsenals leading to nuclear disarmament, agreed at the 2000 Review Conference of the Parties to the Treaty on the Non-Proliferation of Nuclear Weapons,[3] and the action points agreed at the 2010 Review Conference of the Parties to the Treaty on the Non-Proliferation

---

[1] United Nations, *Treaty Series*, vol. 729, No. 10485.

[2] *1995 Review and Extension Conference of the Parties to the Treaty on the Non-Proliferation of Nuclear Weapons, Final Document, Part I* (NPT/CONF.1995/32 (Part I) and Corr.2), annex, decision 2.

[3] See *2000 Review Conference of the Parties to the Treaty on the Non-Proliferation of Nuclear Weapons, Final Document*, vol. I (NPT/CONF.2000/28 (Parts I and II)), part I, section entitled "Article VI and eighth to twelfth preambular paragraphs", para. 15.

of Nuclear Weapons as part of the conclusions and recommendations for follow-on actions on nuclear disarmament,[4]

Sharing the deep concern at the catastrophic humanitarian consequences of any use of nuclear weapons, and in this context reaffirming the need for all States at all times to comply with applicable international law, including international humanitarian law,

Calling upon all nuclear-weapon States to undertake concrete disarmament efforts, and stressing that all States need to make special efforts to achieve and maintain a world without nuclear weapons,

Noting the five-point proposal for nuclear disarmament of the Secretary-General,[5] in which he proposes, inter alia, the consideration of negotiations on a nuclear weapons convention or agreement on a framework of separate mutually reinforcing instruments, backed by a strong system of verification,

Recalling the adoption of the Comprehensive Nuclear-Test-Ban Treaty in its resolution 50/245 of 10 September 1996, and expressing its satisfaction at the increasing number of States that have signed and ratified the Treaty,

Recognizing with satisfaction that the Antarctic Treaty,[6] the treaties of Tlatelolco,[7] Rarotonga,[8] Bangkok[9] and Pelindaba[10] and the Treaty on a Nuclear-Weapon-Free Zone in Central Asia, as well as Mongolia's nuclear-weapon-free status, are gradually freeing the entire southern hemisphere and adjacent areas covered by those treaties from nuclear weapons,

Recognizing the need for a multilaterally negotiated and legally binding instrument to assure non-nuclear-weapon States against the threat or use of nuclear weapons pending the total elimination of nuclear weapons,

Reaffirming the central role of the Conference on Disarmament as the sole multilateral disarmament negotiating forum,

Emphasizing the need for the Conference on Disarmament to commence negotiations on a phased programme for the complete elimination of nuclear weapons with a specified framework of time,

Stressing the urgent need for the nuclear-weapon States to accelerate concrete progress on the thirteen practical steps to implement article VI of the Treaty on the Non-Proliferation of Nuclear Weapons leading to

---

[4] See *2010 Review Conference of the Parties to the Treaty on the Non-Proliferation of Nuclear Weapons, Final Document*, vols. I–III (NPT/CONF.2010/50 (Vols. I–III)), vol. I, part I.

[5] Available from www.un.org/disarmament/WMD/Nuclear/sg5point.

[6] United Nations, *Treaty Series*, vol. 402, No. 5778.

[7] Ibid., vol. 634, No. 9068.

[8] See *The United Nations Disarmament Yearbook*, vol. 10: 1985 (United Nations publication, Sales No. E.86.IX.7), appendix VII.

[9] United Nations, *Treaty Series*, vol. 1981, No. 33873.

[10] A/50/426, annex.

nuclear disarmament, contained in the Final Document of the 2000 Review Conference,[3]

Taking note of the Model Nuclear Weapons Convention that was submitted to the Secretary-General by Costa Rica and Malaysia in 2007 and circulated by the Secretary-General,[11]

Desiring to achieve the objective of a legally binding prohibition of the development, production, testing, deployment, stockpiling, threat or use of nuclear weapons and their destruction under effective international control,

Recalling the advisory opinion of the International Court of Justice on the *Legality of the Threat or Use of Nuclear Weapons*, issued on 8 July 1996,[12]

1.   *Underlines once again* the unanimous conclusion of the International Court of Justice that there exists an obligation to pursue in good faith and bring to a conclusion negotiations leading to nuclear disarmament in all its aspects under strict and effective international control;

2.   *Calls once again upon* all States immediately to fulfil that obligation by commencing multilateral negotiations leading to an early conclusion of a nuclear weapons convention prohibiting the development, production, testing, deployment, stockpiling, transfer, threat or use of nuclear weapons and providing for their elimination;

3.   *Requests* all States to inform the Secretary-General of the efforts and measures they have taken with respect to the implementation of the present resolution and nuclear disarmament, and requests the Secretary-General to apprise the General Assembly of that information at its sixty-seventh session;

4.   *Decides* to include in the provisional agenda of its sixty-seventh session the item entitled "Follow-up to the advisory opinion of the International Court of Justice on the *Legality of the Threat or Use of Nuclear Weapons*".

Action by the General Assembly

Date: 2 December 2011   Meeting: 71st plenary meeting
Vote: 130-26-23   Report: A/66/412

Sponsors

Algeria, Bangladesh, Belize, Benin, Brazil, Brunei Darussalam, Burkina Faso, Cambodia, Chile, Comoros, Costa Rica, Cuba, Democratic People's Republic of Korea, Dominican Republic, Ecuador, Egypt, Fiji, Guatemala, Guyana, Haiti, Honduras, India, Indonesia, Iran (Islamic Republic of), Iraq, Jamaica, Kenya, Lao People's Democratic Republic,

---

[11] See A/62/650, annex.
[12] A/51/218, annex; see also *Legality of the Threat or Use of Nuclear Weapons, Advisory Opinion, I.C.J. Reports 1996*, p. 226.

Lesotho, Libyan Arab Jamahiriya, Madagascar, **Malaysia**, Mexico, Myanmar, Nepal, Nicaragua, Nigeria, Peru, Philippines, Samoa, Senegal, Sierra Leone, Singapore, Sri Lanka, Sudan, Syrian Arab Republic, Thailand, Trinidad and Tobago, United Republic of Tanzania, Uruguay, Viet Nam, Zimbabwe

Co-sponsors

Congo, Saint Vincent and the Grenadines, Venezuela (Bolivarian Republic of)

Recorded vote

In favour:

Afghanistan, Algeria, Angola, Antigua and Barbuda, Argentina, Austria, Azerbaijan, Bahamas, Bahrain, Bangladesh, Barbados, Belize, Benin, Bhutan, Bolivia (Plurinational State of), Bosnia and Herzegovina, Botswana, Brazil, Brunei Darussalam, Burkina Faso, Cambodia, Cape Verde, Chad, Chile, China, Colombia, Comoros, Congo, Costa Rica, Côte d'Ivoire, Cuba, Democratic People's Republic of Korea, Djibouti, Dominican Republic, Ecuador, Egypt, El Salvador, Eritrea, Ethiopia, Fiji, Ghana, Grenada, Guatemala, Guinea, Guinea-Bissau, Guyana, Haiti, Honduras, India, Indonesia, Iran (Islamic Republic of), Iraq, Ireland, Jamaica, Jordan, Kazakhstan, Kenya, Kuwait, Lao People's Democratic Republic, Lebanon, Lesotho, Liberia, Libyan Arab Jamahiriya, Madagascar, Malawi, Malaysia, Maldives, Mali, Malta, Mauritania, Mauritius, Mexico, Mongolia, Morocco, Mozambique, Myanmar, Namibia, Nepal, New Zealand, Nicaragua, Niger, Nigeria, Oman, Pakistan, Panama, Papua New Guinea, Paraguay, Peru, Philippines, Qatar, Saint Kitts and Nevis, Saint Lucia, Saint Vincent and the Grenadines, Samoa, San Marino, Sao Tome and Principe, Saudi Arabia, Senegal, Serbia, Seychelles, Sierra Leone, Singapore, Solomon Islands, South Africa, Sri Lanka, Sudan, Suriname, Swaziland, Sweden, Switzerland, Syrian Arab Republic, Thailand, Timor-Leste, Togo, Tonga, Trinidad and Tobago, Tunisia, Turkmenistan, Tuvalu, Uganda, Ukraine, United Arab Emirates, United Republic of Tanzania, Uruguay, Vanuatu, Venezuela (Bolivarian Republic of), Viet Nam, Yemen, Zambia, Zimbabwe

Against:

Albania, Belgium, Bulgaria, Czech Republic, Denmark, Estonia, France, Germany, Greece, Hungary, Israel, Italy, Latvia, Lithuania, Luxembourg, Netherlands, Palau, Poland, Portugal, Russian Federation, Slovakia, Slovenia, Spain, Turkey, United Kingdom, United States

Abstaining:

Andorra, Armenia, Australia, Belarus, Canada, Croatia, Cyprus, Finland, Georgia, Iceland, Japan, Kyrgyzstan, Liechtenstein, Marshall Islands, Micronesia (Federated States of), Montenegro, Norway, Republic of Korea, Republic of Moldova, Romania, Tajikistan, the former Yugoslav Republic of Macedonia, Uzbekistan

Action by the First Committee

Date: 27 October 2011   Meeting: 22nd meeting
Vote: 127-25-22   Draft resolution: A/C.1/66/L.42

Agenda item 98

66/47 The illicit trade in small arms and light weapons in all its aspects

Text

> *The General Assembly,*
>
> *Recalling* its resolution 65/64 of 8 December 2010, as well as all previous resolutions entitled "The illicit trade in small arms and light weapons in all its aspects", including resolution 56/24 V of 24 December 2001,
>
> *Emphasizing* the importance of the continued and full implementation of the Programme of Action to Prevent, Combat and Eradicate the Illicit Trade in Small Arms and Light Weapons in All Its Aspects, adopted by the United Nations Conference on the Illicit Trade in Small Arms and Light Weapons in All Its Aspects,[1]
>
> *Welcoming* the tenth anniversary of the adoption of the Programme of Action, and recognizing its important contribution to international efforts on this matter,
>
> *Emphasizing* the importance of the continued and full implementation of the International Instrument to Enable States to Identify and Trace, in a Timely and Reliable Manner, Illicit Small Arms and Light Weapons (the International Tracing Instrument),[2]
>
> *Recalling* the commitment of States to the Programme of Action as the main framework for measures within the activities of the international community to prevent, combat and eradicate the illicit trade in small arms and light weapons in all its aspects,
>
> *Underlining* the need for States to enhance their efforts to build national capacity for the effective implementation of the Programme of Action and the International Tracing Instrument,
>
> *Welcoming* the Open-ended Meeting of Governmental Experts on the Implementation of the Programme of Action to Prevent, Combat and Eradicate the Illicit Trade in Small Arms and Light Weapons in All Its Aspects, held in New York from 9 to 13 May 2011,
>
> *Welcoming also* the early designation of Nigeria as the Chair of the second conference to review progress made in the implementation of the Programme of Action, to be held in 2012, and of its preparatory committee,

---

[1] See *Report of the United Nations Conference on the Illicit Trade in Small Arms and Light Weapons in All Its Aspects, New York, 9–20 July 2001* (A/CONF.192/15), chap. IV, para. 24.

[2] A/60/88 and Corr.2, annex; see also decision 60/519.

Stressing the importance of voluntary national reporting to follow up on the Programme of Action as a means of assessing overall implementation efforts, including implementation challenges and opportunities, and which could greatly facilitate the rendering of international cooperation and assistance to affected States,

Noting that tools developed by the Office for Disarmament Affairs of the Secretariat, including the Programme of Action Implementation Support System, and those developed by Member States could be used to assess progress made in the implementation of the Programme of Action,

Welcoming the coordinated efforts within the United Nations to implement the Programme of Action, including by developing the Programme of Action Implementation Support System, which forms an integrated clearing house for international cooperation and assistance for capacity-building in the area of small arms and light weapons,

Taking into account the importance of regional approaches to the implementation of the Programme of Action,

Noting with satisfaction regional and subregional efforts being undertaken in support of the implementation of the Programme of Action, and commending the progress that has already been made in this regard, including tackling both supply and demand factors that are relevant to addressing the illicit trade in small arms and light weapons,

Reiterating that illicit brokering in small arms and light weapons is a serious problem that the international community should address urgently,

Recognizing the efforts undertaken by non-governmental organizations in the provision of assistance to States for the implementation of the Programme of Action,

Taking note of the report of the Secretary-General,[3] which includes an overview of the implementation of resolution 65/64,

1.   *Underlines* the fact that the issue of the illicit trade in small arms and light weapons in all its aspects requires concerted efforts at the national, regional and international levels to prevent, combat and eradicate the illicit manufacture, transfer and circulation of small arms and light weapons, and that their uncontrolled spread in many regions of the world has a wide range of humanitarian and socio-economic consequences and poses a serious threat to peace, reconciliation, safety, security, stability and sustainable development at the individual, local, national, regional and international levels;

2.   *Encourages* all initiatives, including those of the United Nations, other international organizations, regional and subregional organizations,

---

[3] A/66/177.

non-governmental organizations and civil society, for the successful implementation of the Programme of Action to Prevent, Combat and Eradicate the Illicit Trade in Small Arms and Light Weapons in All Its Aspects,[1] and calls upon all Member States to contribute towards the continued implementation of the Programme of Action at the national, regional and global levels;

3.   *Encourages* States to implement the recommendations contained in the report of the Group of Governmental Experts established pursuant to resolution 60/81 to consider further steps to enhance international cooperation in preventing, combating and eradicating illicit brokering in small arms and light weapons;[4]

4.   *Recalls* its endorsement of the report adopted at the fourth biennial meeting of States to consider the implementation of the Programme of Action,[5] and encourages all States to implement, as appropriate, the measures highlighted in the section of the report entitled "The way forward";

5.   *Endorses* the report adopted at the Open-ended Meeting of Governmental Experts on the Implementation of the Programme of Action to Prevent, Combat and Eradicate the Illicit Trade in Small Arms and Light Weapons in All Its Aspects,[6] and takes note with appreciation of the Chair's summary of discussions,[7] prepared under his own responsibility, reflecting his interpretation of the main points under discussion;

6.   *Decides* that, pursuant to resolution 65/64, the second conference to review progress made in the implementation of the Programme of Action will be held in New York, from 27 August to 7 September 2012;

7.   *Also decides* that the preparatory committee for the review conference will be convened in New York, from 19 to 23 March 2012;

8.   *Encourages* all efforts to build national capacity for the effective implementation of the Programme of Action, including those highlighted in the report of the fourth biennial meeting of States, and, inter alia, through the strengthening of national coordination agencies or bodies and institutional infrastructure;

9.   *Encourages* States to submit, on a voluntary basis, national reports on their implementation of the Programme of Action,[8] notes that States will submit national reports on their implementation of the International Tracing

---

[4] See A/62/163 and Corr.1.
[5] See A/CONF.192/BMS/2010/3, sect. IV, para. 23.
[6] A/CONF.192/MGE/2011/1.
[7] A/66/157, annex.
[8] See *Report of the United Nations Conference on the Illicit Trade in Small Arms and Light Weapons in All Its Aspects, New York, 9–20 July 2001* (A/CONF.192/15), chap. IV (sect. II, para. 33, of the quoted text).

Instrument,[9] in advance of the convening of the preparatory committee but, to the extent possible, by the end of 2011, and encourages those States in a position to do so to use the reporting template made available by the Office for Disarmament Affairs[10] and to include therein information, as appropriate, on progress made in the implementation of the measures highlighted in the reports of the third and fourth biennial meetings of States;

10. *Also encourages* States, on a voluntary basis, to make increasing use of their national reports as another tool for communicating assistance needs and information on the resources and mechanisms available to address such needs, and encourages States in a position to render such assistance to make use of these national reports;

11. *Encourages* States, relevant international and regional organizations and civil society with the capacity to do so to cooperate with and assist other States, upon request, in the preparation of comprehensive reports on their implementation of the Programme of Action;

12. *Calls upon* all States to implement the International Tracing Instrument by, inter alia, including in their national reports the name and contact information of the national points of contact and information on national marking practices used to indicate country of manufacture and/or country of import, as applicable;

13. *Recognizes* the urgent need to maintain and enhance national controls, in accordance with the Programme of Action, to prevent, combat and eradicate the illicit trade in small arms and light weapons, including their diversion to unauthorized recipients, taking into account, inter alia, their adverse humanitarian and socio-economic consequences on the affected States;

14. *Invites* States, at the second review conference, to review progress made in the implementation of the Programme of Action, and, subject to the agenda of the conference to be agreed by the preparatory committee, encourages them to explore ways to strengthen its implementation, including consideration of the possibility of convening a further open-ended meeting of governmental experts;

15. *Encourages* States in a position to do so to provide financial assistance, through a voluntary sponsorship fund, that could be distributed, upon request, to States otherwise unable to participate in meetings on the Programme of Action;

16. *Encourages* interested States and relevant international and regional organizations in a position to do so to convene regional meetings to consider and advance the implementation of the Programme of Action, as well

---

[9] See A/60/88 and Corr.2, annex, para. 36.

[10] Available from www.poa-iss.org/reporting.

as the International Tracing Instrument, in preparation for the meetings on the Programme of Action;

17. *Emphasizes* the fact that initiatives by the international community with respect to international cooperation and assistance remain essential and complementary to national implementation efforts, as well as to those at the regional and global levels;

18. *Encourages* States to consider ways to enhance cooperation and assistance and to assess their effectiveness in order to ensure the implementation of the Programme of Action;

19. *Recognizes* the necessity for interested States to develop effective coordination mechanisms, where they do not exist, in order to match the needs of States with existing resources to enhance the implementation of the Programme of Action and to make international cooperation and assistance more effective, and in this regard encourages States to make use, as appropriate, of the Programme of Action Implementation Support System;

20. *Encourages* States to consider, among other mechanisms, the coherent identification of needs, priorities, national plans and programmes that may require international cooperation and assistance from States and regional and international organizations in a position to do so;

21. *Encourages* civil society and relevant organizations to strengthen their cooperation and work with States at the respective national and regional levels to achieve the implementation of the Programme of Action;

22. *Requests* the Secretary-General to report to the General Assembly at its sixty-seventh session on the implementation of the present resolution;

23. *Decides* to include in the provisional agenda of its sixty-seventh session the item entitled "The illicit trade in small arms and light weapons in all its aspects".

Action by the General Assembly

Date: 2 December 2011   Meeting: 71st plenary meeting
Vote: Adopted without a vote   Report: A/66/412

Sponsors

Argentina, Australia, Bosnia and Herzegovina, Chad, Colombia, Costa Rica, Croatia, Czech Republic, Ethiopia, Finland, France, Ireland, Italy, **Japan**, Kazakhstan, Kenya, Lesotho, Liechtenstein, Luxembourg, Mali, Montenegro, Morocco, New Zealand, Nigeria, Panama, Peru, Philippines, Portugal, Republic of Korea, Republic of Moldova, Senegal, Slovakia, Slovenia, South Africa, Sweden, Switzerland, Thailand, the former Yugoslav Republic of Macedonia, Turkey, United Kingdom, United States

Co-sponsors

Afghanistan, Albania, Armenia, Austria, Bangladesh, Belgium, Belize, Benin, Botswana, Brazil, Bulgaria, Congo, Cyprus, Democratic Republic of the Congo, Denmark, Eritrea, Estonia, Georgia, Germany, Greece, Guatemala, Guyana, Haiti, Honduras, Hungary, India, Jamaica, Kyrgyzstan, Latvia, Lithuania, Malta, Mongolia, Netherlands, Papua New Guinea, Paraguay, Poland, Romania, Saint Lucia, Samoa, San Marino, Serbia, Swaziland, Trinidad and Tobago

Action by the First Committee

Date: 27 October 2011   Meeting: 22nd meeting
Vote: Adopted without a vote   Draft resolution: A/C.1/66/L.43

Agenda item 98

66/48   Reducing nuclear danger

Text

The General Assembly,

Bearing in mind that the use of nuclear weapons poses the most serious threat to mankind and to the survival of civilization,

Reaffirming that any use or threat of use of nuclear weapons would constitute a violation of the Charter of the United Nations,

Convinced that the proliferation of nuclear weapons in all its aspects would seriously enhance the danger of nuclear war,

Convinced also that nuclear disarmament and the complete elimination of nuclear weapons are essential to remove the danger of nuclear war,

Considering that, until nuclear weapons cease to exist, it is imperative on the part of the nuclear-weapon States to adopt measures that assure non-nuclear-weapon States against the use or threat of use of nuclear weapons,

Considering also that the hair-trigger alert of nuclear weapons carries unacceptable risks of unintentional or accidental use of nuclear weapons, which would have catastrophic consequences for all mankind,

Emphasizing the need to adopt measures to avoid accidental, unauthorized or unexplained incidents arising from computer anomaly or other technical malfunctions,

Conscious that limited steps relating to de-alerting and de-targeting have been taken by the nuclear-weapon States and that further practical, realistic and mutually reinforcing steps are necessary to contribute to the improvement in the international climate for negotiations leading to the elimination of nuclear weapons,

Mindful that a diminishing role for nuclear weapons in the security policies of nuclear-weapon States would positively impact on international peace and security and improve the conditions for the further reduction and the elimination of nuclear weapons,

Reiterating the highest priority accorded to nuclear disarmament in the Final Document of the Tenth Special Session of the General Assembly[1] and by the international community,

Recalling the advisory opinion of the International Court of Justice on the *Legality of the Threat or Use of Nuclear Weapons*[2] that there exists an obligation for all States to pursue in good faith and bring to a conclusion

---

[1] Resolution S-10/2.

[2] A/51/218, annex; see also *Legality of the Threat or Use of Nuclear Weapons, Advisory Opinion, I.C.J. Reports 1996*, p. 226.

negotiations leading to nuclear disarmament in all its aspects under strict and effective international control,

Recalling also the call in the United Nations Millennium Declaration[3] to seek to eliminate the dangers posed by weapons of mass destruction and the resolve to strive for the elimination of weapons of mass destruction, particularly nuclear weapons, including the possibility of convening an international conference to identify ways of eliminating nuclear dangers,

1.   *Calls for* a review of nuclear doctrines and, in this context, immediate and urgent steps to reduce the risks of unintentional and accidental use of nuclear weapons, including through de-alerting and de-targeting nuclear weapons;

2.   *Requests* the five nuclear-weapon States to take measures towards the implementation of paragraph 1 above;

3.   *Calls upon* Member States to take the necessary measures to prevent the proliferation of nuclear weapons in all its aspects and to promote nuclear disarmament, with the objective of eliminating nuclear weapons;

4.   *Takes note* of the report of the Secretary-General submitted pursuant to paragraph 5 of its resolution 65/60 of 8 December 2010;[4]

5.   *Requests* the Secretary-General to intensify efforts and support initiatives that would contribute towards the full implementation of the seven recommendations identified in the report of the Advisory Board on Disarmament Matters that would significantly reduce the risk of nuclear war,[5] and also to continue to encourage Member States to consider the convening of an international conference, as proposed in the United Nations Millennium Declaration,[3] to identify ways of eliminating nuclear dangers, and to report thereon to the General Assembly at its sixty-seventh session;

6.   *Decides* to include in the provisional agenda of its sixty-seventh session the item entitled "Reducing nuclear danger".

Action by the General Assembly

Date: 2 December 2011   Meeting: 71st plenary meeting
Vote: 117-49-13   Report: A/66/412

Sponsors

Afghanistan, Bangladesh, Bhutan, Cambodia, Chile, Congo, Cuba, Democratic Republic of the Congo, Gabon, Haiti, India, Indonesia, Libyan Arab Jamahiriya, Malaysia, Mauritius, Myanmar, Nepal, Nicaragua, Sri Lanka, Sudan, Viet Nam, Zambia*

---

[3] See resolution 55/2.
[4] A/66/132 and Add.1.
[5] See A/56/400, para. 3.
* The draft resolution was submitted by the sponsors.

Co-sponsors

Belize, Comoros, El Salvador, Jamaica, Jordan, Venezuela (Bolivarian Republic of)

Recorded vote

In favour:

Afghanistan, Algeria, Angola, Antigua and Barbuda, Azerbaijan, Bahamas, Bahrain, Bangladesh, Barbados, Belize, Benin, Bhutan, Bolivia (Plurinational State of), Botswana, Brazil, Brunei Darussalam, Burkina Faso, Cambodia, Cameroon, Cape Verde, Chad, Chile, Colombia, Comoros, Congo, Costa Rica, Côte d'Ivoire, Cuba, Democratic People's Republic of Korea, Djibouti, Dominican Republic, Ecuador, Egypt, El Salvador, Eritrea, Ethiopia, Fiji, Ghana, Grenada, Guatemala, Guinea, Guinea-Bissau, Guyana, Haiti, Honduras, India, Indonesia, Iran (Islamic Republic of), Iraq, Jamaica, Jordan, Kazakhstan, Kenya, Kuwait, Kyrgyzstan, Lao People's Democratic Republic, Lebanon, Lesotho, Liberia, Libya, Madagascar, Malaysia, Maldives, Mali, Mauritania, Mauritius, Mexico, Mongolia, Morocco, Mozambique, Myanmar, Namibia, Nepal, Nicaragua, Niger, Nigeria, Oman, Pakistan, Panama, Papua New Guinea, Paraguay, Peru, Philippines, Qatar, Saint Kitts and Nevis, Saint Lucia, Saint Vincent and the Grenadines, Samoa, Sao Tome and Principe, Saudi Arabia, Senegal, Seychelles, Sierra Leone, Singapore, Solomon Islands, South Africa, Sri Lanka, Sudan, Suriname, Swaziland, Syrian Arab Republic, Thailand, Togo, Tonga, Trinidad and Tobago, Tunisia, Turkmenistan, Uganda, United Arab Emirates, United Republic of Tanzania, Uruguay, Vanuatu, Venezuela (Bolivarian Republic of), Viet Nam, Yemen, Zambia, Zimbabwe.

Against:

Albania, Andorra, Australia, Austria, Belgium, Bosnia and Herzegovina, Bulgaria, Canada, Croatia, Cyprus, Czech Republic, Denmark, Estonia, Finland, France, Germany, Greece, Hungary, Iceland, Ireland, Israel, Italy, Latvia, Liechtenstein, Lithuania, Luxembourg, Malta, Micronesia (Federated States of), Monaco, Montenegro, Netherlands, New Zealand, Norway, Palau, Poland, Portugal, Republic of Moldova, Romania, San Marino, Slovakia, Slovenia, Spain, Sweden, Switzerland, the former Yugoslav Republic of Macedonia, Turkey, Ukraine, United Kingdom, United States

Abstaining:

Argentina, Armenia, Belarus, China, Georgia, Japan, Marshall Islands, Republic of Korea, Russian Federation, Serbia, Tajikistan, Timor-Leste, Uzbekistan

Action by the First Committee

Date: 26 October 2011　　Meeting:　21st meeting
Vote: 110-48-12　　Draft resolution: A/C.1/66/L.45

Agenda item 98

66/49   Compliance with non-proliferation, arms limitation and disarmament agreements and commitments

Text

The General Assembly,

Recalling its resolution 63/59 of 2 December 2008 and other relevant resolutions on the question,

Recognizing the abiding concern of all Member States for ensuring respect for the rights and obligations arising from treaties to which they are parties and from other sources of international law,

Convinced that observance by Member States of the Charter of the United Nations and compliance with non-proliferation, arms limitation and disarmament agreements to which they are parties and with other agreed obligations are essential for regional and global peace, security and stability,

Stressing that failure by States parties to comply with such agreements and with other agreed obligations not only adversely affects the security of States parties but also can create security risks for other States relying on the constraints and commitments stipulated in those agreements,

Stressing also that the viability and effectiveness of non-proliferation, arms limitation and disarmament agreements and of other agreed obligations require that those agreements be fully complied with and enforced,

Concerned by non-compliance by some States with their respective obligations,

Noting that verification and compliance, and enforcement in a manner consistent with the Charter, are integrally related,

Recognizing the importance of and support for effective national, regional and international capacities for such verification, compliance and enforcement,

Recognizing also that full compliance by States with all their respective non-proliferation, arms limitation and disarmament agreements and with other agreed obligations they have undertaken contributes to efforts to prevent the development and proliferation, contrary to international obligations, of weapons of mass destruction, related technologies and means of delivery, as well as to efforts to deny non-State actors access to such capabilities,

1.   *Underscores* the contribution that compliance with non-proliferation, arms limitation and disarmament agreements and with other agreed obligations makes to enhancing confidence and to strengthening international security and stability;

2.   *Urges* all States to implement and to comply fully with their respective obligations;

3.   *Welcomes* efforts by all States to pursue additional areas of cooperation, as appropriate, that can increase confidence in compliance with existing non-proliferation, arms limitation and disarmament agreements and commitments and reduce the possibility of misinterpretation and misunderstanding;

4.   *Calls upon* all Member States to encourage and, for those States in a position to do so, to appropriately assist States which request assistance to increase their capacity to implement fully their obligations;

5.   *Calls upon* Member States to support efforts aimed at the resolution of compliance questions by means consistent with such agreements and with international law;

6.   *Welcomes* the role that the United Nations has played and continues to play in restoring the integrity of, and fostering negotiations on, certain arms limitation and disarmament and non-proliferation agreements and in the removal of threats to peace;

7.   *Calls upon* all concerned States to take concerted action, in a manner consistent with relevant international law, to encourage, through bilateral and multilateral means, the compliance by all States with their respective non-proliferation, arms limitation and disarmament agreements and with other agreed obligations, and to hold those not in compliance with such agreements accountable for their non-compliance in a manner consistent with the Charter of the United Nations;

8.   *Urges* those States not currently in compliance with their respective obligations and commitments to make the strategic decision to come back into compliance;

9.   *Encourages* efforts by all States, the United Nations and other international organizations, pursuant to their respective mandates, to take action, consistent with the Charter, to prevent serious damage to international security and stability arising from non-compliance by States with their existing non-proliferation, arms limitation and disarmament obligations;

10.   *Decides* to include in the provisional agenda of its sixty-ninth session an item entitled "Compliance with non-proliferation, arms limitation and disarmament agreements and commitments".

Action by the General Assembly

Date: 2 December 2011   Meeting: 71st plenary meeting
Vote: 161-0-18   Report: A/66/412

Sponsors

Afghanistan, Albania, Andorra, Australia, Austria, Belgium, Bosnia and Herzegovina, Bulgaria, Cameroon, Canada, Chile, Colombia, Costa Rica, Croatia, Cyprus, Czech Republic, Democratic Republic of the Congo, Denmark, El Salvador, Estonia, Finland, France, Georgia, Germany, Greece, Hungary, Iceland, Ireland, Israel, Italy, Japan, Latvia, Lesotho, Liechtenstein, Lithuania, Luxembourg, Malta, Monaco, Montenegro, Netherlands, New Zealand, Nigeria, Norway, Palau, Panama, Poland, Portugal, Republic of Korea, Republic of Moldova, Romania, San Marino, Serbia, Slovakia, Slovenia, Spain, Sweden, Switzerland, the former Yugoslav Republic of Macedonia, Timor-Leste, Trinidad and Tobago, Turkey, Ukraine, United Kingdom, United Republic of Tanzania, **United States**, Uruguay

Recorded vote

In favour:

Afghanistan, Albania, Algeria, Andorra, Angola, Antigua and Barbuda, Argentina, Armenia, Australia, Austria, Azerbaijan, Bahamas, Bangladesh, Barbados, Belgium, Belize, Benin, Bhutan, Bosnia and Herzegovina, Botswana, Brazil, Brunei Darussalam, Bulgaria, Burkina Faso, Cambodia, Cameroon, Canada, Cape Verde, Chad, Chile, China, Colombia, Comoros, Congo, Costa Rica, Côte d'Ivoire, Croatia, Cyprus, Czech Republic, Denmark, Djibouti, Dominican Republic, El Salvador, Eritrea, Estonia, Ethiopia, Fiji, Finland, France, Gabon, Georgia, Germany, Ghana, Greece, Grenada, Guatemala, Guinea, Guinea-Bissau, Guyana, Haiti, Honduras, Hungary, Iceland, India, Indonesia, Iraq, Ireland, Israel, Italy, Jamaica, Japan, Jordan, Kazakhstan, Kenya, Kyrgyzstan, Latvia, Lesotho, Liberia, Libya, Liechtenstein, Lithuania, Luxembourg, Madagascar, Malawi, Malaysia, Maldives, Mali, Malta, Marshall Islands, Mauritania, Mauritius, Mexico, Micronesia (Federated States of), Monaco, Mongolia, Montenegro, Morocco, Mozambique, Myanmar, Namibia, Nepal, Netherlands, New Zealand, Niger, Nigeria, Norway, Palau, Panama, Papua New Guinea, Paraguay, Peru, Philippines, Poland, Portugal, Republic of Korea, Republic of Moldova, Romania, Russian Federation, Saint Kitts and Nevis, Saint Lucia, Saint Vincent and the Grenadines, Samoa, San Marino, Sao Tome and Principe, Senegal, Serbia, Seychelles, Sierra Leone, Singapore, Slovakia, Slovenia, Solomon Islands, South Africa, Spain, Sri Lanka, Suriname, Swaziland, Sweden, Switzerland, Tajikistan, Thailand, the former Yugoslav Republic of Macedonia, Timor-Leste, Togo, Tonga, Trinidad and Tobago, Tunisia, Turkey, Turkmenistan, Tuvalu, Uganda, Ukraine, United Arab Emirates, United Kingdom, United Republic of Tanzania, United States, Uruguay, Vanuatu, Viet Nam, Zambia, Zimbabwe

Against:
  None.

Abstaining:
  Bahrain, Belarus, Bolivia (Plurinational State of), Cuba, Ecuador, Egypt, Iran (Islamic Republic of), Kuwait, Lebanon, Nicaragua, Oman, Pakistan, Qatar, Saudi Arabia, Sudan, Syrian Arab Republic, Venezuela (Bolivarian Republic of), Yemen

Action by the First Committee

Date: 27 October 2011   Meeting: 22nd meeting
Vote: 157-0-18   Draft resolution: A/C.1/66/L.47/Rev.1

Agenda item 98

66/50   Measures to prevent terrorists from acquiring weapons of mass destruction

Text

The General Assembly,

Recalling its resolution 65/62 of 8 December 2010,

Recognizing the determination of the international community to combat terrorism, as evidenced in relevant General Assembly and Security Council resolutions,

Deeply concerned by the growing risk of linkages between terrorism and weapons of mass destruction, and in particular by the fact that terrorists may seek to acquire weapons of mass destruction,

Cognizant of the steps taken by States to implement Security Council resolution 1540 (2004) on the non-proliferation of weapons of mass destruction, adopted on 28 April 2004,

Recalling the entry into force on 7 July 2007 of the International Convention for the Suppression of Acts of Nuclear Terrorism,[1]

Recalling also the adoption, by consensus, of amendments to strengthen the Convention on the Physical Protection of Nuclear Material[2] by the International Atomic Energy Agency on 8 July 2005,

Noting the support expressed in the final document of the Fifteenth Summit Conference of Heads of State and Government of the Movement of Non-Aligned Countries, which was held in Sharm el-Sheikh, Egypt, from 11 to 16 July 2009,[3] for measures to prevent terrorists from acquiring weapons of mass destruction,

Noting also that the Group of Eight, the European Union, the Regional Forum of the Association of Southeast Asian Nations and others have taken into account in their deliberations the dangers posed by the likely acquisition by terrorists of weapons of mass destruction and the need for international cooperation in combating it, and that the Global Initiative to Combat Nuclear Terrorism has been launched jointly by the Russian Federation and the United States of America,

Noting further the holding of the Nuclear Security Summit on 12 and 13 April 2010 in Washington, D.C.,

---

[1] United Nations, *Treaty Series*, vol. 2445, No. 44004.
[2] Ibid., vol. 1456, No. 24631.
[3] See A/63/965-S/2009/514, annex.

Noting the holding of the High-level Meeting on Nuclear Safety and Security, in New York on 22 September 2011,

Acknowledging the consideration of issues relating to terrorism and weapons of mass destruction by the Advisory Board on Disarmament Matters,[4]

Taking note of the relevant resolutions adopted by the General Conference of the International Atomic Energy Agency at its fifty-fifth regular session,[5]

Taking note also of the 2005 World Summit Outcome adopted at the high-level plenary meeting of the General Assembly in September 2005[6] and the adoption of the United Nations Global Counter-Terrorism Strategy on 8 September 2006,[7]

Taking note further of the report of the Secretary-General submitted pursuant to paragraph 5 of resolution 65/62,[8]

Mindful of the urgent need for addressing, within the United Nations framework and through international cooperation, this threat to humanity,

Emphasizing that progress is urgently needed in the area of disarmament and non-proliferation in order to maintain international peace and security and to contribute to global efforts against terrorism,

1.   *Calls upon* all Member States to support international efforts to prevent terrorists from acquiring weapons of mass destruction and their means of delivery;

2.   *Appeals* to all Member States to consider early accession to and ratification of the International Convention for the Suppression of Acts of Nuclear Terrorism;[1]

3.   *Urges* all Member States to take and strengthen national measures, as appropriate, to prevent terrorists from acquiring weapons of mass destruction, their means of delivery and materials and technologies related to their manufacture;

4.   *Encourages* cooperation among and between Member States and relevant regional and international organizations for strengthening national capacities in this regard;

5.   *Requests* the Secretary-General to compile a report on measures already taken by international organizations on issues relating to the linkage between the fight against terrorism and the proliferation of weapons of mass

---

[4] See A/59/361.
[5] See International Atomic Energy Agency, *Resolutions and Other Decisions of the General Conference, Fifty-fifth Regular Session, 19–23 September 2011* (GC(55)/RES/DEC(2011)).
[6] See resolution 60/1.
[7] Resolution 60/288.
[8] A/66/115 and Add.1.

destruction and to seek the views of Member States on additional relevant measures, including national measures, for tackling the global threat posed by the acquisition by terrorists of weapons of mass destruction and to report to the General Assembly at its sixty-seventh session;

6.   *Decides* to include in the provisional agenda of its sixty-seventh session the item entitled "Measures to prevent terrorists from acquiring weapons of mass destruction".

Action by the General Assembly

> Date: 2 December 2011   Meeting: 71st plenary meeting
> Vote: Adopted without a vote   Report: A/66/412

Sponsors

> Afghanistan, Argentina, Armenia, Australia, Azerbaijan, Bangladesh, Belgium, Belize, Bhutan, Bosnia and Herzegovina, Bulgaria, Cambodia, Canada, Chile, Congo, Croatia, Cyprus, Czech Republic, Democratic Republic of the Congo, Denmark, Estonia, Finland, France, Germany, Honduras, Hungary, **India**, Ireland, Italy, Latvia, Lithuania, Luxembourg, Malta, Mauritius, Monaco, Montenegro, Myanmar, Nepal, Norway, Philippines, Poland, Portugal, Republic of Moldova, Romania, Russian Federation, Saint Vincent and the Grenadines, Serbia, Singapore, Slovakia, Slovenia, Sri Lanka, Thailand, the former Yugoslav Republic of Macedonia, Turkey, United Kingdom, United States

Co-sponsors

> Albania, Austria, El Salvador, Georgia, Greece, Guatemala, Guyana, Haiti, Iceland, Jamaica, Kuwait, Netherlands, Spain, Sweden, Zambia

Action by the First Committee

> Date: 26 October 2011   Meeting: 21st meeting
> Vote: Adopted without a vote   Draft resolution: A/C.1/66/L.48

Agenda item 98

66/51   Nuclear disarmament

Text

The General Assembly,

Recalling its resolution 49/75 E of 15 December 1994 on a step-by-step reduction of the nuclear threat, and its resolutions 50/70 P of 12 December 1995, 51/45 O of 10 December 1996, 52/38 L of 9 December 1997, 53/77 X of 4 December 1998, 54/54 P of 1 December 1999, 55/33 T of 20 November 2000, 56/24 R of 29 November 2001, 57/79 of 22 November 2002, 58/56 of 8 December 2003, 59/77 of 3 December 2004, 60/70 of 8 December 2005, 61/78 of 6 December 2006, 62/42 of 5 December 2007, 63/46 of 2 December 2008, 64/53 of 2 December 2009 and 65/56 of 8 December 2010 on nuclear disarmament,

Reaffirming the commitment of the international community to the goal of the total elimination of nuclear weapons and the establishment of a nuclear-weapon-free world,

Bearing in mind that the Convention on the Prohibition of the Development, Production and Stockpiling of Bacteriological (Biological) and Toxin Weapons and on Their Destruction of 1972[1] and the Convention on the Prohibition of the Development, Production, Stockpiling and Use of Chemical Weapons and on Their Destruction of 1993[2] have already established legal regimes on the complete prohibition of biological and chemical weapons, respectively, and determined to achieve a nuclear weapons convention on the prohibition of the development, testing, production, stockpiling, loan, transfer, use and threat of use of nuclear weapons and on their destruction, and to conclude such an international convention at an early date,

Recognizing that there now exist conditions for the establishment of a world free of nuclear weapons, and stressing the need to take concrete practical steps towards achieving this goal,

Bearing in mind paragraph 50 of the Final Document of the Tenth Special Session of the General Assembly, the first special session devoted to disarmament,[3] calling for the urgent negotiation of agreements for the cessation of the qualitative improvement and development of nuclear-weapon systems, and for a comprehensive and phased programme with agreed time frames, wherever feasible, for the progressive and balanced reduction of nuclear weapons and their means of delivery, leading to their ultimate and complete elimination at the earliest possible time,

---

[1] United Nations, *Treaty Series*, vol. 1015, No. 14860.
[2] Ibid., vol. 1974, No. 33757.
[3] Resolution S-10/2.

Reaffirming the conviction of the States parties to the Treaty on the Non-Proliferation of Nuclear Weapons[4] that the Treaty is a cornerstone of nuclear non-proliferation and nuclear disarmament, and the importance of the decision on strengthening the review process for the Treaty, the decision on principles and objectives for nuclear non-proliferation and disarmament, the decision on the extension of the Treaty and the resolution on the Middle East, adopted by the 1995 Review and Extension Conference of the Parties to the Treaty on the Non-Proliferation of Nuclear Weapons,[5]

Stressing the importance of the thirteen steps for the systematic and progressive efforts to achieve the objective of nuclear disarmament leading to the total elimination of nuclear weapons, as agreed to by the States parties in the Final Document of the 2000 Review Conference of the Parties to the Treaty on the Non-Proliferation of Nuclear Weapons,[6]

Recognizing the important work done at the 2010 Review Conference of the Parties to the Treaty on the Non-Proliferation of Nuclear Weapons,[7] and affirming its action plan as an impetus to intensify work aimed at beginning negotiations for a nuclear weapons convention,

Reiterating the highest priority accorded to nuclear disarmament in the Final Document of the Tenth Special Session of the General Assembly and by the international community,

Reiterating its call for an early entry into force of the Comprehensive Nuclear-Test-Ban Treaty,[8]

Taking note of the entry into force of the new strategic arms reduction treaty between the Russian Federation and the United States of America, in order to achieve further deep cuts in their strategic and tactical nuclear weapons, and stressing that such cuts should be irreversible, verifiable and transparent,

Recalling the entry into force of the Treaty on Strategic Offensive Reductions ("the Moscow Treaty") between the United States of America and the Russian Federation[9] as a significant step towards reducing their deployed strategic nuclear weapons, while calling for further irreversible deep cuts in their nuclear arsenals,

---

[4] United Nations, *Treaty Series*, vol. 729, No. 10485.

[5] See *1995 Review and Extension Conference of the Parties to the Treaty on the Non-Proliferation of Nuclear Weapons, Final Document, Part I* (NPT/CONF.1995/32 (Part I) and Corr.2), annex.

[6] See *2000 Review Conference of the Parties to the Treaty on the Non-Proliferation of Nuclear Weapons, Final Document*, vol. I (NPT/CONF.2000/28 (Parts I and II)), part I, section entitled "Article VI and eighth to twelfth preambular paragraphs", para. 15.

[7] See *2010 Review Conference of the Parties to the Treaty on the Non-Proliferation of Nuclear Weapons, Final Document*, vols. I–III (NPT/CONF.2010/50 (Vols. I–III)).

[8] See resolution 50/245.

[9] See CD/1674.

Noting the positive statements by nuclear-weapon States of their intention to pursue actions in achieving a world free of nuclear weapons, while reaffirming the need for urgent concrete actions by nuclear-weapon States to achieve this goal within a specified framework of time, and urging them to take further measures for progress on nuclear disarmament,

Recognizing the complementarity of bilateral, plurilateral and multilateral negotiations on nuclear disarmament, and that bilateral negotiations can never replace multilateral negotiations in this respect,

Noting the support expressed in the Conference on Disarmament and in the General Assembly for the elaboration of an international convention to assure non-nuclear-weapon States against the use or threat of use of nuclear weapons, and the multilateral efforts in the Conference on Disarmament to reach agreement on such an international convention at an early date,

Recalling the advisory opinion of the International Court of Justice on the *Legality of the Threat or Use of Nuclear Weapons*, issued on 8 July 1996,[10] and welcoming the unanimous reaffirmation by all Judges of the Court that there exists an obligation for all States to pursue in good faith and bring to a conclusion negotiations leading to nuclear disarmament in all its aspects under strict and effective international control,

Mindful of paragraph 102 of the Final Document of the Coordinating Bureau of the Non-Aligned Movement at its Ministerial Meeting, held in Havana from 27 to 30 April 2009,[11]

Recalling paragraph 112 and other relevant recommendations in the Final Document of the Fifteenth Summit Conference of Heads of State and Government of the Movement of Non-Aligned Countries, held in Sharm el-Sheikh, Egypt, from 11 to 16 July 2009,[12] calling upon the Conference on Disarmament to establish, as soon as possible and as the highest priority, an ad hoc committee on nuclear disarmament and to commence negotiations on a phased programme for the complete elimination of nuclear weapons within a specified framework of time, including a nuclear weapons convention,

Noting the adoption of the programme of work for the 2009 session by the Conference on Disarmament on 29 May 2009,[13] after years of stalemate, while regretting that the Conference has not been able to undertake substantive work on its agenda in 2011,

Reaffirming the importance and validity of the Conference on Disarmament as the sole multilateral negotiating forum on disarmament, and expressing the need to adopt and implement a balanced and comprehensive

---

[10] A/51/218, annex; see also *Legality of the Threat or Use of Nuclear Weapons, Advisory Opinion, I.C.J. Reports 1996*, p. 226.

[11] See A/63/858.

[12] See A/63/965-S/2009/514, annex.

[13] See CD/1864.

programme of work on the basis of its agenda and dealing with, inter alia, four core issues, in accordance with the rules of procedure,[14] and by taking into consideration the security concerns of all States,

Reaffirming also the specific mandate conferred upon the Disarmament Commission by the General Assembly, in its decision 52/492 of 8 September 1998, to discuss the subject of nuclear disarmament as one of its main substantive agenda items,

Recalling the United Nations Millennium Declaration,[15] in which Heads of State and Government resolved to strive for the elimination of weapons of mass destruction, in particular nuclear weapons, and to keep all options open for achieving this aim, including the possibility of convening an international conference to identify ways of eliminating nuclear dangers,

Recalling also the statement on the total elimination of nuclear weapons, adopted by the Sixteenth Ministerial Conference and Commemorative Meeting of the Movement of Non-Aligned Countries, held in Bali, Indonesia, from 23 to 27 May 2011, in which the Non-Aligned Movement reiterated its call for an international conference to identify ways and means of eliminating nuclear weapons, at the earliest possible date,[16]

Reaffirming that, in accordance with the Charter of the United Nations, States should refrain from the use or threat of use of nuclear weapons in settling their disputes in international relations,

Seized of the danger of the use of weapons of mass destruction, particularly nuclear weapons, in terrorist acts and the urgent need for concerted international efforts to control and overcome it,

1. *Recognizes* that the time is now opportune for all the nuclear-weapon States to take effective disarmament measures to achieve the total elimination of these weapons at the earliest possible time;

2. *Reaffirms* that nuclear disarmament and nuclear non-proliferation are substantively interrelated and mutually reinforcing, that the two processes must go hand in hand and that there is a genuine need for a systematic and progressive process of nuclear disarmament;

3. *Welcomes and encourages* the efforts to establish new nuclear-weapon-free zones in different parts of the world, including the establishment of a Middle East zone free of nuclear weapons, on the basis of agreements or arrangements freely arrived at among the States of the regions concerned, which is an effective measure for limiting the further spread of nuclear weapons geographically and contributes to the cause of nuclear disarmament;

---

[14] CD/8/Rev.9.
[15] See resolution 55/2.
[16] See A/65/896-S/2011/407, annex V.

4. *Welcomes* the ongoing efforts between the States members of the Association of Southeast Asian Nations and the nuclear-weapon States, and encourages the nuclear-weapon States in their early signing of the Protocol to the Treaty on the South-East Asia Nuclear-Weapon-Free Zone; [17]

5. *Recognizes* that there is a genuine need to diminish the role of nuclear weapons in strategic doctrines and security policies to minimize the risk that these weapons will ever be used and to facilitate the process of their total elimination;

6. *Urges* the nuclear-weapon States to stop immediately the qualitative improvement, development, production and stockpiling of nuclear warheads and their delivery systems;

7. *Also urges* the nuclear-weapon States, as an interim measure, to de-alert and deactivate immediately their nuclear weapons and to take other concrete measures to reduce further the operational status of their nuclear-weapon systems, while stressing that reductions in deployments and in operational status cannot substitute for irreversible cuts in, and the total elimination of, nuclear weapons;

8. *Reiterates its call upon* the nuclear-weapon States to undertake the step-by-step reduction of the nuclear threat and to carry out effective nuclear disarmament measures with a view to achieving the total elimination of these weapons within a specified framework of time;

9. *Calls upon* the nuclear-weapon States, pending the achievement of the total elimination of nuclear weapons, to agree on an internationally and legally binding instrument on a joint undertaking not to be the first to use nuclear weapons, and calls upon all States to conclude an internationally and legally binding instrument on security assurances of non-use and non-threat of use of nuclear weapons against non-nuclear-weapon States;

10. *Urges* the nuclear-weapon States to commence plurilateral negotiations among themselves at an appropriate stage on further deep reductions of nuclear weapons as an effective measure of nuclear disarmament;

11. *Underlines* the importance of applying the principles of transparency, irreversibility and verifiability to the process of nuclear disarmament and to nuclear and other related arms control and reduction measures;

12. *Also underlines* the importance of the unequivocal undertaking by the nuclear-weapon States, in the Final Document of the 2000 Review Conference of the Parties to the Treaty on the Non-Proliferation of Nuclear Weapons, to accomplish the total elimination of their nuclear arsenals leading to nuclear disarmament, to which all States parties are committed under

---

[17] United Nations, *Treaty Series*, vol. 1981, No. 33873.

article VI of the Treaty,[6] and the reaffirmation by the States parties that the total elimination of nuclear weapons is the only absolute guarantee against the use or threat of use of nuclear weapons;[18]

13. *Calls for* the full and effective implementation of the thirteen practical steps for nuclear disarmament contained in the Final Document of the 2000 Review Conference;[6]

14. *Also calls for* the full implementation of the action plan as set out in the conclusions and recommendations for follow-on actions of the Final Document of the 2010 Review Conference of the Parties to the Treaty on the Non-Proliferation of Nuclear Weapons, particularly the 22-point action plan on nuclear disarmament;[7]

15. *Urges* the nuclear-weapon States to carry out further reductions of non-strategic nuclear weapons, based on unilateral initiatives and as an integral part of the nuclear arms reduction and disarmament process;

16. *Calls for* the immediate commencement of negotiations in the Conference on Disarmament on a non-discriminatory, multilateral and internationally and effectively verifiable treaty banning the production of fissile material for nuclear weapons or other nuclear explosive devices on the basis of the report of the Special Coordinator[19] and the mandate contained therein;

17. *Urges* the Conference on Disarmament to commence as early as possible its substantive work during its 2012 session, on the basis of a comprehensive and balanced programme of work that takes into consideration all the real and existing priorities in the field of disarmament and arms control, including the immediate commencement of negotiations on such a treaty with a view to their conclusion within five years;

18. *Calls for* the conclusion of an international legal instrument or instruments on adequate and unconditional security assurances to non-nuclear-weapon States;

19. *Also calls for* the early entry into force and strict observance of the Comprehensive Nuclear-Test-Ban Treaty;[8]

20. *Expresses its regret* that the Conference on Disarmament was unable to establish an ad hoc committee to deal with nuclear disarmament early in 2011, as called for by the General Assembly in its resolution 65/56;

21. *Reiterates its call upon* the Conference on Disarmament to establish, as soon as possible and as the highest priority, an ad hoc committee on nuclear disarmament early in 2012 and to commence negotiations on a

---

[18] *2000 Review Conference of the Parties to the Treaty on the Non-Proliferation of Nuclear Weapons, Final Document*, vol. I (NPT/CONF.2000/28 (Parts I and II)), part I, section entitled "Article VII and the security of non-nuclear-weapon States", para. 2.

[19] CD/1299.

phased programme of nuclear disarmament leading to the total elimination of nuclear weapons within a specified framework of time;

22. *Calls for* the convening of an international conference on nuclear disarmament in all its aspects at an early date to identify and deal with concrete measures of nuclear disarmament;

23. *Requests* the Secretary-General to submit to the General Assembly at its sixty-seventh session a report on the implementation of the present resolution;

24. *Decides* to include in the provisional agenda of its sixty-seventh session the item entitled "Nuclear disarmament".

Action by the General Assembly

Date: 2 December 2011   Meeting: 71st plenary meeting
Vote: 117-45-18   Report: A/66/412
      162-0-14, o.p. 14
      172-1-7, o.p. 16

Sponsors

Algeria, Bangladesh, Bhutan, Bolivia (Plurinational State of), Brunei Darussalam, Cambodia, Congo, Cuba, Dominican Republic, Indonesia, Iran (Islamic Republic of), Jordan, Kenya, Lao People's Democratic Republic, Libyan Arab Jamahiriya, Malaysia, **Myanmar**, Nepal, Nicaragua, Philippines, Samoa, Senegal, Sierra Leone, Singapore, Sri Lanka, Sudan, Thailand, Timor-Leste, Uganda, Venezuela (Bolivarian Republic of), Viet Nam, Zambia

Co-sponsors

Ecuador, Fiji, Kuwait, Mongolia, Suriname

Recorded vote

As a whole

In favour:

Afghanistan, Algeria, Angola, Antigua and Barbuda, Argentina, Azerbaijan, Bahamas, Bahrain, Bangladesh, Barbados, Belize, Benin, Bhutan, Bolivia (Plurinational State of), Botswana, Brazil, Brunei Darussalam, Burkina Faso, Cambodia, Cameroon, Cape Verde, Chad, Chile, China, Colombia, Comoros, Congo, Costa Rica, Côte d'Ivoire, Cuba, Democratic People's Republic of Korea, Djibouti, Dominican Republic, Ecuador, Egypt, El Salvador, Eritrea, Ethiopia, Fiji, Ghana, Grenada, Guatemala, Guinea, Guinea-Bissau, Guyana, Haiti, Honduras, Indonesia, Iran (Islamic Republic of), Iraq, Jamaica, Jordan, Kazakhstan, Kenya, Kuwait, Lao People's Democratic Republic, Lebanon, Lesotho,

Liberia, Libya, Madagascar, Malawi, Malaysia, Maldives, Mali, Mauritania, Mexico, Mongolia, Morocco, Mozambique, Myanmar, Namibia, Nepal, Nicaragua, Niger, Nigeria, Oman, Panama, Papua New Guinea, Paraguay, Peru, Philippines, Qatar, Saint Kitts and Nevis, Saint Lucia, Saint Vincent and the Grenadines, Samoa, Sao Tome and Principe, Saudi Arabia, Senegal, Seychelles, Sierra Leone, Singapore, Solomon Islands, South Africa, Sri Lanka, Sudan, Suriname, Swaziland, Syrian Arab Republic, Thailand, Timor-Leste, Togo, Tonga, Trinidad and Tobago, Tunisia, Tuvalu, Uganda, United Arab Emirates, United Republic of Tanzania, Uruguay, Vanuatu, Venezuela (Bolivarian Republic of), Viet Nam, Yemen, Zambia, Zimbabwe

Against:

Albania, Andorra, Australia, Belgium, Bosnia and Herzegovina, Bulgaria, Canada, Croatia, Cyprus, Czech Republic, Denmark, Estonia, Finland, France, Georgia, Germany, Greece, Hungary, Iceland, Israel, Italy, Latvia, Liechtenstein, Lithuania, Luxembourg, Micronesia (Federated States of), Monaco, Montenegro, Netherlands, Norway, Palau, Poland, Portugal, Republic of Moldova, Romania, San Marino, Slovakia, Slovenia, Spain, Switzerland, the former Yugoslav Republic of Macedonia, Turkey, Ukraine, United Kingdom, United States

Abstaining:

Armenia, Austria, Belarus, India, Ireland, Japan, Kyrgyzstan, Malta, Marshall Islands, Mauritius, New Zealand, Pakistan, Republic of Korea, Russian Federation, Serbia, Sweden, Tajikistan, Uzbekistan

Operative paragraph 14

In favour:

Afghanistan, Albania, Algeria, Andorra, Angola, Antigua and Barbuda, Argentina, Australia, Austria, Azerbaijan, Bahamas, Bahrain, Bangladesh, Barbados, Belarus, Belgium, Belize, Benin, Bhutan, Bolivia (Plurinational State of), Bosnia and Herzegovina, Botswana, Brazil, Brunei Darussalam, Bulgaria, Burkina Faso, Cambodia, Cameroon, Canada, Cape Verde, Chad, Chile, China, Colombia, Comoros, Congo, Costa Rica, Côte d'Ivoire, Croatia, Cuba, Cyprus, Czech Republic, Democratic People's Republic of Korea, Denmark, Djibouti, Dominican Republic, Ecuador, Egypt, Eritrea, Estonia, Ethiopia, Fiji, Finland, Gabon, Georgia, Germany, Ghana, Greece, Grenada, Guatemala, Guinea, Guinea-Bissau, Guyana, Haiti, Honduras, Hungary, Iceland, Indonesia, Iran (Islamic Republic of), Iraq, Ireland, Jamaica, Japan, Jordan, Kazakhstan, Kenya, Kuwait, Kyrgyzstan, Lao People's Democratic Republic, Latvia, Lebanon, Lesotho, Liberia, Libya, Liechtenstein, Lithuania, Luxembourg, Madagascar, Malawi, Malaysia, Maldives, Mali, Malta, Mauritania, Mauritius, Mexico, Monaco, Mongolia,

Montenegro, Morocco, Mozambique, Myanmar, Namibia, Nepal, New Zealand, Nicaragua, Niger, Nigeria, Norway, Oman, Panama, Papua New Guinea, Paraguay, Peru, Philippines, Poland, Portugal, Qatar, Republic of Moldova, Romania, Russian Federation, Saint Kitts and Nevis, Saint Lucia, Saint Vincent and the Grenadines, Samoa, San Marino, Sao Tome and Principe, Saudi Arabia, Senegal, Serbia, Seychelles, Sierra Leone, Singapore, Slovakia, Solomon Islands, South Africa, Spain, Sri Lanka, Sudan, Suriname, Swaziland, Sweden, Switzerland, Syrian Arab Republic, Thailand, the former Yugoslav Republic of Macedonia, Timor-Leste, Togo, Tonga, Trinidad and Tobago, Tunisia, Tuvalu, Uganda, United Arab Emirates, United Republic of Tanzania, Uruguay, Vanuatu, Venezuela (Bolivarian Republic of), Viet Nam, Yemen, Zambia, Zimbabwe

Against:

None.

Abstaining:

Armenia, El Salvador, France, India, Israel, Italy, Netherlands, Pakistan, Slovenia, Turkey, Ukraine, United Kingdom, United States, Uzbekistan

Operative paragraph 16*

In favour:

Afghanistan, Albania, Algeria, Andorra, Angola, Antigua and Barbuda, Argentina, Australia, Austria, Azerbaijan, Bahamas, Bahrain, Bangladesh, Barbados, Belarus, Belgium, Belize, Benin, Bhutan, Bolivia (Plurinational State of), Bosnia and Herzegovina, Botswana, Brunei Darussalam, Bulgaria, Burkina Faso, Cambodia, Cameroon, Canada, Cape Verde, Chad, Chile, China, Colombia, Comoros, Congo, Costa Rica, Côte d'Ivoire, Croatia, Cuba, Cyprus, Democratic People's Republic of Korea, Denmark, Djibouti, Dominican Republic, Ecuador, Egypt, El Salvador, Eritrea, Estonia, Ethiopia, Fiji, Finland, Gabon, Georgia, Germany, Ghana, Greece, Grenada, Guatemala, Guinea, Guinea-Bissau, Guyana, Haiti, Honduras, Hungary, Iceland, India, Indonesia, Iran (Islamic Republic of), Iraq, Ireland, Italy, Jamaica, Japan, Jordan, Kazakhstan, Kenya, Kuwait, Kyrgyzstan, Lao People's Democratic Republic, Latvia, Lebanon, Lesotho, Liberia, Libya, Liechtenstein, Lithuania, Luxembourg, Madagascar, Malawi, Malaysia, Maldives, Mali, Malta, Marshall Islands, Mauritania, Mauritius, Mexico, Micronesia (Federated States of), Monaco, Mongolia, Montenegro, Morocco, Mozambique, Myanmar, Namibia, Nepal, Netherlands, New Zealand, Nicaragua, Niger, Nigeria, Norway, Oman, Palau, Panama,

---

* Subsequently, the delegations of Brazil and the Czech Republic advised the Secretariat that they had intended to vote in favour. The voting tally above does not reflect this information.

Papua New Guinea, Paraguay, Peru, Philippines, Poland, Portugal, Qatar, Republic of Korea, Republic of Moldova, Romania, Russian Federation, Saint Kitts and Nevis, Saint Lucia, Saint Vincent and the Grenadines, Samoa, San Marino, Sao Tome and Principe, Saudi Arabia, Senegal, Serbia, Seychelles, Sierra Leone, Singapore, Slovakia, Slovenia, Solomon Islands, South Africa, Spain, Sri Lanka, Sudan, Suriname, Swaziland, Sweden, Switzerland, Syrian Arab Republic, Tajikistan, Thailand, the former Yugoslav Republic of Macedonia, Timor-Leste, Togo, Tonga, Trinidad and Tobago, Tunisia, Turkey, Tuvalu, Uganda, United Arab Emirates, United Republic of Tanzania, United States of America, Uruguay, Vanuatu, Venezuela (Bolivarian Republic of), Viet Nam, Yemen, Zambia, Zimbabwe

Against:
Pakistan

Abstaining:
Armenia, Czech Republic, France, Israel, Ukraine, United Kingdom, Uzbekistan

Action by the First Committee

Date: 27 October 2011   Meeting: 22nd meeting
Vote: 113-44-18   Draft resolution: A/C.1/66/L.49
      157-0-14, o.p. 14
      164-1-6, o.p. 16

Agenda item 98

66/52   Prohibition of the dumping of radioactive wastes

Text

The General Assembly,

Bearing in mind resolutions CM/Res.1153 (XLVIII) of 1988[1] and CM/Res.1225 (L) of 1989,[2] adopted by the Council of Ministers of the Organization of African Unity, concerning the dumping of nuclear and industrial wastes in Africa,

Welcoming resolution GC(XXXIV)/RES/530 establishing a Code of Practice on the International Transboundary Movement of Radioactive Waste, adopted on 21 September 1990 by the General Conference of the International Atomic Energy Agency at its thirty-fourth regular session,[3]

Taking note of the commitment by the participants in the Summit on Nuclear Safety and Security, held in Moscow on 19 and 20 April 1996, to ban the dumping at sea of radioactive wastes,[4]

Considering its resolution 2602 C (XXIV) of 16 December 1969, in which it requested the Conference of the Committee on Disarmament,[5] inter alia, to consider effective methods of control against the use of radiological methods of warfare,

Aware of the potential hazards underlying any use of radioactive wastes that would constitute radiological warfare and its implications for regional and international security, in particular for the security of developing countries,

Recalling all its resolutions on the matter since its forty-third session in 1988, including its resolution 51/45 J of 10 December 1996,

Recalling also resolution GC(45)/RES/10 adopted by consensus on 21 September 2001 by the General Conference of the International Atomic Energy Agency at its forty-fifth regular session,[6] in which States shipping radioactive materials are invited to provide, as appropriate, assurances

---

[1] See A/43/398, annex I.

[2] See A/44/603, annex I.

[3] See International Atomic Energy Agency, *Resolutions and Other Decisions of the General Conference, Thirty-fourth Regular Session, 17–21 September 1990* (GC(XXXIV)/RESOLUTIONS (1990)).

[4] A/51/131, annex I, para. 20.

[5] The Conference of the Committee on Disarmament became the Committee on Disarmament as from the tenth special session of the General Assembly. The Committee on Disarmament was redesignated the Conference on Disarmament as from 7 February 1984.

[6] See International Atomic Energy Agency, *Resolutions and Other Decisions of the General Conference, Forty-fifth Regular Session, 17–21 September 2001* (GC(45)/RES/DEC(2001)).

to concerned States, upon their request, that the national regulations of the shipping State take into account the Agency's transport regulations and to provide them with relevant information relating to the shipment of such materials; the information provided should in no case be contradictory to the measures of physical security and safety,

Welcoming the adoption at Vienna, on 5 September 1997, of the Joint Convention on the Safety of Spent Fuel Management and on the Safety of Radioactive Waste Management,[7] as recommended by the participants in the Summit on Nuclear Safety and Security,

Welcoming also the convening by the International Atomic Energy Agency of the Ministerial Conference on Nuclear Safety, held in Vienna from 20 to 24 June 2011, and its outcome, the Declaration of the International Atomic Energy Agency Ministerial Conference on Nuclear Safety,[8] as well as the Action Plan on Nuclear Safety, endorsed by the General Conference of the Agency at its fifty-fifth regular session,[9]

Noting the convening by the Secretary-General of the High-level Meeting on Nuclear Safety and Security, in New York on 22 September 2011,

Noting with satisfaction that the Joint Convention entered into force on 18 June 2001,

Noting that the first Review Meeting of the Contracting Parties to the Joint Convention on the Safety of Spent Fuel Management and on the Safety of Radioactive Waste Management was convened in Vienna from 3 to 14 November 2003,

Desirous of promoting the implementation of paragraph 76 of the Final Document of the Tenth Special Session of the General Assembly, the first special session devoted to disarmament,[10]

1. *Takes note* of the part of the report of the Conference on Disarmament relating to radiological weapons;[11]

2. *Also takes note* of the Declaration of the International Atomic Energy Agency Ministerial Conference on Nuclear Safety,[8] the Action Plan on Nuclear Safety[9] and the High-level Meeting on Nuclear Safety and Security, convened by the Secretary-General;

3. *Expresses grave concern* regarding any use of nuclear wastes that would constitute radiological warfare and have grave implications for the national security of all States;

---

[7] United Nations, *Treaty Series*, vol. 2153, No. 37605.

[8] Available from www.iaea.org/Publications/Documents/Infcircs/2011/infcirc821.pdf.

[9] See International Atomic Energy Agency, document GOV/2011/59-GC(55)/14.

[10] Resolution S-10/2.

[11] See *Official Records of the General Assembly, Sixty-fourth Session, Supplement No. 27* (A/64/27), chap. III, sect. E.

4.	*Calls upon* all States to take appropriate measures with a view to preventing any dumping of nuclear or radioactive wastes that would infringe upon the sovereignty of States;

5.	*Requests* the Conference on Disarmament to take into account, in the negotiations for a convention on the prohibition of radiological weapons, radioactive wastes as part of the scope of such a convention;

6.	*Also requests* the Conference on Disarmament to intensify efforts towards an early conclusion of such a convention and to include in its report to the General Assembly at its sixty-eighth session the progress recorded in the negotiations on this subject;

7.	*Takes note* of resolution CM/Res.1356 (LIV) of 1991, adopted by the Council of Ministers of the Organization of African Unity,[12] on the Bamako Convention on the Ban on the Import of Hazardous Wastes into Africa and on the Control of Their Transboundary Movements within Africa;

8.	*Expresses the hope* that the effective implementation of the International Atomic Energy Agency Code of Practice on the International Transboundary Movement of Radioactive Waste will enhance the protection of all States from the dumping of radioactive wastes on their territories;

9.	*Appeals* to all Member States that have not yet taken the necessary steps to become party to the Joint Convention on the Safety of Spent Fuel Management and on the Safety of Radioactive Waste Management[7] to do so as soon as possible;

10.	*Decides* to include in the provisional agenda of its sixty-eighth session the item entitled "Prohibition of the dumping of radioactive wastes".

Action by the General Assembly

Date: 2 December 2011	Meeting: 71st plenary meeting
Vote: Adopted without a vote	Report:	A/66/412

Sponsors

Nigeria, on behalf of the States Members of the United Nations that are members of the Group of African States

Co-sponsors

El Salvador

Action by the First Committee

Date: 27 October 2011	Meeting:	22nd meeting
Vote: Adopted without a vote	Draft resolution: A/C.1/66/L.53

---

[12] See A/46/390, annex I.

Agenda item 99

66/53 United Nations regional centres for peace and disarmament

Text

The General Assembly,

Recalling its resolutions 60/83 of 8 December 2005, 61/90 of 6 December 2006, 62/50 of 5 December 2007, 63/76 of 2 December 2008, 64/58 of 2 December 2009 and 65/78 of 8 December 2010 regarding the maintenance and revitalization of the three United Nations regional centres for peace and disarmament,

Recalling also the reports of the Secretary-General on the United Nations Regional Centre for Peace and Disarmament in Africa,[1] the United Nations Regional Centre for Peace and Disarmament in Asia and the Pacific[2] and the United Nations Regional Centre for Peace, Disarmament and Development in Latin America and the Caribbean,[3]

Reaffirming its decision, taken in 1982 at its twelfth special session, to establish the United Nations Disarmament Information Programme, the purpose of which is to inform, educate and generate public understanding and support for the objectives of the United Nations in the field of arms control and disarmament,[4]

Bearing in mind its resolutions 40/151 G of 16 December 1985, 41/60 J of 3 December 1986, 42/39 D of 30 November 1987 and 44/117 F of 15 December 1989 on the regional centres for peace and disarmament in Nepal, Peru and Togo,

Recognizing that the changes that have taken place in the world have created new opportunities and posed new challenges for the pursuit of disarmament, and bearing in mind in this regard that the regional centres for peace and disarmament can contribute substantially to understanding and cooperation among States in each particular region in the areas of peace, disarmament and development,

Recalling that, in paragraph 127 of the Final Document of the Fifteenth Summit Conference of Heads of State and Government of the Movement of Non-Aligned Countries, held in Sharm el-Sheikh, Egypt, from 11 to 16 July 2009,[5] and in paragraph 162 of the Final Document of the Sixteenth Ministerial Conference and Commemorative Meeting of the Movement of

---

[1] A/66/159.

[2] A/66/113.

[3] A/66/140.

[4] See *Official Records of the General Assembly, Twelfth Special Session, Plenary Meetings*, 1st meeting, paras. 110 and 111.

[5] A/63/965-S/2009/514, annex.

Non-Aligned Countries, held in Bali, Indonesia, from 23 to 27 May 2011,[6] the Movement of Non-Aligned Countries emphasized the importance of United Nations activities at the regional level to increase the stability and security of its Member States, which could be promoted in a substantive manner by the maintenance and revitalization of the three regional centres for peace and disarmament,

1.   *Reiterates* the importance of United Nations activities at the regional level to advance disarmament and to increase the stability and security of its Member States, which could be promoted in a substantive manner by the maintenance and revitalization of the three regional centres for peace and disarmament;

2.   *Reaffirms* that, in order to achieve positive results, it is useful for the three regional centres to carry out dissemination and educational programmes that promote regional peace and security and that are aimed at changing basic attitudes with respect to peace and security and disarmament so as to support the achievement of the purposes and principles of the United Nations;

3.   *Appeals* to Member States in each region that are able to do so, as well as to international governmental and non-governmental organizations and foundations, to make voluntary contributions to the regional centres in their respective regions in order to strengthen their activities and initiatives;

4.   *Emphasizes* the importance of the activities of the Regional Disarmament Branch of the Office for Disarmament Affairs of the Secretariat;

5.   *Requests* the Secretary-General to provide all necessary support, within existing resources, to the regional centres in carrying out their programmes of activities;

6.   *Decides* to include in the provisional agenda of its sixty-seventh session the item entitled "United Nations regional centres for peace and disarmament".

Action by the General Assembly

Date: 2 December 2011   Meeting: 71st plenary meeting
Vote: Adopted without a vote   Report: A/66/413

Sponsors

Indonesia, on behalf of the States Members of the United Nations that are members of the Movement of Non-Aligned Countries

Action by the First Committee

Date: 27 October 2011   Meeting: 22nd meeting
Vote: Adopted without a vote   Draft resolution: A/C.1/66/L.9

---

[6] A/65/896-S/2011/407, annex I.

Agenda item 99

**66/54   United Nations Regional Centre for Peace,
Disarmament and Development in
Latin America and the Caribbean**

Text

The General Assembly,

Recalling its resolutions 41/60 J of 3 December 1986, 42/39 K of 30 November 1987 and 43/76 H of 7 December 1988 on the United Nations Regional Centre for Peace, Disarmament and Development in Latin America and the Caribbean, with headquarters in Lima,

Recalling also its resolutions 46/37 F of 9 December 1991, 48/76 E of 16 December 1993, 49/76 D of 15 December 1994, 50/71 C of 12 December 1995, 52/220 of 22 December 1997, 53/78 F of 4 December 1998, 54/55 F of 1 December 1999, 55/34 E of 20 November 2000, 56/25 E of 29 November 2001, 57/89 of 22 November 2002, 58/60 of 8 December 2003, 59/99 of 3 December 2004, 60/84 of 8 December 2005, 61/92 of 6 December 2006, 62/49 of 5 December 2007, 63/74 of 2 December 2008, 64/60 of 2 December 2009 and 65/79 of 8 December 2010,

Recognizing that the Regional Centre has continued to provide substantive support for the implementation of regional and subregional initiatives and has intensified its contribution to the coordination of United Nations efforts towards peace and disarmament and for the promotion of economic and social development,

Reaffirming the mandate of the Regional Centre to provide, on request, substantive support for the initiatives and other activities of the Member States of the region for the implementation of measures for peace and disarmament and for the promotion of economic and social development,

Taking note of the report of the Secretary-General,[1] and expressing its appreciation for the important assistance provided by the Regional Centre to many countries in the region, including through capacity-building and technical assistance programmes as well as outreach activities, for the development of plans to reduce and prevent armed violence from an arms control perspective, for promoting the implementation of relevant agreements and treaties and for capacity-building initiatives aimed at bolstering the efforts of the law enforcement community to combat illicit firearms trafficking,

Welcoming the support provided by the Regional Centre to Member States in the implementation of disarmament and non-proliferation instruments,

---

[1] A/66/140.

Emphasizing the need for the Regional Centre to develop and strengthen its activities and programmes in a comprehensive and balanced manner, in accordance with its mandate,

Welcoming the ongoing support provided by the Regional Centre to Member States in the implementation of the Programme of Action to Prevent, Combat and Eradicate the Illicit Trade in Small Arms and Light Weapons in All Its Aspects,[2]

Welcoming also the initiative of the Regional Centre to conduct its first course specifically for women, in line with efforts to implement gender mainstreaming in promoting disarmament, non-proliferation and arms control, as called for in General Assembly resolution 65/69 of 8 December 2010,

Recalling the report of the Group of Governmental Experts on the relationship between disarmament and development, referred to in General Assembly resolution 59/78 of 3 December 2004,[3] which is of utmost interest with regard to the role that the Regional Centre plays in promoting the issue in the region in pursuit of its mandate to promote economic and social development related to peace and disarmament,

Noting that security and disarmament issues have always been recognized as significant topics in Latin America and the Caribbean, the first inhabited region in the world to be declared a nuclear-weapon-free zone,

Emphasizing the importance of maintaining the support provided by the Regional Centre for strengthening the nuclear-weapon-free zone established by the Treaty for the Prohibition of Nuclear Weapons in Latin America and the Caribbean (Treaty of Tlatelolco),[4] and its efforts in promoting peace and disarmament education,

Bearing in mind the important role of the Regional Centre in promoting confidence-building measures, arms control and limitation, disarmament and development at the regional level,

Bearing in mind also the importance of information, research, education and training for peace, disarmament and development in order to achieve understanding and cooperation among States,

1. *Reiterates its strong support* for the role of the United Nations Regional Centre for Peace, Disarmament and Development in Latin America and the Caribbean in the promotion of United Nations activities at the regional and subregional levels to strengthen peace, disarmament, stability, security and development among its member States;

2. *Expresses its satisfaction* for the activities carried out in the past year by the Regional Centre, and requests the Centre to continue to take into

---

[2] See *Report of the United Nations Conference on the Illicit Trade in Small Arms and Light Weapons in All Its Aspects, New York, 9–20 July 2001* (A/CONF.192/15), chap. IV, para. 24.
[3] See A/59/119.
[4] United Nations, *Treaty Series*, vol. 634, No. 9068.

account the proposals to be submitted by the countries of the region for the promotion of, inter alia, confidence-building measures, arms control and limitation, transparency, the reduction and prevention of armed violence, disarmament and development at the regional and subregional levels;

3. *Expresses its appreciation* for the political support for and financial contributions to the Regional Centre, which are essential for its continued operation;

4. *Appeals* to Member States, in particular those within the Latin American and Caribbean region, and to international governmental and non-governmental organizations and foundations to make and to increase voluntary contributions in order to strengthen the Regional Centre, its programme of activities and the implementation thereof;

5. *Invites* all States of the region to continue to take part in the activities of the Regional Centre, proposing items for inclusion in its programme of activities and making greater and better use of the potential of the Centre to meet the current challenges facing the international community, with a view to fulfilling the aims of the Charter of the United Nations in the areas of peace, disarmament and development;

6. *Recognizes* that the Regional Centre has an important role in the promotion and development of regional and subregional initiatives agreed upon by the countries of Latin America and the Caribbean in the field of weapons of mass destruction, in particular nuclear weapons, and conventional arms, including small arms and light weapons, as well as in the relationship between disarmament and development;

7. *Encourages* the Regional Centre to further develop activities in all countries of the region in the important areas of peace, disarmament and development;

8. *Requests* the Secretary-General to report to the General Assembly at its sixty-seventh session on the implementation of the present resolution;

9. *Decides* to include in the provisional agenda of its sixty-seventh session the sub-item entitled "United Nations Regional Centre for Peace, Disarmament and Development in Latin America and the Caribbean".

Action by the General Assembly

Date: 2 December 2011	Meeting: 71st plenary meeting
Vote: Adopted without a vote	Report: A/66/413

Sponsors

Peru, on behalf of the States Members of the United Nations that are members of the Group of Latin American and Caribbean States

Action by the First Committee

Date: 31 October 2011	Meeting: 19th meeting
Vote: Adopted without a vote	Draft resolution: A/C.1/66/L.16

Agenda item 99

66/55   Regional confidence-building measures: activities of the United Nations Standing Advisory Committee on Security Questions in Central Africa

Text

The General Assembly,

Recalling its previous relevant resolutions, in particular resolution 65/84 of 8 December 2010,

Recalling also the guidelines for general and complete disarmament adopted at its tenth special session, the first special session devoted to disarmament,

Bearing in mind the establishment by the Secretary-General on 28 May 1992 of the United Nations Standing Advisory Committee on Security Questions in Central Africa, the purpose of which is to encourage arms limitation, disarmament, non-proliferation and development in the subregion,

Reaffirming that the purpose of the Standing Advisory Committee is to conduct reconstruction and confidence-building activities in Central Africa among its member States, including through confidence-building and arms limitation measures,

Taking note of the Sao Tome Declaration on a Central African Common Position on the Arms Trade Treaty, adopted by the States members of the Standing Advisory Committee on 16 March 2011 at their thirty-second ministerial meeting, held in Sao Tome from 12 to 16 March 2011,[1]

Convinced that the resources released by disarmament, including regional disarmament, can be devoted to economic and social development and to the protection of the environment for the benefit of all peoples, in particular those of developing countries,

Considering the importance and effectiveness of confidence-building measures taken on the initiative and with the participation of all States concerned and taking into account the specific characteristics of each region, since such measures can contribute to regional stability and to international peace and security,

Convinced that development can be achieved only in a climate of peace, security and mutual confidence both within and among States,

Recalling the Brazzaville Declaration on Cooperation for Peace and Security in Central Africa,[2] the Bata Declaration for the Promotion of Lasting

---

[1] See A/66/72-S/2011/225, annex.
[2] A/50/474, annex I.

Democracy, Peace and Development in Central Africa[3] and the Yaoundé Declaration on Peace, Security and Stability in Central Africa,[4]

Bearing in mind resolutions 1196 (1998) and 1197 (1998), adopted by the Security Council on 16 and 18 September 1998, respectively, following its consideration of the report of the Secretary-General on the causes of conflict and the promotion of durable peace and sustainable development in Africa,[5]

Emphasizing the need to strengthen the capacity for conflict prevention and peacekeeping in Africa, and welcoming the close cooperation established between the United Nations and the Economic Community of Central African States for that purpose,

Taking note with interest of the increasing focus of the Standing Advisory Committee on human security questions, such as trafficking in persons, especially in women and children, as an important consideration for subregional peace, stability and conflict prevention,

Expressing concern about the increasing impact of cross-border criminality, in particular the activities of the Lord's Resistance Army and increasing incidents of piracy in the Gulf of Guinea, on peace, security and development in Central Africa,

Considering the urgent need to prevent the possible movement of illicit weapons and mercenaries from the conflict in Libya into the neighbouring countries in the Central African region,

1. *Reaffirms its support* for efforts aimed at promoting confidence-building measures at the regional and subregional levels in order to ease tensions and conflicts in Central Africa and to further sustainable peace, stability and development in the subregion;

2. *Reaffirms* the importance of disarmament and arms limitation programmes in Central Africa carried out by the States of the subregion with the support of the United Nations, the African Union and other international partners;

3. *Renews its encouragement* to the States members of the United Nations Standing Advisory Committee on Security Questions in Central Africa and other interested States to provide financial support for the implementation of the Central African Convention for the Control of Small Arms and Light Weapons, Their Ammunition and All Parts and Components That Can Be Used for Their Manufacture, Repair and Assembly (Kinshasa Convention), adopted on 30 April 2010, at the thirtieth ministerial meeting of the Standing Advisory Committee, held in Kinshasa from 26 to 30 April 2010;[6]

---

[3] A/53/258-S/1998/763, annex II, appendix I.
[4] A/53/868-S/1999/303, annex II.
[5] A/52/871-S/1998/318.
[6] See A/65/517-S/2010/534, annex.

4.   *Welcomes* the adoption by the States members of the Standing Advisory Committee of the Sao Tome Declaration on a Central African Common Position on the Arms Trade Treaty,[1] encourages the Committee to take the necessary measures for the implementation of the steps identified in the Declaration, towards the continued active participation of its member States in the process for the arms trade treaty, and requests the United Nations Regional Office for Central Africa and international partners to support those measures;

5.   *Also welcomes* the active participation of experts of States members of the Standing Advisory Committee in the open-ended meeting of governmental experts on the Implementation of the Programme of Action to Prevent, Combat and Eradicate the Illicit Trade in Small Arms and Light Weapons in All Its Aspects, held in New York from 9 to 13 May 2011;

6.   *Encourages* the States members of the Standing Advisory Committee to carry out the programmes of activities adopted at their ministerial meetings;

7.   *Also encourages* the States members of the Standing Advisory Committee to continue their efforts to render the early warning mechanism for Central Africa fully operational as an instrument for analysing and monitoring the political situation in the subregion within the framework of the prevention of crises and armed conflicts, and requests the Secretary-General to provide the assistance necessary for its smooth functioning;

8.   *Welcomes* the signing of the Kinshasa Convention by all eleven States members of the Standing Advisory Committee, and appeals to them to ratify the Convention in a timely manner in order to facilitate its early entry into force and implementation;

9.   *Appeals* to the international community to support the efforts undertaken by the States concerned to implement disarmament, demobilization and reintegration programmes;

10.   *Requests* the United Nations Regional Office for Central Africa, in collaboration with the United Nations Regional Centre for Peace and Disarmament in Africa, to facilitate the efforts undertaken by the States members of the Standing Advisory Committee, in particular for their execution of the Implementation Plan for the Kinshasa Convention, as adopted on 19 November 2010 at their thirty-first ministerial meeting, held in Brazzaville from 15 to 19 November 2010;[7]

11.   *Requests* the Secretary-General and the Office of the United Nations High Commissioner for Refugees to continue to assist the countries of Central Africa in tackling the problems of refugees and displaced persons in their territories;

---

[7]   See A/65/717-S/2011/53, annex.

12. *Requests* the Secretary-General and the United Nations High Commissioner for Human Rights to continue to provide their full assistance for the proper functioning of the Subregional Centre for Human Rights and Democracy in Central Africa;

13. *Reminds* the States members of the Standing Advisory Committee of the commitments they undertook at the adoption of the Declaration on the Trust Fund of the United Nations Standing Advisory Committee on Security Questions in Central Africa (Libreville Declaration) on 8 May 2009,[8] and invites those States members of the Committee that have not already done so to contribute to the Trust Fund;

14. *Urges* other Member States and intergovernmental and non-governmental organizations to support the activities of the Standing Advisory Committee effectively through voluntary contributions to the Trust Fund;

15. *Urges* the States members of the Standing Advisory Committee, in accordance with Security Council resolution 1325 (2000) of 31 October 2000, to strengthen the gender component of the various meetings of the Committee relating to disarmament and international security;

16. *Expresses its satisfaction* to the Secretary-General for his support for the effective inauguration of the United Nations Regional Office for Central Africa in Libreville, welcomes the efforts made by the Office since its opening, and strongly encourages the States members of the Standing Advisory Committee and international partners to support the work of the Office;

17. *Welcomes* the efforts of the Standing Advisory Committee towards addressing cross-border security threats in Central Africa, including the fallout from the situation in Libya, and welcomes the role of the United Nations Regional Office for Central Africa in coordinating those efforts, working closely with the Economic Community of Central African States, the African Union and all relevant regional and international partners;

18. *Expresses its satisfaction* to the Secretary-General for his support for the revitalization of the activities of the Standing Advisory Committee, and requests him to continue to provide the assistance needed to ensure the success of its regular biannual meetings;

19. *Calls upon* the Secretary-General to submit to the General Assembly at its sixty-seventh session a report on the implementation of the present resolution;

20. *Decides* to include in the provisional agenda of its sixty-seventh session the sub-item entitled "Regional confidence-building measures:

---

[8] See A/64/85-S/2009/288, annex.

activities of the United Nations Standing Advisory Committee on Security Questions in Central Africa".

Action by the General Assembly

    Date: 2 December 2011   Meeting: 71st plenary meeting

    Vote: Adopted without a vote   Report: A/66/413

Sponsors

Angola, Burundi, Central African Republic, Cameroon, Chad, **Congo,** Democratic Republic of the Congo, Equatorial Guinea, Gabon, Rwanda, Sao Tome and Principe

Co-sponsors

Kenya, Niger

Action by the First Committee

    Date: 28 October 2011   Meeting: 23rd meeting

    Vote: Adopted without a vote   Draft resolution: A/C.1/66/L.23

Agenda item 99

66/56 United Nations Regional Centre for Peace and Disarmament in Asia and the Pacific

Text

The General Assembly,

Recalling its resolutions 42/39 D of 30 November 1987 and 44/117 F of 15 December 1989, by which it established the United Nations Regional Centre for Peace and Disarmament in Asia and renamed it the United Nations Regional Centre for Peace and Disarmament in Asia and the Pacific, with headquarters in Kathmandu and with the mandate of providing, on request, substantive support for the initiatives and other activities mutually agreed upon by the Member States of the Asia-Pacific region for the implementation of measures for peace and disarmament, through appropriate utilization of available resources,

Welcoming the physical operation of the Regional Centre from Kathmandu in accordance with General Assembly resolution 62/52 of 5 December 2007,

Recalling the mandate of the Regional Centre to provide, on request, substantive support for the initiatives and other activities mutually agreed upon by the Member States of the Asia-Pacific region for the implementation of measures for peace and disarmament,

Taking note of the report of the Secretary-General[1] and expressing its appreciation to the Regional Centre for its important work in promoting confidence-building measures through the organization of meetings, conferences and workshops in the region, including conferences held on Jeju Island, Republic of Korea, on 2 and 3 December 2010 and in Matsumoto, Japan, from 27 to 29 July 2011, a regional workshop on strengthening the media's capacity in promoting disarmament held in Beijing on 20 and 21 January 2011 and a regional seminar on armed violence prevention held in Kathmandu from 16 to 18 March 2011,

Appreciating the timely execution by Nepal of its financial commitments for the physical operation of the Regional Centre,

1. *Expresses its satisfaction* for the activities carried out in the past year by the United Nations Regional Centre for Peace and Disarmament in Asia and the Pacific, and invites all States of the region to continue to support the activities of the Centre, including by continuing to take part in them, where possible, and by proposing items for inclusion in the programme of activities

---

[1] A/66/113.

of the Centre, in order to contribute to the implementation of measures for peace and disarmament;

2. *Expresses its gratitude* to the Government of Nepal for its cooperation and financial support, which has enabled the Regional Centre to operate from Kathmandu;

3. *Expresses its appreciation* to the Secretary-General and the Office for Disarmament Affairs of the Secretariat for providing necessary support with a view to ensuring the smooth operation of the Regional Centre from Kathmandu and to enabling the Centre to function effectively;

4. *Appeals* to Member States, in particular those within the Asia-Pacific region, as well as to international governmental and non-governmental organizations and foundations, to make voluntary contributions, the only resources of the Regional Centre, to strengthen the programme of activities of the Centre and the implementation thereof;

5. *Reaffirms its strong support* for the role of the Regional Centre in the promotion of United Nations activities at the regional level to strengthen peace, stability and security among its Member States;

6. *Underlines* the importance of the Kathmandu process for the development of the practice of region-wide security and disarmament dialogues;

7. *Requests* the Secretary-General to report to the General Assembly at its sixty-seventh session on the implementation of the present resolution;

8. *Decides* to include in the provisional agenda of its sixty-seventh session the sub-item entitled "United Nations Regional Centre for Peace and Disarmament in Asia and the Pacific".

Action by the General Assembly

Date: 2 December 2011   Meeting: 71st plenary meeting
Vote: Adopted without a vote   Report: A/66/413

Sponsors

Afghanistan, Australia, Bangladesh, Bhutan, China, India, Indonesia, Japan, Kazakhstan, Maldives, Micronesia (Federated States of), Mongolia, Myanmar, **Nepal**, New Zealand, Republic of Korea, Samoa, Thailand, Viet Nam

Co-sponsors

Congo, Kyrgyzstan, Pakistan, Papua New Guinea, Timor-Leste

Action by the First Committee

Date: 31 October 2011   Meeting: 24th meeting
Vote: Adopted without a vote   Draft resolution: A/C.1/66/L.34

Agenda item 99

66/57 Convention on the Prohibition of the Use of Nuclear Weapons

Text

The General Assembly,

Convinced that the use of nuclear weapons poses the most serious threat to the survival of mankind,

Bearing in mind the advisory opinion of the International Court of Justice of 8 July 1996 on the *Legality of the Threat or Use of Nuclear Weapons*,[1]

Convinced that a multilateral, universal and binding agreement prohibiting the use or threat of use of nuclear weapons would contribute to the elimination of the nuclear threat and to the climate for negotiations leading to the ultimate elimination of nuclear weapons, thereby strengthening international peace and security,

Conscious that some steps taken by the Russian Federation and the United States of America towards a reduction of their nuclear weapons and the improvement in the international climate can contribute towards the goal of the complete elimination of nuclear weapons,

Recalling that paragraph 58 of the Final Document of the Tenth Special Session of the General Assembly[2] states that all States should actively participate in efforts to bring about conditions in international relations among States in which a code of peaceful conduct of nations in international affairs could be agreed upon and that would preclude the use or threat of use of nuclear weapons,

Reaffirming that any use of nuclear weapons would be a violation of the Charter of the United Nations and a crime against humanity, as declared in its resolutions 1653 (XVI) of 24 November 1961, 33/71 B of 14 December 1978, 34/83 G of 11 December 1979, 35/152 D of 12 December 1980 and 36/92 I of 9 December 1981,

Determined to achieve an international convention prohibiting the development, production, stockpiling and use of nuclear weapons, leading to their ultimate destruction,

Stressing that an international convention on the prohibition of the use of nuclear weapons would be an important step in a phased programme towards the complete elimination of nuclear weapons, with a specified framework of time,

---

[1] A/51/218, annex; see also *Legality of the Threat or Use of Nuclear Weapons, Advisory Opinion, I.C.J. Reports 1996*, p. 226.

[2] Resolution S-10/2.

Noting with regret that the Conference on Disarmament, during its 2011 session, was unable to undertake negotiations on this subject as called for in General Assembly resolution 65/80 of 8 December 2010,

1.	*Reiterates its request* to the Conference on Disarmament to commence negotiations in order to reach agreement on an international convention prohibiting the use or threat of use of nuclear weapons under any circumstances;

2.	*Requests* the Conference on Disarmament to report to the General Assembly on the results of those negotiations.

Action by the General Assembly

Date: 2 December 2011	Meeting: 71st plenary meeting
Vote: 117-48-12	Report: A/66/413

Sponsors*

Afghanistan, Bangladesh, Bhutan, Cambodia, Chile, Congo, Cuba, Democratic Republic of the Congo, Ecuador, Egypt, Haiti, Honduras, India, Indonesia, Iran (Islamic Republic of), Libyan Arab Jamahiriya, Malaysia, Mauritius, Myanmar, Nepal, Nicaragua, Sri Lanka, Sudan, Viet Nam, Zambia

Co-sponsors

El Salvador, Jordan, Kuwait, Paraguay, Trinidad and Tobago, Venezuela (Bolivarian Republic of)

Recorded vote**

In favour:

Afghanistan, Algeria, Angola, Antigua and Barbuda, Argentina, Azerbaijan, Bahamas, Bahrain, Bangladesh, Barbados, Belize, Benin, Bhutan, Bolivia (Plurinational State of), Botswana, Brazil, Brunei Darussalam, Burkina Faso, Cambodia, Cameroon, Cape Verde, Chad, Chile, China, Colombia, Comoros, Congo, Costa Rica, Côte d'Ivoire, Cuba, Democratic People's Republic of Korea, Djibouti, Dominican Republic, Ecuador, Egypt, Eritrea, Ethiopia, Fiji, Ghana, Grenada, Guatemala, Guinea, Guinea-Bissau, Guyana, Haiti, Honduras, India, Indonesia, Iran (Islamic Republic of), Iraq, Jamaica, Jordan, Kazakhstan, Kenya, Kuwait, Lao People's Democratic Republic, Lebanon, Lesotho, Liberia, Libyan Arab Jamahiriya, Madagascar, Malawi, Malaysia, Maldives, Mali, Mauritania, Mauritius, Mexico, Mongolia, Morocco, Mozambique, Myanmar, Namibia, Nepal, Nicaragua, Niger, Nigeria, Oman, Pakistan, Panama, Papua New Guinea, Paraguay, Peru,

---

*	The draft resolution was submitted by the sponsors.
**	Subsequently the delegation of Montenegro advised the Secretariat that it had intended to vote against.

Philippines, Qatar, Saint Kitts and Nevis, Saint Lucia, Saint Vincent and the Grenadines, Samoa, Sao Tome and Principe, Saudi Arabia, Senegal, Seychelles, Sierra Leone, Singapore, Solomon Islands, South Africa, Sri Lanka, Sudan, Suriname, Swaziland, Syrian Arab Republic, Thailand, Togo, Tonga, Trinidad and Tobago, Tunisia, Turkmenistan, Uganda, United Arab Emirates, United Republic of Tanzania, Uruguay, Venezuela (Bolivarian Republic of), Viet Nam, Yemen, Zambia, Zimbabwe

Against:

Albania, Andorra, Australia, Austria, Belgium, Bosnia and Herzegovina, Bulgaria, Canada, Croatia, Cyprus, Czech Republic, Denmark, Estonia, Finland, France, Germany, Greece, Hungary, Iceland, Ireland, Israel, Italy, Latvia, Liechtenstein, Lithuania, Luxembourg, Malta, Micronesia (Federated States of), Monaco, Netherlands, New Zealand, Norway, Palau, Poland, Portugal, Republic of Moldova, Romania, San Marino, Slovakia, Slovenia, Spain, Sweden, Switzerland, the former Yugoslav Republic of Macedonia, Turkey, Ukraine, United Kingdom, United States

Abstaining:

Armenia, Belarus, El Salvador, Georgia, Japan, Kyrgyzstan, Marshall Islands, Republic of Korea, Russian Federation, Serbia, Tajikistan, Uzbekistan

Action by the First Committee

Date: 26 October 2011   Meeting: 21st meeting
Vote: 113-48-10   Draft resolution: A/C.1/66/L.46

Agenda item 99

66/58　United Nations Regional Centre for Peace and Disarmament in Africa

Text

The General Assembly,

Mindful of the provisions of Article 11, paragraph 1, of the Charter of the United Nations stipulating that a function of the General Assembly is to consider the general principles of cooperation in the maintenance of international peace and security, including the principles governing disarmament and arms limitation,

Recalling its resolutions 40/151 G of 16 December 1985, 41/60 D of 3 December 1986, 42/39 J of 30 November 1987 and 43/76 D of 7 December 1988 on the United Nations Regional Centre for Peace and Disarmament in Africa and its resolutions 46/36 F of 6 December 1991 and 47/52 G of 9 December 1992 on regional disarmament, including confidence-building measures,

Recalling also its resolutions 48/76 E of 16 December 1993, 49/76 D of 15 December 1994, 50/71 C of 12 December 1995, 51/46 E of 10 December 1996, 52/220 of 22 December 1997, 53/78 C of 4 December 1998, 54/55 B of 1 December 1999, 55/34 D of 20 November 2000, 56/25 D of 29 November 2001, 57/91 of 22 November 2002, 58/61 of 8 December 2003, 59/101 of 3 December 2004, 60/86 of 8 December 2005, 61/93 of 6 December 2006, 62/216 of 22 December 2007, 63/80 of 2 December 2008 and 64/62 of 2 December 2009,

Reaffirming the role of the Regional Centre in promoting disarmament, peace and security at the regional level,

Welcoming the continuing and deepening cooperation between the Regional Centre and the African Union, in particular its institutions in the fields of disarmament, peace and security, as well as between the Centre and relevant United Nations bodies and programmes in Africa, and considering the communiqué adopted by the Peace and Security Council of the African Union at its two-hundredth meeting, held in Addis Ababa on 21 August 2009,

Recalling the decision taken by the Executive Council of the African Union at its eighth ordinary session, held in Khartoum from 16 to 21 January 2006,[1] in which the Council called upon member States to make voluntary contributions to the Regional Centre to maintain its operations,

---

[1]　A/60/693, annex II, decision EX.CL/Dec.263 (VIII).

Recalling also the call by the Secretary-General for continued financial and in kind support from Member States,[2] which would enable the Regional Centre to discharge its mandate in full and to respond more effectively to requests for assistance from African States,

1. *Takes note* of the report of the Secretary-General;[3]

2. *Welcomes* the continental dimension of the activities of the United Nations Regional Centre for Peace and Disarmament in Africa in response to the evolving needs of African Member States in the areas of disarmament, peace and security;

3. *Also welcomes* the undertaking by the Regional Centre to provide capacity-building, technical assistance programmes and advisory services to the African Union Commission and subregional organizations on the control of small arms and light weapons, including on stockpile management and destruction, the proposed arms trade treaty and issues related to weapons of mass destruction, as detailed in the report of the Secretary-General;

4. *Further welcomes* the contribution of the Regional Centre to continental disarmament, peace and security, in particular its assistance to the African Union Commission in the elaboration of the African Union Strategy on the Control of Illicit Proliferation, Circulation and Trafficking of Small Arms and Light Weapons and the ongoing process of seeking an African common position on the proposed arms trade treaty, and to the African Commission on Nuclear Energy in its implementation of the African Nuclear-Weapon-Free Zone Treaty (Treaty of Pelindaba);[4]

5. *Notes with appreciation* the tangible achievements and impact of the Regional Centre at the regional level, including its assistance to Central African States in their elaboration of the Central African Convention for the Control of Small Arms and Light Weapons, Their Ammunition and All Parts and Components That Can Be Used for Their Manufacture, Repair and Assembly (Kinshasa Convention),[5] to Central and West African States in the elaboration of their respective common positions on the proposed arms trade treaty, to West Africa on security sector reform initiatives, and to East Africa on programmes to control brokering of small arms and light weapons;

6. *Also notes with appreciation* the contribution of the Regional Centre to the "One United Nations" approach and to United Nations inter-agency mechanisms, including the United Nations Development Assistance Framework, the common country assessments and the poverty reduction strategy papers, in a number of African countries;

---

[2] See A/66/159, para. 58.
[3] A/66/159.
[4] See A/50/426, annex.
[5] See A/65/517-S/2010/534, annex.

7. *Urges* all States, as well as international governmental and non-governmental organizations and foundations, to make voluntary contributions to enable the Regional Centre to carry out its programmes and activities and meet the needs of the African States;

8. *Urges*, in particular, States members of the African Union to make voluntary contributions to the Trust Fund for the United Nations Regional Centre for Peace and Disarmament in Africa in conformity with the decision taken by the Executive Council of the African Union in Khartoum in January 2006;[1]

9. *Requests* the Secretary-General to continue to facilitate close cooperation between the Regional Centre and the African Union, in particular in the areas of disarmament, peace and security;

10. *Also requests* the Secretary-General to continue to provide the necessary support to the Regional Centre for greater achievements and results;

11. *Further requests* the Secretary-General to report to the General Assembly at its sixty-seventh session on the implementation of the present resolution;

12. *Decides* to include in the provisional agenda of its sixty-seventh session the sub-item entitled "United Nations Regional Centre for Peace and Disarmament in Africa".

Action by the General Assembly

Date: 2 December 2011   Meeting: 71st plenary meeting
Vote: Adopted without a vote   Report: A/66/413

Sponsors

Nigeria, on behalf of the States Members of the United Nations that are members of the Group of African States

Action by the First Committee

Date: 28 October 2011   Meeting: 24th meeting
Vote: Adopted without a vote   Draft resolution: A/C.1/66/L.52

Agenda item 100

66/59   Report of the Conference on Disarmament

Text

The General Assembly,

Having considered the report of the Conference on Disarmament,[1]

Convinced that the Conference on Disarmament, as the sole multilateral disarmament negotiating forum of the international community, has the primary role in substantive negotiations on priority questions of disarmament,

Recognizing the addresses of the President of the General Assembly and the Secretary-General of the United Nations, as well as the addresses of Ministers for Foreign Affairs and other high-level officials in the Conference on Disarmament, as expressions of support for the endeavours of the Conference,

Recognizing also the need to conduct multilateral negotiations with the aim of reaching agreement on concrete issues, and considering that the present international climate should give additional impetus to multilateral negotiations,

Recalling, in this respect, that the Conference on Disarmament has a number of urgent and important issues for negotiation,

Noting the follow-up discussions to the high-level meeting on revitalizing the work of the Conference on Disarmament and taking forward multilateral negotiations, held on 24 September 2010 at the initiative of the Secretary-General, and acknowledging the continued support for the Conference expressed by high-level officials in 2011,

Noting with renewed concern that the Conference on Disarmament has been unable to commence its substantive work, including negotiations, for over a decade, as envisaged by the General Assembly in its resolution 65/85 of 8 December 2010, or to agree on a programme of work,

Welcoming the renewed overwhelming call for greater flexibility with respect to commencing the substantive work of the Conference on Disarmament without further delay, on the basis of a balanced and comprehensive programme of work,

Appreciating the continued cooperation among the States members of the Conference on Disarmament as well as the six successive Presidents of the Conference at its 2011 session,

Noting with appreciation the significant contributions made during the 2011 session to promote substantive discussions on issues on the agenda, as

---

[1] *Official Records of the General Assembly, Sixty-sixth Session, Supplement No. 27* (A/66/27).

well as the discussions held on other issues that could also be relevant to the current international security environment,

Welcoming the enhanced engagement between civil society and the Conference on Disarmament at its 2011 session according to decisions taken by the Conference,

Stressing the urgent need for the Conference on Disarmament to commence its substantive work at the beginning of its 2012 session,

1. *Reaffirms* the role of the Conference on Disarmament as the sole multilateral disarmament negotiating forum of the international community;

2. *Calls upon* the Conference on Disarmament to further intensify consultations and explore possibilities with a view to adopting a balanced and comprehensive programme of work at the earliest possible date during its 2012 session, bearing in mind the decision on the programme of work adopted by the Conference on 29 May 2009;[2]

3. *Expresses its appreciation* for the strong support expressed for the Conference on Disarmament during its 2011 session by Ministers for Foreign Affairs and other high-level officials, and takes into account their calls for greater flexibility with respect to commencing the substantive work of the Conference without further delay;

4. *Welcomes* the decision of the Conference on Disarmament to request the current President and the incoming President to conduct consultations during the intersessional period and, if possible, make recommendations, taking into account all relevant proposals, past, present and future, including those submitted as documents of the Conference, views presented and discussions held, and to endeavour to keep the membership of the Conference informed, as appropriate, of their consultations;

5. *Requests* all States members of the Conference on Disarmament to cooperate with the current President and successive Presidents in their efforts to guide the Conference to the early commencement of its substantive work, including negotiations, in its 2012 session;

6. *Recognizes* the importance of continuing consultations on the question of the expansion of the membership of the Conference on Disarmament;

7. *Requests* the Secretary-General to continue to ensure and strengthen, if needed, the provision to the Conference on Disarmament of all necessary administrative, substantive and conference support services;

8. *Requests* the Conference on Disarmament to submit to the General Assembly at its sixty-seventh session a report on its work;

---

[2] CD/1864.

9.   *Decides* to include in the provisional agenda of its sixty-seventh session the sub-item entitled "Report of the Conference on Disarmament".

Action by the General Assembly

Date: 2 December 2011   Meeting: 71st plenary meeting
Vote: Adopted without a vote   Report: A/66/414

Sponsors

China, **Cuba,** Democratic People's Republic of Korea

Action by the First Committee

Date: 27 October 2011   Meeting: 22nd meeting
Vote: Adopted without a vote   Draft resolution: A/C.1/66/L.13/Rev.1

Agenda item 100

66/60   Report of the Disarmament Commission

Text

The General Assembly,

Having considered the report of the Disarmament Commission,[1]

Recalling its resolutions 47/54 A of 9 December 1992, 47/54 G of 8 April 1993, 48/77 A of 16 December 1993, 49/77 A of 15 December 1994, 50/72 D of 12 December 1995, 51/47 B of 10 December 1996, 52/40 B of 9 December 1997, 53/79 A of 4 December 1998, 54/56 A of 1 December 1999, 55/35 C of 20 November 2000, 56/26 A of 29 November 2001, 57/95 of 22 November 2002, 58/67 of 8 December 2003, 59/105 of 3 December 2004, 60/91 of 8 December 2005, 61/98 of 6 December 2006, 62/54 of 5 December 2007, 63/83 of 2 December 2008, 64/65 of 2 December 2009 and 65/86 of 8 December 2010,

Considering the role that the Disarmament Commission has been called upon to play and the contribution that it should make in examining and submitting recommendations on various problems in the field of disarmament and in promoting the implementation of the relevant decisions adopted by the General Assembly at its tenth special session,

1.   *Takes note* of the report of the Disarmament Commission;[1]

2.   *Reaffirms* the validity of its decision 52/492 of 8 September 1998 concerning the efficient functioning of the Disarmament Commission;

3.   *Recalls* its resolution 61/98, in which it adopted additional measures for improving the effectiveness of the Disarmament Commission's methods of work;

4.   *Reaffirms* the mandate of the Disarmament Commission as the specialized, deliberative body within the United Nations multilateral disarmament machinery that allows for in-depth deliberations on specific disarmament issues, leading to the submission of concrete recommendations on those issues;

5.   *Also reaffirms* the importance of further enhancing the dialogue and cooperation among the First Committee, the Disarmament Commission and the Conference on Disarmament;

6.   *Requests* the Disarmament Commission to continue its work in accordance with its mandate, as set forth in paragraph 118 of the Final Document of the Tenth Special Session of the General Assembly,[2] and with

---

[1]   *Official Records of the General Assembly, Sixty-sixth Session, Supplement No. 42* (A/66/42).
[2]   Resolution S-10/2.

paragraph 3 of Assembly resolution 37/78 H of 9 December 1982, and to that end to make every effort to achieve specific recommendations on the items on its agenda, taking into account the adopted "Ways and means to enhance the functioning of the Disarmament Commission";[3]

7. *Recommends* that the Disarmament Commission intensify consultations with a view to reaching agreement on the items on its agenda, in accordance with decision 52/492, before the start of its substantive session of 2012;

8. *Requests* the Disarmament Commission to meet for a period not exceeding three weeks during 2012, namely from 2 to 20 April, and to submit a substantive report to the General Assembly at its sixty-seventh session;

9. *Requests* the Secretary-General to transmit to the Disarmament Commission the annual report of the Conference on Disarmament,[4] together with all the official records of the sixty-sixth session of the General Assembly relating to disarmament matters, and to render all assistance that the Commission may require for implementing the present resolution;

10. *Also requests* the Secretary-General to ensure full provision to the Disarmament Commission and its subsidiary bodies of interpretation and translation facilities in the official languages and to assign, as a matter of priority, all the necessary resources and services, including verbatim records, to that end;

11. *Decides* to include in the provisional agenda of its sixty-seventh session the sub-item entitled "Report of the Disarmament Commission".

Action by the General Assembly

Date: 2 December 2011   Meeting: 71st plenary meeting
Vote: Adopted without a vote   Report: A/66/414

Sponsors

Iraq, on behalf of members of the extended Bureau of the Disarmament Commission

Action by the First Committee

Date: 27 October 2011   Meeting: 22nd meeting
Vote: Adopted without a vote   Draft resolution: A/C.1/66/L.20

---

[3] A/CN.10/137.
[4] *Official Records of the General Assembly, Sixty-sixth Session, Supplement No. 27* (A/66/27).

Agenda item 101

66/61   The risk of nuclear proliferation in the Middle East

Text

The General Assembly,

Bearing in mind its relevant resolutions,

Taking note of the relevant resolutions adopted by the General Conference of the International Atomic Energy Agency, the latest of which is resolution GC(55)/RES/14, adopted on 23 September 2011,[1]

Cognizant that the proliferation of nuclear weapons in the region of the Middle East would pose a serious threat to international peace and security,

Mindful of the immediate need for placing all nuclear facilities in the region of the Middle East under full-scope safeguards of the Agency,

Recalling the decision on principles and objectives for nuclear non-proliferation and disarmament adopted by the 1995 Review and Extension Conference of the Parties to the Treaty on the Non-Proliferation of Nuclear Weapons on 11 May 1995,[2] in which the Conference urged universal adherence to the Treaty[3] as an urgent priority and called upon all States not yet parties to the Treaty to accede to it at the earliest date, particularly those States that operate unsafeguarded nuclear facilities,

Recognizing with satisfaction that, in the Final Document of the 2000 Review Conference of the Parties to the Treaty on the Non-Proliferation of Nuclear Weapons,[4] the Conference undertook to make determined efforts towards the achievement of the goal of universality of the Treaty, called upon those remaining States not parties to the Treaty to accede to it, thereby accepting an international legally binding commitment not to acquire nuclear weapons or nuclear explosive devices and to accept Agency safeguards on all their nuclear activities, and underlined the necessity of universal adherence to the Treaty and of strict compliance by all parties with their obligations under the Treaty,

Recalling the resolution on the Middle East adopted by the 1995 Review and Extension Conference on 11 May 1995,[2] in which the Conference noted

---

[1] See International Atomic Energy Agency, *Resolutions and Other Decisions of the General Conference, Fifty-fifth Regular Session, 19–23 September 2011* (GC(55)/RES/DEC(2011)).

[2] See *1995 Review and Extension Conference of the Parties to the Treaty on the Non-Proliferation of Nuclear Weapons, Final Document, Part I* (NPT/CONF.1995/32 (Part I) and Corr.2), annex.

[3] United Nations, *Treaty Series*, vol. 729, No. 10485.

[4] *2000 Review Conference of the Parties to the Treaty on the Non-Proliferation of Nuclear Weapons, Final Document*, vols. I-III (NPT/CONF.2000/28 (Parts I-IV)).

with concern the continued existence in the Middle East of unsafeguarded nuclear facilities, reaffirmed the importance of the early realization of universal adherence to the Treaty and called upon all States in the Middle East that had not yet done so, without exception, to accede to the Treaty as soon as possible and to place all their nuclear facilities under full-scope Agency safeguards,

Noting with satisfaction that, in the Final Document of the 2010 Review Conference of the Parties to the Treaty on the Non-Proliferation of Nuclear Weapons,[5] the Conference emphasized the importance of a process leading to full implementation of the 1995 resolution on the Middle East and decided, inter alia, that the Secretary-General of the United Nations and the co-sponsors of the 1995 resolution, in consultation with the States of the region, would convene a conference in 2012, to be attended by all States of the Middle East, on the establishment of a Middle East zone free of nuclear weapons and all other weapons of mass destruction, on the basis of arrangements freely arrived at by the States of the region and with the full support and engagement of the nuclear-weapon States,

Recalling that Israel remains the only State in the Middle East that has not yet become a party to the Treaty,

Concerned about the threats posed by the proliferation of nuclear weapons to the security and stability of the Middle East region,

Stressing the importance of taking confidence-building measures, in particular the establishment of a nuclear-weapon-free zone in the Middle East, in order to enhance peace and security in the region and to consolidate the global non-proliferation regime,

Emphasizing the need for all parties directly concerned to seriously consider taking the practical and urgent steps required for the implementation of the proposal to establish a nuclear-weapon-free zone in the region of the Middle East in accordance with the relevant resolutions of the General Assembly and, as a means of promoting this objective, inviting the countries concerned to adhere to the Treaty and, pending the establishment of the zone, to agree to place all their nuclear activities under Agency safeguards,

Noting that one hundred and eighty-two States have signed the Comprehensive Nuclear-Test-Ban Treaty,[6] including a number of States in the region,

---

[5] *2010 Review Conference of the Parties to the Treaty on the Non-Proliferation of Nuclear Weapons, Final Document*, vols. I-III (NPT/CONF.2010/50 (Vols. I-III)).
[6] See resolution 50/245.

1.   *Welcomes* the conclusions on the Middle East of the 2010 Review Conference of the Parties to the Treaty on the Non-Proliferation of Nuclear Weapons;[7]

2.   *Reaffirms* the importance of Israel's accession to the Treaty on the Non-Proliferation of Nuclear Weapons[3] and placement of all its nuclear facilities under comprehensive International Atomic Energy Agency safeguards, in realizing the goal of universal adherence to the Treaty in the Middle East;

3.   *Calls upon* that State to accede to the Treaty without further delay, not to develop, produce, test or otherwise acquire nuclear weapons, to renounce possession of nuclear weapons and to place all its unsafeguarded nuclear facilities under full-scope Agency safeguards as an important confidence-building measure among all States of the region and as a step towards enhancing peace and security;

4.   *Requests* the Secretary-General to report to the General Assembly at its sixty-seventh session on the implementation of the present resolution;

5.   *Decides* to include in the provisional agenda of its sixty-seventh session the item entitled "The risk of nuclear proliferation in the Middle East".

Action by the General Assembly

Date: 2 December 2011   Meeting: 71st plenary meeting
Vote: 167-6-5   Report: A/66/415
        170-2-2, p.p. 5
        171-2-2, p.p. 6
        173-1-2, p.p. 7

Sponsors

Algeria, Bahrain, Bangladesh, Comoros, Djibouti, **Egypt**, Iraq, Jordan, Kuwait, Lebanon, Libyan Arab Jamahiriya, Mauritania, Morocco, Oman, Palestine, Qatar, Saudi Arabia, Somalia, Sudan, Syrian Arab Republic, Tunisia, United Arab Emirates, Venezuela (Bolivarian Republic of), Yemen

Recorded vote

As a whole

In favour:

Afghanistan, Albania, Algeria, Andorra, Angola, Antigua and Barbuda, Argentina, Armenia, Austria, Azerbaijan, Bahamas, Bahrain, Bangladesh, Barbados, Belarus, Belgium, Belize, Benin, Bhutan,

---

[7]   *2010 Review Conference of the Parties to the Treaty on the Non-Proliferation of Nuclear Weapons, Final Document*, vol. I (NPT/CONF.2010/50 (Vol. I)), part I, *Conclusions and recommendations for follow-on actions*, sect. IV.

Bolivia (Plurinational State of), Bosnia and Herzegovina, Botswana, Brazil, Brunei Darussalam, Bulgaria, Burkina Faso, Cambodia, Cape Verde, Chad, Chile, China, Colombia, Comoros, Congo, Costa Rica, Côte d'Ivoire, Croatia, Cuba, Cyprus, Czech Republic, Democratic People's Republic of Korea, Denmark, Djibouti, Dominican Republic, Ecuador, Egypt, El Salvador, Eritrea, Estonia, Fiji, Finland, France, Gabon, Georgia, Germany, Ghana, Greece, Grenada, Guatemala, Guinea, Guinea-Bissau, Guyana, Haiti, Honduras, Hungary, Iceland, Indonesia, Iran (Islamic Republic of), Iraq, Ireland, Italy, Jamaica, Japan, Jordan, Kazakhstan, Kenya, Kuwait, Kyrgyzstan, Lao People's Democratic Republic, Latvia, Lebanon, Lesotho, Liberia, Libyan Arab Jamahiriya, Liechtenstein, Lithuania, Luxembourg, Madagascar, Malawi, Malaysia, Maldives, Malta, Mauritania, Mauritius, Mexico, Monaco, Mongolia, Montenegro, Morocco, Mozambique, Myanmar, Namibia, Nepal, Netherlands, New Zealand, Nicaragua, Nigeria, Norway, Oman, Pakistan, Papua New Guinea, Paraguay, Peru, Philippines, Poland, Portugal, Qatar, Republic of Korea, Republic of Moldova, Romania, Russian Federation, Saint Kitts and Nevis, Saint Lucia, Saint Vincent and the Grenadines, Samoa, San Marino, Sao Tome and Principe, Saudi Arabia, Senegal, Serbia, Seychelles, Sierra Leone, Singapore, Slovakia, Slovenia, Solomon Islands, South Africa, Spain, Sri Lanka, Sudan, Suriname, Swaziland, Sweden, Switzerland, Syrian Arab Republic, Tajikistan, Thailand, the former Yugoslav Republic of Macedonia, Timor-Leste, Togo, Trinidad and Tobago, Tunisia, Turkey, Turkmenistan, Tuvalu, Uganda, Ukraine, United Arab Emirates, United Kingdom, United Republic of Tanzania, Uruguay, Uzbekistan, Venezuela (Bolivarian Republic of), Viet Nam, Yemen, Zambia, Zimbabwe

Against:

Canada, Israel, Marshall Islands, Micronesia (Federated States of), Palau, United States

Abstaining:

Australia, Cameroon, Ethiopia, India, Panama

Fifth preambular paragraph

In favour:

Afghanistan, Albania, Algeria, Andorra, Angola, Antigua and Barbuda, Argentina, Armenia, Australia, Austria, Azerbaijan, Bahamas, Bahrain, Bangladesh, Barbados, Belarus, Belgium, Belize, Benin, Bolivia (Plurinational State of), Bosnia and Herzegovina, Botswana, Brazil, Brunei Darussalam, Bulgaria, Burkina Faso, Cambodia, Canada, Cape Verde, Chad, Chile, China, Colombia, Comoros, Congo, Costa Rica, Côte d'Ivoire, Croatia, Cuba, Cyprus, Czech Republic, Democratic People's Republic of Korea, Denmark, Djibouti, Dominican Republic,

Ecuador, Egypt, El Salvador, Eritrea, Estonia, Ethiopia, Fiji, Finland, France, Gabon, Georgia, Germany, Ghana, Greece, Grenada, Guatemala, Guinea, Guinea-Bissau, Guyana, Haiti, Honduras, Hungary, Iceland, Indonesia, Iran (Islamic Republic of), Iraq, Ireland, Italy, Jamaica, Japan, Jordan, Kazakhstan, Kuwait, Kyrgyzstan, Lao People's Democratic Republic, Latvia, Lebanon, Lesotho, Liberia, Libyan Arab Jamahiriya, Liechtenstein, Lithuania, Luxembourg, Madagascar, Malawi, Malaysia, Maldives, Mali, Malta, Mauritania, Mexico, Monaco, Mongolia, Montenegro, Morocco, Mozambique, Myanmar, Namibia, Nepal, Netherlands, New Zealand, Nicaragua, Nigeria, Norway, Oman, Palau, Panama, Papua New Guinea, Paraguay, Peru, Philippines, Poland, Portugal, Qatar, Republic of Korea, Republic of Moldova, Romania, Russian Federation, Saint Kitts and Nevis, Saint Lucia, Saint Vincent and the Grenadines, Samoa, San Marino, Sao Tome and Principe, Saudi Arabia, Senegal, Serbia, Seychelles, Sierra Leone, Singapore, Slovakia, Slovenia, Solomon Islands, South Africa, Spain, Sri Lanka, Sudan, Suriname, Swaziland, Sweden, Switzerland, Syrian Arab Republic, Tajikistan, Thailand, the former Yugoslav Republic of Macedonia, Togo, Tonga, Trinidad and Tobago, Tunisia, Turkey, Turkmenistan, Tuvalu, Uganda, Ukraine, United Arab Emirates, United Kingdom, United Republic of Tanzania, United States, Uruguay, Uzbekistan, Venezuela (Bolivarian Republic of), Viet Nam, Yemen, Zambia, Zimbabwe

Against:

India, Israel

Abstaining:

Bhutan, Pakistan

Sixth preambular paragraph

In favour:

Afghanistan, Albania, Algeria, Andorra, Angola, Antigua and Barbuda, Argentina, Armenia, Australia, Austria, Azerbaijan, Bahamas, Bahrain, Bangladesh, Barbados, Belarus, Belgium, Belize, Benin, Bolivia (Plurinational State of), Bosnia and Herzegovina, Botswana, Brazil, Brunei Darussalam, Bulgaria, Burkina Faso, Cambodia, Canada, Cape Verde, Chad, Chile, China, Colombia, Comoros, Congo, Costa Rica, Côte d'Ivoire, Croatia, Cuba, Cyprus, Czech Republic, Democratic People's Republic of Korea, Denmark, Djibouti, Dominican Republic, Ecuador, Egypt, El Salvador, Eritrea, Estonia, Ethiopia, Fiji, Finland, France, Gabon, Georgia, Germany, Ghana, Greece, Grenada, Guatemala, Guinea, Guinea-Bissau, Guyana, Haiti, Honduras, Hungary, Iceland, Indonesia, Iran (Islamic Republic of), Iraq, Ireland, Italy, Jamaica, Japan, Jordan, Kazakhstan, Kenya, Kuwait, Kyrgyzstan, Lao People's Democratic Republic, Latvia, Lebanon, Lesotho, Liberia, Libyan

Arab Jamahiriya, Liechtenstein, Lithuania, Luxembourg, Madagascar, Malawi, Malaysia, Maldives, Mali, Malta, Mauritania, Mexico, Monaco, Mongolia, Montenegro, Morocco, Mozambique, Myanmar, Namibia, Nepal, Netherlands, New Zealand, Nicaragua, Nigeria, Norway, Oman, Palau, Panama, Papua New Guinea, Paraguay, Peru, Philippines, Poland, Portugal, Qatar, Republic of Korea, Republic of Moldova, Romania, Russian Federation, Saint Kitts and Nevis, Saint Lucia, Saint Vincent and the Grenadines, Samoa, San Marino, Sao Tome and Principe, Saudi Arabia, Senegal, Serbia, Seychelles, Sierra Leone, Singapore, Slovakia, Slovenia, Solomon Islands, South Africa, Spain, Sri Lanka, Sudan, Suriname, Swaziland, Sweden, Switzerland, Syrian Arab Republic, Tajikistan, Thailand, the former Yugoslav Republic of Macedonia, Togo, Tonga, Trinidad and Tobago, Tunisia, Turkey, Turkmenistan, Tuvalu, Uganda, Ukraine, United Arab Emirates, United Kingdom, United Republic of Tanzania, United States, Uruguay, Uzbekistan, Venezuela (Bolivarian Republic of), Viet Nam, Yemen, Zambia, Zimbabwe

Against:

India, Israel

Abstaining:

Bhutan, Pakistan

Seventh preambular paragraph

In favour:

Afghanistan, Albania, Algeria, Andorra, Angola, Antigua and Barbuda, Argentina, Armenia, Australia, Austria, Azerbaijan, Bahamas, Bahrain, Bangladesh, Barbados, Belarus, Belgium, Belize, Benin, Bhutan, Bolivia (Plurinational State of), Bosnia and Herzegovina, Botswana, Brazil, Brunei Darussalam, Bulgaria, Burkina Faso, Cambodia, Canada, Cape Verde, Chad, Chile, China, Colombia, Comoros, Congo, Costa Rica, Côte d'Ivoire, Croatia, Cuba, Cyprus, Czech Republic, Democratic People's Republic of Korea, Denmark, Djibouti, Dominican Republic, Ecuador, Egypt, El Salvador, Eritrea, Estonia, Ethiopia, Fiji, Finland, France, Gabon, Georgia, Germany, Ghana, Greece, Grenada, Guatemala, Guinea, Guinea-Bissau, Guyana, Haiti, Honduras, Hungary, Iceland, Indonesia, Iran (Islamic Republic of), Iraq, Ireland, Italy, Jamaica, Japan, Jordan, Kazakhstan, Kenya, Kuwait, Kyrgyzstan, Lao People's Democratic Republic, Latvia, Lebanon, Lesotho, Liberia, Libyan Arab Jamahiriya, Liechtenstein, Lithuania, Luxembourg, Madagascar, Malawi, Malaysia, Maldives, Mali, Malta, Mauritania, Mauritius, Mexico, Monaco, Mongolia, Montenegro, Morocco, Mozambique, Myanmar, Namibia, Nepal, Netherlands, New Zealand, Nicaragua, Nigeria, Norway, Oman, Palau, Panama, Papua New Guinea, Paraguay, Peru, Philippines, Poland, Portugal, Qatar, Republic of Korea, Republic of Moldova, Romania,

Russian Federation, Saint Kitts and Nevis, Saint Lucia, Saint Vincent and the Grenadines, Samoa, San Marino, Sao Tome and Principe, Saudi Arabia, Senegal, Serbia, Seychelles, Sierra Leone, Singapore, Slovakia, Slovenia, Solomon Islands, South Africa, Spain, Sri Lanka, Sudan, Suriname, Swaziland, Sweden, Switzerland, Syrian Arab Republic, Tajikistan, Thailand, the former Yugoslav Republic of Macedonia, Togo, Tonga, Trinidad and Tobago, Tunisia, Turkey, Turkmenistan, Tuvalu, Uganda, Ukraine, United Arab Emirates, United Kingdom, United Republic of Tanzania, United States, Uruguay, Uzbekistan, Venezuela (Bolivarian Republic of), Viet Nam, Yemen, Zambia, Zimbabwe

Against:
Israel

Abstaining:
India, Pakistan

Action by the First Committee

Date: 26 October 2011   Meeting: 21st meeting
Vote: 157-5-6   Draft resolution: A/C.1/66/L.2
   155-2-4, p.p. 5
   160-2-2, p.p. 6
   163-1-2, p.p. 7

Agenda item 102

66/62   Convention on Prohibitions or Restrictions on the Use of Certain Conventional Weapons Which May Be Deemed to Be Excessively Injurious or to Have Indiscriminate Effects

Text

The General Assembly,

Recalling its resolution 65/89 of 8 December 2010,

Recalling with satisfaction the adoption and the entry into force of the Convention on Prohibitions or Restrictions on the Use of Certain Conventional Weapons Which May Be Deemed to Be Excessively Injurious or to Have Indiscriminate Effects[1] and its amended article 1,[2] the Protocol on Non-Detectable Fragments (Protocol I),[1] the Protocol on Prohibitions or Restrictions on the Use of Mines, Booby Traps and Other Devices (Protocol II)[1] and its amended version,[3] the Protocol on Prohibitions or Restrictions on the Use of Incendiary Weapons (Protocol III),[1] the Protocol on Blinding Laser Weapons (Protocol IV)[4] and the Protocol on Explosive Remnants of War (Protocol V),[5]

Welcoming the results of the Third Review Conference of the High Contracting Parties to the Convention on Prohibitions or Restrictions on the Use of Certain Conventional Weapons Which May Be Deemed to Be Excessively Injurious or to Have Indiscriminate Effects, held in Geneva from 7 to 17 November 2006,

Welcoming also the results of the 2010 Meeting of the High Contracting Parties to the Convention, held in Geneva on 25 and 26 November 2010,

Welcoming further the results of the Twelfth Annual Conference of the High Contracting Parties to Amended Protocol II, held in Geneva on 24 November 2010,

Welcoming the results of the Fourth Conference of the High Contracting Parties to Protocol V, held in Geneva on 22 and 23 November 2010,

Recalling the role played by the International Committee of the Red Cross in the elaboration of the Convention and the Protocols thereto, and welcoming the particular efforts of various international, non-governmental

---

[1] United Nations, *Treaty Series*, vol. 1342, No. 22495.
[2] Ibid., vol. 2260, No. 22495.
[3] Ibid., vol. 2048, No. 22495.
[4] Ibid., vol. 2024, No. 22495.
[5] Ibid., vol. 2399, No. 22495.

and other organizations in raising awareness of the humanitarian consequences of explosive remnants of war,

1.   *Calls upon* all States that have not yet done so to take all measures to become parties, as soon as possible, to the Convention on Prohibitions or Restrictions on the Use of Certain Conventional Weapons Which May Be Deemed to Be Excessively Injurious or to Have Indiscriminate Effects[1] and the Protocols thereto, as amended, with a view to achieving the widest possible adherence to these instruments at an early date and so as to ultimately achieve their universality;

2.   *Calls upon* all States parties to the Convention that have not yet done so to express their consent to be bound by the Protocols to the Convention and the amendment extending the scope of the Convention and the Protocols thereto to include armed conflicts of a non-international character;

3.   *Emphasizes* the importance of the universalization of the Protocol on Explosive Remnants of War (Protocol V);[5]

4.   *Welcomes* the additional ratifications and acceptances of or accessions to the Convention, as well as the consents to be bound by the Protocols thereto;

5.   *Also welcomes* the adoption by the Third Review Conference of the High Contracting Parties to the Convention of a plan of action to promote universality of the Convention and the Protocols thereto,[6] and expresses appreciation for the continued efforts of the Secretary-General, as depositary of the Convention and the Protocols thereto, the Chair of the Meeting of the High Contracting Parties to the Convention, the President of the Fourth Conference of the High Contracting Parties to Protocol V and the President of the Twelfth Annual Conference of the High Contracting Parties to Amended Protocol II, on behalf of the High Contracting Parties, to achieve the goal of universality;

6.   *Recalls* the decision of the Third Review Conference of the High Contracting Parties to the Convention to establish a sponsorship programme within the framework of the Convention,[7] and, with recognition of the value and importance of the programme, encourages States to contribute to the Sponsorship Programme;

7.   *Welcomes* the decision of the 2010 Meeting of the High Contracting Parties to the Convention to convene the Fourth Review Conference of the High Contracting Parties to the Convention in Geneva from 14 to 25 November 2011;

8.   *Acknowledges* the work of the Implementation Support Unit within the Geneva Branch of the Office for Disarmament Affairs of the Secretariat,

---

[6] See CCW/CONF.III/11 (Part II), annex III.
[7] Ibid., annex IV.

which was established following a decision of the 2009 Meeting of the High Contracting Parties to the Convention;

9.   *Welcomes* the commitment by States parties to continue to address the humanitarian problems caused by certain specific types of munitions in all their aspects, including cluster munitions, with a view to minimizing the humanitarian impact of these munitions;

10.   *Also welcomes* the preparatory work for the Fourth Review Conference conducted by the Group of Governmental Experts of the High Contracting Parties to the Convention, acting under the overall responsibility of the President-designate, and notes that the issue of urgently addressing the humanitarian impact of cluster munitions, while striking a balance between military and humanitarian considerations, will be further addressed at the Fourth Review Conference in November 2011;

11.   *Further welcomes* the commitment of States parties to the Protocol on Explosive Remnants of War (Protocol V) to the effective and efficient implementation of the Protocol and the implementation of the decisions of the First and Second Conferences of the High Contracting Parties to the Protocol establishing a comprehensive framework for the exchange of information and cooperation,[8] and also welcomes the holding of the Meeting of Experts of the High Contracting Parties to the Protocol, in Geneva from 6 to 8 April 2011, as a mechanism for consultation and cooperation among the States parties;

12.   *Notes* the decision of the Tenth Annual Conference of the High Contracting Parties to Amended Protocol II to establish an informal open-ended group of experts,[9] and welcomes the holding of the third session of the Group of Experts of the High Contracting Parties to Amended Protocol II, in Geneva on 4 and 5 April 2011, to exchange national practices and experiences and to assess the implementation of the Protocol;

13.   *Also notes* that, in conformity with article 8 of the Convention, conferences may be convened to examine amendments to the Convention or to any of the Protocols thereto, to examine additional protocols concerning other categories of conventional weapons not covered by existing Protocols or to review the scope and application of the Convention and the Protocols thereto and to examine any proposed amendments or additional protocols;

14.   *Requests* the Secretary-General to render the necessary assistance and to provide such services, including summary records, as may be required for the Fourth Review Conference of the High Contracting Parties to the Convention, to be held from 14 to 25 November 2011, and other annual conferences and expert meetings of the High Contracting Parties to Amended

---

[8]   See CCW/P.V/CONF/2007/1 and Corr.1 and 2 and CCW/P.V/CONF/2008/12.
[9]   See CCW/AP.II/CONF.10/2, para. 23.

Protocol II and Protocol V, as well as for any continuation of the work after the meetings;

15. *Also requests* the Secretary-General, in his capacity as depositary of the Convention and the Protocols thereto, to continue to inform the General Assembly periodically, by electronic means, of ratifications and acceptances of and accessions to the Convention, its amended article 1[2] and the Protocols thereto;

16. *Decides* to include in the provisional agenda of its sixty-seventh session the item entitled "Convention on Prohibitions or Restrictions on the Use of Certain Conventional Weapons Which May Be Deemed to Be Excessively Injurious or to Have Indiscriminate Effects".

Action by the General Assembly

Date: 2 December 2011   Meeting: 71st plenary meeting
Vote: Adopted without a vote   Report: A/66/416

Sponsors

Bulgaria, **Sweden**

Action by the First Committee

Date: 27 October 2011   Meeting: 22nd meeting
Vote: Adopted without a vote   Draft resolution: A/C.1/66/L.17

Agenda item 103

66/63 Strengthening of security and cooperation in the Mediterranean region

Text

The General Assembly,

Recalling its previous resolutions on the subject, including resolution 65/90 of 8 December 2010,

Reaffirming the primary role of the Mediterranean countries in strengthening and promoting peace, security and cooperation in the Mediterranean region,

Welcoming the efforts deployed by the Euro-Mediterranean countries to strengthen their cooperation in combating terrorism, in particular through the adoption of the Euro-Mediterranean Code of Conduct on Countering Terrorism by the Euro-Mediterranean Summit, held in Barcelona, Spain, on 27 and 28 November 2005,

Bearing in mind all the previous declarations and commitments, as well as all the initiatives taken by the riparian countries at the recent summits, ministerial meetings and various forums concerning the question of the Mediterranean region,

Recalling, in this regard, the adoption on 13 July 2008 of the Joint Declaration of the Paris Summit for the Mediterranean, which launched a reinforced partnership, named the "Barcelona Process: Union for the Mediterranean", and the common political will to revive efforts to transform the Mediterranean into an area of peace, democracy, cooperation and prosperity,

Welcoming the entry into force of the African Nuclear-Weapon-Free Zone Treaty (Treaty of Pelindaba)[1] as a contribution to the strengthening of peace and security both regionally and internationally,

Recognizing the indivisible character of security in the Mediterranean and that the enhancement of cooperation among Mediterranean countries with a view to promoting the economic and social development of all peoples of the region will contribute significantly to stability, peace and security in the region,

Recognizing also the efforts made so far and the determination of the Mediterranean countries to intensify the process of dialogue and consultations with a view to resolving the problems existing in the Mediterranean region and to eliminating the causes of tension and the consequent threat to peace

---

[1] See A/50/426, annex.

and security, as well as their growing awareness of the need for further joint efforts to strengthen economic, social, cultural and environmental cooperation in the region,

Recognizing further that prospects for closer Euro-Mediterranean cooperation in all spheres can be enhanced by positive developments worldwide, in particular in Europe, in the Maghreb and in the Middle East,

Reaffirming the responsibility of all States to contribute to the stability and prosperity of the Mediterranean region and their commitment to respecting the purposes and principles of the Charter of the United Nations as well as the provisions of the Declaration on Principles of International Law concerning Friendly Relations and Cooperation among States in accordance with the Charter of the United Nations,[2]

Noting the peace negotiations in the Middle East, which should be of a comprehensive nature and represent an appropriate framework for the peaceful settlement of contentious issues in the region,

Expressing its concern at the persistent tension and continuing military activities in parts of the Mediterranean that hinder efforts to strengthen security and cooperation in the region,

Taking note of the report of the Secretary-General,[3]

1.   *Reaffirms* that security in the Mediterranean is closely linked to European security as well as to international peace and security;

2.   *Expresses its satisfaction* at the continuing efforts by Mediterranean countries to contribute actively to the elimination of all causes of tension in the region and to the promotion of just and lasting solutions to the persistent problems of the region through peaceful means, thus ensuring the withdrawal of foreign forces of occupation and respecting the sovereignty, independence and territorial integrity of all countries of the Mediterranean and the right of peoples to self-determination, and therefore calls for full adherence to the principles of non-interference, non-intervention, non-use of force or threat of use of force and the inadmissibility of the acquisition of territory by force, in accordance with the Charter and the relevant resolutions of the United Nations;

3.   *Commends* the Mediterranean countries for their efforts in meeting common challenges through coordinated overall responses, based on a spirit of multilateral partnership, towards the general objective of turning the Mediterranean basin into an area of dialogue, exchanges and cooperation, guaranteeing peace, stability and prosperity, encourages them to strengthen such efforts through, inter alia, a lasting multilateral and action-oriented

---

[2] Resolution 2625 (XXV), annex.
[3] A/66/122.

cooperative dialogue among States of the region, and recognizes the role of the United Nations in promoting regional and international peace and security;

4. *Recognizes* that the elimination of the economic and social disparities in levels of development and other obstacles, as well as respect and greater understanding among cultures in the Mediterranean area, will contribute to enhancing peace, security and cooperation among Mediterranean countries through the existing forums;

5. *Calls upon* all States of the Mediterranean region that have not yet done so to adhere to all the multilaterally negotiated legal instruments related to the field of disarmament and non-proliferation, thus creating the conditions necessary for strengthening peace and cooperation in the region;

6. *Encourages* all States of the region to favour the conditions necessary for strengthening the confidence-building measures among them by promoting genuine openness and transparency on all military matters, by participating, inter alia, in the United Nations system for the standardized reporting of military expenditures and by providing accurate data and information to the United Nations Register of Conventional Arms;[4]

7. *Encourages* the Mediterranean countries to strengthen further their cooperation in combating terrorism in all its forms and manifestations, including the possible resort by terrorists to weapons of mass destruction, taking into account the relevant resolutions of the United Nations, and in combating international crime and illicit arms transfers and illicit drug production, consumption and trafficking, which pose a serious threat to peace, security and stability in the region and therefore to the improvement of the current political, economic and social situation and which jeopardize friendly relations among States, hinder the development of international cooperation and result in the destruction of human rights, fundamental freedoms and the democratic basis of pluralistic society;

8. *Requests* the Secretary-General to submit a report on means to strengthen security and cooperation in the Mediterranean region;

9. *Decides* to include in the provisional agenda of its sixty-seventh session the item entitled "Strengthening of security and cooperation in the Mediterranean region".

Action by the General Assembly

Date: 2 December 2011   Meeting: 71st plenary meeting
Vote: Adopted without a vote   Report: A/66/417

---

[4] See resolution 46/36 L.

Sponsors

Albania, **Algeria**, Andorra, Angola, Australia, Austria, Belgium, Bulgaria, Croatia, Cyprus, Czech Republic, Denmark, Egypt, Estonia, Finland, France, Germany, Greece, Hungary, Ireland, Italy, Jordan, Kazakhstan, Latvia, Lithuania, Luxembourg, Malta, Montenegro, Morocco, Poland, Portugal, Republic of Moldova, Romania, Serbia, Slovakia, Slovenia, Spain, Sudan, Sweden, Tunisia, United Kingdom

Co-sponsors

Bosnia and Herzegovina, Iceland, Mali, Mauritania, Monaco, Netherlands, Norway, San Marino, the former Yugoslav Republic of Macedonia, Turkey

Action by the First Committee

Date: 27 October 2011   Meeting: 22nd meeting
Vote: Adopted without a vote   Draft resolution: A/C.1/66/L.22

Agenda item 104

66/64   Comprehensive Nuclear-Test-Ban Treaty

Text

The General Assembly,

Reiterating that the cessation of nuclear-weapon test explosions or any other nuclear explosions constitutes an effective nuclear disarmament and non-proliferation measure, and convinced that this is a meaningful step in the realization of a systematic process for achieving nuclear disarmament,

Recalling that the Comprehensive Nuclear-Test-Ban Treaty, adopted by its resolution 50/245 of 10 September 1996, was opened for signature on 24 September 1996,

Stressing that a universal and effectively verifiable Treaty constitutes a fundamental instrument in the field of nuclear disarmament and non-proliferation and that, after more than fifteen years, its entry into force is more urgent than ever before,

Encouraged by the signing of the Treaty by one hundred and eighty-two States, including forty-one of the forty-four whose ratification is needed for its entry into force, and welcoming the ratification of the Treaty by one hundred and fifty-five States, including thirty-five of the forty-four whose ratification is needed for its entry into force, among which there are three nuclear-weapon States,

Recalling its resolution 65/91 of 8 December 2010,

Welcoming the adoption by consensus of the conclusions and recommendations for follow-on actions of the 2010 Review Conference of the Parties to the Treaty on the Non-Proliferation of Nuclear Weapons,[1] which, inter alia, reaffirmed the vital importance of the entry into force of the Comprehensive Nuclear-Test-Ban Treaty as a core element of the international nuclear disarmament and non-proliferation regime and included specific actions to be taken in support of the entry into force of the Treaty,

Welcoming also the Joint Ministerial Statement on the Comprehensive Nuclear-Test-Ban Treaty, adopted at the ministerial meeting held in New York on 23 September 2010,[2]

Recalling the Final Declaration adopted by the seventh Conference on Facilitating the Entry into Force of the Comprehensive Nuclear-Test-Ban

---

[1] *2010 Review Conference of the Parties to the Treaty on the Non-Proliferation of Nuclear Weapons, Final Document,* vol. I (NPT/CONF.2010/50 (Vol. I)), part I, *Conclusions and recommendations for follow-on actions.*

[2] A/65/675, annex.

Treaty, held in New York on 23 September 2011,[3] convened pursuant to article XIV of the Treaty, and noting the improved prospects for ratification in several Annex 2 countries,

1.   *Stresses* the vital importance and urgency of signature and ratification, without delay and without conditions, in order to achieve the earliest entry into force of the Comprehensive Nuclear-Test-Ban Treaty;[4]

2.   *Welcomes* the contributions by the States signatories to the work of the Preparatory Commission for the Comprehensive Nuclear-Test-Ban Treaty Organization, in particular its efforts to ensure that the verification regime of the Treaty will be capable of meeting the verification requirements of the Treaty upon its entry into force, in accordance with article IV of the Treaty;

3.   *Underlines* the need to maintain momentum towards completion of all elements of the verification regime;

4.   *Urges* all States not to carry out nuclear-weapon test explosions or any other nuclear explosions, to maintain their moratoriums in this regard and to refrain from acts that would defeat the object and purpose of the Treaty, while stressing that these measures do not have the same permanent and legally binding effect as the entry into force of the Treaty;

5.   *Recalls* Security Council resolutions 1718 (2006) of 14 October 2006 and 1874 (2009) of 12 June 2009, emphasizes the importance of their implementation, and reaffirms its firm support for the Six-Party Talks;

6.   *Urges* all States that have not yet signed the Treaty, in particular those whose ratification is needed for its entry into force, to sign and ratify it as soon as possible;

7.   *Urges* all States that have signed but not yet ratified the Treaty, in particular those whose ratification is needed for its entry into force, to accelerate their ratification processes with a view to ensuring their earliest successful conclusion;

8.   *Welcomes,* since its previous resolution on the subject, the ratification of the Treaty by Ghana and Guinea as a significant step towards the early entry into force of the Treaty;

9.   *Also welcomes* the recent expressions by a number of the remaining States whose ratification is needed for the Treaty to enter into force of their intention to pursue and complete the ratification process;

10.   *Urges* all States to remain seized of the issue at the highest political level and, where in a position to do so, to promote adherence to the Treaty through bilateral and joint outreach, seminars and other means;

---

[3] See CTBT-Art.XIV/2011/6.
[4] See resolution 50/245.

11. *Requests* the Secretary-General, in consultation with the Preparatory Commission for the Comprehensive Nuclear-Test-Ban Treaty Organization, to prepare a report on the efforts of States that have ratified the Treaty towards its universalization and possibilities for providing assistance on ratification procedures to States that so request it, and to submit such a report to the General Assembly at its sixty-seventh session;

12. *Decides* to include in the provisional agenda of its sixty-seventh session the item entitled "Comprehensive Nuclear-Test-Ban Treaty".

Action by the General Assembly

Date: 2 December 2011   Meeting: 71st plenary meeting
Vote: 175-1-3   Report: A/66/418
      174-1-3, p.p. 6

Sponsors

Afghanistan, Andorra, Argentina, Australia, Austria, Belgium, Brazil, Bulgaria, Burkina Faso, Cambodia, Chile, China, Colombia, Costa Rica, Croatia, Cyprus, Czech Republic, Denmark, Eritrea, Estonia, Finland, France, Germany, Greece, Hungary, Indonesia, Ireland, Italy, Jamaica, Japan, Kazakhstan, Kenya, Latvia, Lithuania, Luxembourg, Malaysia, Malta, **Mexico**, Micronesia (Federated States of), Montenegro, Netherlands, New Zealand, Norway, Peru, Poland, Portugal, Republic of Korea, Republic of Moldova, Romania, Russian Federation, Samoa, Serbia, Slovakia, Slovenia, South Africa, Spain, Sweden, Switzerland, Turkey, Ukraine, United Kingdom, United States

Co-sponsors

Albania, Armenia, Azerbaijan, Bahamas, Bangladesh, Belize, Canada, Congo, Georgia, Guyana, Haiti, Lesotho, Liechtenstein, Monaco, Mongolia, Morocco, Paraguay, Papua New Guinea, Philippines, San Marino, Tajikistan, Thailand, the former Yugoslav Republic of Macedonia, Trinidad and Tobago

Recorded vote

As a whole

In favour:

Afghanistan, Albania, Algeria, Andorra, Angola, Antigua and Barbuda, Argentina, Armenia, Australia, Austria, Azerbaijan, Bahamas, Bahrain, Bangladesh, Barbados, Belarus, Belgium, Belize, Benin, Bhutan, Bolivia (Plurinational State of), Bosnia and Herzegovina, Botswana, Brazil, Brunei Darussalam, Bulgaria, Burkina Faso, Cambodia, Cameroon, Canada, Chad, Chile, China, Colombia, Comoros, Congo, Costa Rica, Côte d'Ivoire, Croatia, Cuba, Cyprus, Czech Republic, Denmark,

Djibouti, Dominican Republic, Ecuador, Egypt, El Salvador, Eritrea, Estonia, Ethiopia, Fiji, Finland, France, Georgia, Germany, Ghana, Greece, Grenada, Guatemala, Guinea, Guinea-Bissau, Guyana, Haiti, Honduras, Hungary, Iceland, Indonesia, Iran (Islamic Republic of), Iraq, Ireland, Israel, Italy, Jamaica, Japan, Jordan, Kazakhstan, Kenya, Kuwait, Kyrgyzstan, Lao People's Democratic Republic, Latvia, Lebanon, Lesotho, Liberia, Libyan Arab Jamahiriya, Liechtenstein, Lithuania, Luxembourg, Madagascar, Malawi, Malaysia, Maldives, Mali, Malta, Marshall Islands, Mauritania, Mexico, Micronesia (Federated States of), Monaco, Mongolia, Montenegro, Morocco, Mozambique, Myanmar, Namibia, Nepal, Netherlands, New Zealand, Nicaragua, Niger, Nigeria, Norway, Oman, Pakistan, Palau, Panama, Papua New Guinea, Paraguay, Peru, Philippines, Poland, Portugal, Qatar, Republic of Korea, Republic of Moldova, Romania, Russian Federation, Saint Kitts and Nevis, Saint Lucia, Saint Vincent and the Grenadines, Samoa, San Marino, Sao Tome and Principe, Saudi Arabia, Senegal, Serbia, Seychelles, Sierra Leone, Singapore, Slovakia, Slovenia, Solomon Islands, South Africa, Spain, Sri Lanka, Sudan, Suriname, Swaziland, Sweden, Switzerland, Tajikistan, Thailand, the former Yugoslav Republic of Macedonia, Timor-Leste, Togo, Tonga, Trinidad and Tobago, Tunisia, Turkey, Turkmenistan, Tuvalu, Uganda, Ukraine, United Arab Emirates, United Kingdom, United Republic of Tanzania, United States, Uruguay, Uzbekistan, Venezuela (Bolivarian Republic of), Viet Nam, Yemen, Zambia, Zimbabwe

Against:

Democratic People's Republic of Korea

Abstaining:

India, Mauritius, Syrian Arab Republic

Sixth preambular paragraph

In favour:

Afghanistan, Albania, Algeria, Andorra, Angola, Antigua and Barbuda, Argentina, Armenia, Australia, Austria, Azerbaijan, Bahamas, Bahrain, Bangladesh, Barbados, Belarus, Belgium, Belize, Benin, Bhutan, Bolivia (Plurinational State of), Bosnia and Herzegovina, Botswana, Brazil, Brunei Darussalam, Bulgaria, Burkina Faso, Cambodia, Cameroon, Canada, Cape Verde, Chad, Chile, China, Colombia, Comoros, Congo, Costa Rica, Côte d'Ivoire, Croatia, Cuba, Cyprus, Czech Republic, Denmark, Djibouti, Dominican Republic, Ecuador, El Salvador, Eritrea, Estonia, Ethiopia, Fiji, Finland, France, Gabon, Georgia, Germany, Ghana, Greece, Grenada, Guatemala, Guinea, Guinea-Bissau, Guyana, Haiti, Honduras, Hungary, Iceland, Indonesia, Iran (Islamic Republic of), Iraq, Ireland, Italy, Jamaica, Japan, Jordan, Kazakhstan, Kenya, Kuwait, Kyrgyzstan, Lao People's Democratic Republic, Latvia, Lebanon,

Lesotho, Liberia, Libyan Arab Jamahiriya, Liechtenstein, Lithuania, Luxembourg, Madagascar, Malawi, Malaysia, Maldives, Mali, Malta, Marshall Islands, Mauritania, Mexico, Micronesia (Federated States of), Monaco, Mongolia, Montenegro, Morocco, Mozambique, Myanmar, Namibia, Nepal, Netherlands, New Zealand, Nicaragua, Niger, Nigeria, Norway, Oman, Palau, Panama, Papua New Guinea, Paraguay, Peru, Philippines, Poland, Portugal, Qatar, Republic of Korea, Republic of Moldova, Romania, Russian Federation, Saint Kitts and Nevis, Saint Lucia, Saint Vincent and the Grenadines, Samoa, San Marino, Sao Tome and Principe, Saudi Arabia, Senegal, Serbia, Seychelles, Sierra Leone, Singapore, Slovakia, Slovenia, Solomon Islands, South Africa, Spain, Sri Lanka, Sudan, Suriname, Swaziland, Sweden, Switzerland, Tajikistan, Thailand, the former Yugoslav Republic of Macedonia, Timor-Leste, Togo, Tonga, Trinidad and Tobago, Tunisia, Turkey, Turkmenistan, Tuvalu, Uganda, Ukraine, United Arab Emirates, United Kingdom, United Republic of Tanzania, United States, Uruguay, Uzbekistan, Venezuela (Bolivarian Republic of), Viet Nam, Yemen, Zambia, Zimbabwe

Against:
Democratic People's Republic of Korea

Abstaining:
India, Israel, Pakistan

Action by the First Committee

Date: 28 October 2011   Meeting: 23rd meeting
Vote: 170-1-3   Draft resolution: A/C.1/66/L.37
      168-1-3, p.p. 6

Agenda item 105

66/65 Convention on the Prohibition of the Development, Production and Stockpiling of Bacteriological (Biological) and Toxin Weapons and on Their Destruction

Text

The General Assembly,

Recalling its previous resolutions relating to the complete and effective prohibition of bacteriological (biological) and toxin weapons and to their destruction,

Noting with satisfaction that there are one hundred and sixty-five States parties to the Convention on the Prohibition of the Development, Production and Stockpiling of Bacteriological (Biological) and Toxin Weapons and on Their Destruction,[1] including all the permanent members of the Security Council,

Bearing in mind its call upon all States parties to the Convention to participate in the implementation of the recommendations of the review conferences of the parties to the Convention, including the exchange of information and data agreed to in the Final Declaration of the Third Review Conference of the Parties to the Convention on the Prohibition of the Development, Production and Stockpiling of Bacteriological (Biological) and Toxin Weapons and on Their Destruction,[2] and to provide such information and data in conformity with standardized procedure to the Secretary-General on an annual basis and no later than 15 April,

Welcoming the reaffirmation made in the Final Declaration of the Fourth Review Conference that under all circumstances the use of bacteriological (biological) and toxin weapons and their development, production and stockpiling are effectively prohibited under article I of the Convention,[3]

Recalling the decision reached at the Sixth Review Conference to hold four annual meetings of the States parties of one week's duration each year commencing in 2007, prior to the Seventh Review Conference, which is to be held no later than the end of 2011, and to hold a one-week meeting of experts to prepare for each meeting of the States parties,[4]

1.	*Notes with appreciation* that two additional States have acceded to the Convention on the Prohibition of the Development, Production and

---

[1]	United Nations, *Treaty Series*, vol. 1015, No. 14860.
[2]	See BWC/CONF.III/23, part II.
[3]	See BWC/CONF.IV/9, part II.
[4]	See BWC/CONF.VI/6, part III.

Stockpiling of Bacteriological (Biological) and Toxin Weapons and on Their Destruction,[1] reaffirms its call upon all signatory States that have not yet ratified the Convention to do so without delay, and calls upon those States that have not signed the Convention to become parties thereto at the earliest possible date, thus contributing to the achievement of universal adherence to the Convention;

2. *Welcomes* the information and data provided to date, as well as the several measures to update the mechanism for the transmission of information in the framework of confidence-building measures agreed upon at the Sixth Review Conference of the States Parties to the Convention on the Prohibition of the Development, Production and Stockpiling of Bacteriological (Biological) and Toxin Weapons and on Their Destruction, and reiterates its call upon all States parties to the Convention to participate in the exchange of information and data agreed upon at the Third Review Conference;[2]

3. *Recalls* the decisions on all provisions of the Convention reached at the Sixth Review Conference,[4] and calls upon States parties to the Convention to participate in their implementation;

4. *Notes with appreciation* the work of the Implementation Support Unit within the Office for Disarmament Affairs of the Secretariat during the 2007–2010 intersessional process consistent with its mandate and in accordance with the decisions of the Sixth Review Conference;

5. *Welcomes* the successful holding of meetings as part of the 2007–2010 intersessional process, and in this context also welcomes the discussion aimed at the promotion of common understanding and effective action on topics agreed upon at the Sixth Review Conference;

6. *Notes* the success of the meeting of the Preparatory Committee for the Seventh Review Conference, held in Geneva from 13 to 15 April 2011, and welcomes the convening of the Seventh Review Conference in Geneva from 5 to 22 December 2011 pursuant to the decision of the Preparatory Committee;

7. *Recalls* that the Seventh Review Conference is mandated to consider issues identified in the review of the operation of the Convention as provided for in article XII thereof and any possible consensus follow-up action;

8. *Urges* all States parties to continue to work together to achieve a consensus outcome of the Seventh Review Conference which strengthens the Convention;

9. *Notes with appreciation* the events organized by some States parties for exchanges of views on the work of the Seventh Review Conference;

10. *Requests* the Secretary-General to continue to render the necessary assistance to the depositary Governments of the Convention, to provide such services as may be required for the implementation of the decisions

and recommendations of the review conferences and to render the necessary assistance and to provide such services as may be required for the Seventh Review Conference;

11.   *Decides* to include in the provisional agenda of its sixty-seventh session the item entitled "Convention on the Prohibition of the Development, Production and Stockpiling of Bacteriological (Biological) and Toxin Weapons and on Their Destruction".

Action by the General Assembly

Date: 2 December 2011   Meeting: 71st plenary meeting
Vote: Adopted without a vote   Report: A/66/419

Sponsors

Hungary

Action by the First Committee

Date: 26 October 2011   Meeting: 21st meeting
Vote: Adopted without a vote   Draft resolution: A/C.1/66/L.32

Agenda item 106

66/66   Revitalizing the work of the Conference on Disarmament and taking forward multilateral disarmament negotiations

Text

The General Assembly,

Recalling its resolution 65/93 of 8 December 2010,

Reaffirming the importance of disarmament in strengthening global security and promoting international stability,

Recognizing that the political will to advance the disarmament agenda has been strengthened in recent years and that the international political climate is conducive to the promotion of multilateral disarmament and moving towards the goal of a world without nuclear weapons,

Affirming the importance of multilateralism in negotiations in the area of disarmament and non-proliferation,

Mindful of the continuing importance of the Conference on Disarmament as the single multilateral disarmament negotiating forum, as stated during the first special session of the General Assembly devoted to disarmament,

Recalling the past achievements of the Conference on Disarmament in successfully negotiating arms control and disarmament instruments,

Reiterating its grave concern about the current status of the disarmament machinery, including the lack of substantive progress in the Conference on Disarmament for more than a decade, and stressing the need for greater efforts and flexibility to advance multilateral disarmament negotiations,

Welcoming the efforts by Member States to secure progress in multilateral disarmament and the support of the Secretary-General for such efforts, and recalling the high-level meeting on revitalizing the work of the Conference on Disarmament and taking forward multilateral disarmament negotiations, held in New York on 24 September 2010, and the follow-up plenary meeting of the General Assembly, held from 27 to 29 July 2011,

Noting with concern that, despite all efforts, the Conference on Disarmament has not been able to adopt and implement a programme of work during its 2011 session,

Recognizing the contribution of civil society in the area of disarmament, non-proliferation and arms control,

Mindful of the Charter of the United Nations, in particular Article 11 of Chapter IV concerning the functions and powers of the General Assembly in respect of disarmament,

1.   *Welcomes* the opportunity provided by the high-level meeting on revitalizing the work of the Conference on Disarmament and taking forward multilateral disarmament negotiations, convened at the initiative of the Secretary-General in New York on 24 September 2010, and the follow-up plenary meeting of the General Assembly, held from 27 to 29 July 2011, to address the need to advance multilateral disarmament efforts;

2.   *Expresses appreciation* for the support voiced for the urgent need to revitalize the work of multilateral disarmament bodies and to advance multilateral disarmament negotiations;

3.   *Notes with appreciation* the continuing efforts and suggestions made by Member States and the Secretary-General with regard to revitalizing the multilateral disarmament machinery;

4.   *Calls upon* States to intensify efforts aimed at creating an environment conducive to multilateral disarmament negotiations;

5.   *Invites* States, in the appropriate forums, to explore, consider and consolidate options, proposals and elements for revitalization of the United Nations disarmament machinery as a whole, including the Conference on Disarmament;

6.   *Urges* the Conference on Disarmament to adopt and implement a programme of work to enable it to resume substantive work on its agenda early in its 2012 session;

7.   *Recognizes* the need to take stock, during the sixty-sixth session of the General Assembly, of all relevant efforts to take forward multilateral disarmament negotiations;

8.   *Decides* to include in the provisional agenda of its sixty-seventh session the item entitled "Revitalizing the work of the Conference on Disarmament and taking forward multilateral disarmament negotiations", to review progress made in the implementation of the present resolution and, if necessary, to further explore options for taking forward multilateral disarmament negotiations.

Action by the General Assembly

Date: 2 December 2011   Meeting: 71st plenary meeting
Vote: Adopted without a vote   Report: A/66/420

Sponsors

Netherlands, **South Africa**, Switzerland

Co-sponsors

Albania, Australia, Austria, Bangladesh, Belgium, Bulgaria, Chile, Costa Rica, Croatia, Cyprus, Czech Republic, Democratic Republic of the Congo, Denmark, Estonia, Finland, France, Georgia, Germany, Greece, Hungary, Ireland, Italy, Japan, Latvia, Lesotho, Lithuania, Luxembourg, Malaysia, Malta, Mexico, Mongolia, Montenegro, Norway, Philippines, Poland, Portugal, Republic of Korea, Republic of Moldova, Romania, Serbia, Slovakia, Slovenia, Spain, Swaziland, Sweden, Thailand, the former Yugoslav Republic of Macedonia, Trinidad and Tobago, Turkey, United Kingdom, Viet Nam

Action by the First Committee

Date: 28 October 2011	Meeting: 23rd meeting
Vote: Adopted without a vote	Draft resolution: A/C.1/66/L.39

DECISIONS

Agenda item 92

66/514 Review of the implementation of the Declaration on the Strengthening of International Security

Text

The General Assembly decides to include in the provisional agenda of its sixty-eighth session the item entitled "Review of the implementation of the Declaration on the Strengthening of International Security".

Action by the General Assembly

Date: 2 December 2011   Meeting: 71st plenary meeting
Vote: Adopted without a vote   Report: A/66/406

Sponsors

Indonesia, on behalf of the States Members of the United Nations that are members of the Movement of Non-Aligned Countries.

Action by the First Committee

Date: 27 October 2011   Meeting: 22nd meeting
Vote: Adopted without a vote   Draft resolution: A/C.1/66/L.12

Agenda Item 97

66/515 Role of science and technology in the context of international security and disarmament

Text

The General Assembly decides to include in the provisional agenda of its sixty-seventh session the item entitled "Role of science and technology in the context of international security and disarmament".

Action by the General Assembly

Date: 2 December 2011   Meeting: 71st plenary meeting
Vote: Adopted without a vote   Report: A/66/411

Sponsors

India

Action by the First Committee

Date: 27 October 2011   Meeting: 22nd meeting
Vote: Adopted without a vote   Draft resolution: A/C.1/66/L.44

Agenda item 98

66/516 Missiles

Text

The General Assembly, recalling its resolutions 54/54 F of 1 December 1999, 55/33 A of 20 November 2000, 56/24 B of 29 November 2001, 57/71 of 22 November 2002, 58/37 of 8 December 2003, 59/67 of 3 December 2004, 61/59 of 6 December 2006 and 63/55 of 2 December 2008 and its decisions 60/515 of 8 December 2005, 62/514 of 5 December 2007 and 65/517 of 8 December 2010, decides to include in the provisional agenda of its sixty-seventh session the item entitled "Missiles".

Action by the General Assembly

Date: 2 December 2011   Meeting: 71st plenary meeting
Vote: Adopted without a vote   Report: A/66/412

Sponsors

Egypt, Indonesia, **Iran (Islamic Republic of)**

Action by the First Committee

Date: 26 October 2011   Meeting: 21st meeting
Vote: Adopted without a vote   Draft resolution: A/C.1/66/L.10

Agenda item 98

66/517 Transparency and confidence-building measures in outer space activities

Text

The General Assembly, recalling its resolution 65/68 of 8 December 2010 and previous resolutions on this matter, decides to include in the provisional agenda of its sixty-eighth session the item entitled "Transparency and confidence-building measures in outer space activities".

Action by the General Assembly

Date: 2 December 2011 Meeting: 71st plenary meeting
Vote: Adopted without a vote Report: A/66/412

Sponsors

China, **Russian Federation**

Action by the First Committee

Date: 26 October 2011 Meeting: 21st meeting
Vote: Adopted without a vote Draft resolution: A/C.1/66/L.11

Agenda item 98

66/518 The arms trade treaty

Text

The General Assembly,

Recalling its resolution 64/48 of 2 December 2009,

Decides to hold, within existing resources, the final session of the Preparatory Committee for the United Nations Conference on the Arms Trade Treaty from 13 to 17 February 2012 in New York, to conclude the Preparatory Committee's substantive work and to decide on all relevant procedural matters, pursuant to paragraph 8 of resolution 64/48.

Action by the General Assembly

Date: 2 December 2011   Meeting: 71st plenary meeting
Vote: 166-0-13   Report: A/66/412

Sponsors

Argentina, Australia, Costa Rica, Finland, Japan, Kenya, **United Kingdom**

Recorded vote

In favour:

Afghanistan, Albania, Algeria, Andorra, Angola, Antigua and Barbuda, Argentina, Armenia, Australia, Austria, Azerbaijan, Bahamas, Bangladesh, Barbados, Belarus, Belgium, Belize, Benin, Bhutan, Bolivia (Plurinational State of), Bosnia and Herzegovina, Botswana, Brazil, Brunei Darussalam, Bulgaria, Burkina Faso, Cambodia, Cameroon, Canada, Cape Verde, Chad, Chile, China, Colombia, Comoros, Congo, Costa Rica, Côte d'Ivoire, Croatia, Cuba, Cyprus, Czech Republic, Denmark, Djibouti, Dominican Republic, Ecuador, El Salvador, Eritrea, Estonia, Ethiopia, Fiji, Finland, France, Gabon, Georgia, Germany, Ghana, Greece, Grenada, Guatemala, Guinea, Guinea-Bissau, Guyana, Haiti, Honduras, Hungary, Iceland, India, Indonesia, Iraq, Ireland, Israel, Italy, Jamaica, Japan, Jordan, Kazakhstan, Kenya, Kyrgyzstan, Lao People's Democratic Republic, Latvia, Lebanon, Lesotho, Liberia, Liechtenstein, Lithuania, Luxembourg, Madagascar, Malawi, Malaysia, Maldives, Mali, Malta, Marshall Islands, Mauritania, Mauritius, Mexico, Micronesia (Federated States of), Monaco, Mongolia, Montenegro, Morocco, Mozambique, Myanmar, Namibia, Nepal, Netherlands, New Zealand, Nicaragua, Niger, Nigeria, Norway, Palau, Panama, Papua New Guinea, Paraguay, Peru, Philippines, Poland, Portugal, Republic of Korea, Republic of Moldova, Romania, Russian Federation, Saint Kitts and Nevis, Saint Lucia, Saint Vincent and the Grenadines, Samoa, San

Marino, Sao Tome and Principe, Senegal, Serbia, Seychelles, Sierra Leone, Singapore, Slovakia, Slovenia, Solomon Islands, South Africa, Spain, Sri Lanka, Suriname, Swaziland, Sweden, Switzerland, Tajikistan, Thailand, the former Yugoslav Republic of Macedonia, Timor-Leste, Togo, Tonga, Trinidad and Tobago, Tunisia, Turkey, Turkmenistan, Uganda, Ukraine, United Kingdom, United Republic of Tanzania, United States, Uruguay, Vanuatu, Venezuela (Bolivarian Republic of), Viet Nam, Zambia, Zimbabwe

Against:
None.

Abstaining:
Bahrain, Egypt, Iran (Islamic Republic of), Kuwait, Libyan Arab Jamahiriya, Oman, Pakistan, Qatar, Saudi Arabia, Sudan, Syrian Arab Republic, United Arab Emirates, Yemen

Action by the First Committee

Date: 28 October 2011   Meeting: 23rd meeting
Vote: 155-0-13   Draft resolution: A/C.1/66/L.50

ANNEX

List of reports and notes of the Secretary-General

Agenda item 87	**Reduction of military budgets**
(a)	*Reduction of military budgets*
(b)	*Objective information on military matters, including transparency of military expenditures*
A/66/117	Objective information on military matters, including transparency of military expenditures
A/66/89 and Corr.1-3	Group of Governmental Experts on the Operation and Further Development of the United Nations Standardized Instrument for Reporting Military Expenditures
Agenda item 88	**Prohibition on the development and manufacture of new types of weapons of mass destruction and new systems of such weapons: report of the Conference on Disarmament**
Agenda item 89	**Implementation of the Declaration of the Indian Ocean as a Zone of Peace**
Agenda item 90	**African Nuclear-Weapon-Free Zone Treaty**
Agenda item 91	**Verification in all its aspects, including the role of the United Nations in the field of verification**
Agenda item 92	**Review of the implementation of the Declaration on the Strengthening of International Security**
Agenda item 93	**Developments in the field of information and telecommunications in the context of international security**
A/66/359	Letter dated 12 September 2011 from the Permanent Representatives of China, the Russian Federation, Tajikistan and Uzbekistan to the United Nations addressed to the Secretary-General
A/66/152	Developments in the field of information and telecommunications in the context of international security
Agenda item 94	**Establishment of a nuclear-weapon-free zone in the region of the Middle East**
A/66/153 (Part I), Add. 1 and Add.2	Establishment of a nuclear-weapon-free zone in the region of the Middle East

Agenda item 95	**Conclusion of effective international arrangements to assure non-nuclear-weapon States against the use or threat of use of nuclear weapons**
Agenda item 96	**Prevention of an arms race in outer space**
Agenda item 97	**Role of science and technology in the context of international security and disarmament**
Agenda item 98	**General and complete disarmament**
A/66/176 and Add.1	Information on confidence-building measures in the field of conventional arms
A/65/920	Letter dated 1 August 2011 from the Chargé d'affaires a.i. of the Permanent Mission of Pakistan to the United Nations addressed to the Secretary- General
(a)	*Notification of nuclear tests*
(b)	*Follow-up to nuclear disarmament obligations agreed to at the 1995 and 2000 Review Conferences of the Parties to the Treaty on the Non-Proliferation of Nuclear Weapons*
(c)	*Treaty on the South-East Asia Nuclear-Weapon-Free Zone (Bangkok Treaty)*
(d)	*Prohibition of the dumping of radioactive wastes*
(e)	*Towards an arms trade treaty: establishing common international standards for the import, export and transfer of conventional arms*
A/66/166 and Add.1	The arms trade treaty
(f)	*Problems arising from the accumulation of conventional ammunition stockpiles in surplus*
(g)	*Transparency in armaments*
A/66/127 and Add.1	United Nations Register of Conventional Arms
(h)	*Regional disarmament*
(i)	*Conventional arms control at the regional and subregional levels*
A/66/154 and Add.1	Conventional arms control at the regional and subregional levels
(j)	*Confidence-building measures in the regional and subregional context*
A/66/112 and Add.1	Confidence-building measures in the regional and subregional context

(k)	*Assistance to States for curbing the illicit traffic in small arms and light weapons and collecting them*
A/66/177	Assistance to States for curbing the illicit traffic in small arms and light weapons and collecting them
(l)	*Relationship between disarmament and development*
A/66/168	Relationship between disarmament and development
(m)	*Observance of environmental norms in the drafting and implementation of agreements on disarmament and arms control*
A/66/97 and Add.1	Observance of environmental norms in the drafting and implementation of agreements on disarmament and arms control
(n)	*Promotion of multilateralism in the areas of disarmament and non-proliferation*
A/66/111 and Add.1	Promotion of multilateralism in the area of disarmament and non-proliferation
(o)	*Nuclear disarmament*
A/66/132 and Add.1	Nuclear disarmament —Reducing nuclear danger — Follow-up to the advisory opinion of the International Court of Justice on the *Legality of the Threat or Use of Nuclear Weapons*
(p)	*Implementation of the Convention on the Prohibition of the Development, Production, Stockpiling and Use of Chemical Weapons and on Their Destruction*
A/66/171	Note by the Secretary-General transmitting the annual report of the Organization for the Prohibition of Chemical Weapons
(q)	Towards a nuclear-weapon-free world: accelerating the implementation of nuclear disarmament commitment
(r)	*Reducing nuclear danger*
A/66/132 and Add.1	Nuclear disarmament—Reducing nuclear danger — Follow-up to the advisory opinion of the International Court of Justice on the *Legality of the Threat or Use of Nuclear Weapons*
(s)	*Measures to prevent terrorists from acquiring weapons of mass destruction*
A/66/115	Measures to prevent terrorists from acquiring weapons of mass destruction
(t)	*The illicit trade in small arms and light weapons in all its aspects*

A/66/177   Assistance to States for curbing the illicit traffic in small arms and light weapons and collecting them — The illicit trade in small arms and light weapons in all its aspects

A/66/157   Letter dated 14 July 2011 from the Permanent Representative of New Zealand to the United Nations addressed to the Secretary-General

(u)   *Treaty banning the production of fissile material for nuclear weapons or other nuclear explosive devices*

(v)   *Transparency and confidence-building measures in outer space activities*

(w)   *United action towards the total elimination of nuclear weapons*

(x)   *Follow-up to the advisory opinion of the International Court of Justice on the Legality of the Threat or Use of Nuclear Weapons*

A/66/132 and Add.1   Nuclear disarmament — Reducing nuclear danger — Follow-up to the advisory opinion of the International Court of Justice on the *Legality of the Threat or Use of Nuclear Weapons*

(y)   *Missiles*

Agenda item 99   **Review and implementation of the Concluding Document of the Twelfth Special Session of the General Assembly**

(a)   *United Nations Regional Centre for Peace and Disarmament in Africa*

A/66/159   United Nations Regional Centre for Peace and Disarmament in Africa

(b)   *United Nations regional centres for peace and disarmament*

(c)   *United Nations Regional Centre for Peace, Disarmament and Development in Latin America and the Caribbean*

A/66/140   United Nations Regional Centre for Peace, Disarmament and Development in Latin America and the Caribbean

(d)   *Convention on the Prohibition of the Use of Nuclear Weapons*

(e)   *United Nations Regional Centre for Peace and Disarmament in Asia and the Pacific*

A/66/113   United Nations Regional Centre for Peace and Disarmament in Asia and the Pacific

(f)   *Regional confidence-building measures: activities of the United Nations Standing Advisory Committee on Security Questions in Central Africa*

A/66/72-S/2011/225   Letter dated 4 April 2011 from the Permanent Representative of Sao Tome and Principe to the United Nations addressed to the Secretary-General

A/66/163   Regional confidence-building measures: activities of the United Nations Standing Advisory Committee on Security Questions in Central Africa

Agenda item 100   **Review of the implementation of the recommendations and decisions adopted by the General Assembly at its tenth special session**

A/66/125   Work of the Advisory Board on Disarmament Matters

A/66/123 and Corr.1   United Nations Institute for Disarmament Research

(a)   *Report of the Conference on Disarmament*

A/66/27   Report of the Conference on Disarmament

(b)   *Report of the Disarmament Commission*

A/66/42   Report of the Disarmament Commission for 2011

Agenda item 101   **The risk of nuclear proliferation in the Middle East**

Agenda item 102   **Convention on Prohibitions or Restrictions on the Use of Certain Conventional Weapons Which May Be Deemed to Be Excessively Injurious or to Have Indiscriminate Effects**

Agenda item 103   **Strengthening of security and cooperation in the Mediterranean region**

A/66/122 and Add.1   Strengthening of security and cooperation in the Mediterranean region

Agenda item 104   **Comprehensive Nuclear-Test-Ban Treaty**

A/66/165 and Add.1   Note by the Secretary-General transmitting the annual report of the Executive Secretary of the Preparatory Commission for the Comprehensive Nuclear-Test-Ban Treaty Organization

Agenda item 105   **Convention on the Prohibition of the Development, Production and Stockpiling of Bacteriological (Biological) and Toxin Weapons and on Their Destruction**

Agenda item 106   **Revitalizing the work of the Conference on Disarmament and taking forward multilateral disarmament negotiations**